Cycling Europe

Cycling Europe

Budget Bike Touring in the Old World

_____ Nadine Slavinski

Bicycle Books — San Francisco

Printed in the United States of America

Published by:
Bicycle Books, Inc. PO Box 2038, Mill Valley, CA 94942 (USA)

Distributed to the book trade by:
USA: National Book Network, Lanham, MD
UK: Chris Lloyd Sales and Marketing Services,
               Poole, Dorset
Canada: Raincoast Book Distribution, Vancouver, BC

Cover design Kent Lytle, Lytle Design
Cover photograph The Image Bank

All photos by the author, except as credited otherwise
Maps by Meridian Mapping, Oakland, CA

Publisher's Cataloging in Publication Data
Slavinski, Nadine, 1968—
Cycling Europe: Budget Bike Touring in the Old World, includes
index. I Travel, International, Europe, 2. Bicycles and Bicycling,
Touring, I Title,
II. Authorship.

Library of Congress Catalog Card Number 91-77704

ISBN 0-933201-44-3 Paperback original

Nadine Slavinski is a student at Cornell University at Ithaca, NY, majoring in archeology. She has travelled extensively in Europe, including study tours and participation in student exchange programs. During the last several years, she has spent her summers cycle touring in many parts of Europe, researching and test riding the routes and gathering other materials for this book.

There are several other bicycle touring books that include many well-planned trips in Europe. Yet, for all the information that exists, I think there is also room for a different point of view—that of a budget-minded cyclist and solo traveler. All the touring books I used in planning my trip were written by married couples. Their perspective was naturally very different from mine, and I was left somewhat confused and some of my questions were left unanswered. What if you do not have the option, in terms of budget, to stay at an inn when it rains? How do all those friendly locals generally react to a single American woman pedaling by? What do you do when you get to the Alps? What is bicycle touring in a foreign country *really* like?

If you are confronted by some of the challenges I faced—traveling on a tight budget, cycling solo, and long-term 'marathon' touring—this book will help answer more specific questions. Even if you are not a single, budget-conscious traveler, this book will still be useful to you in terms of basic information applicable to any cyclist, such as road directions and regional conditions.

Cycling is a rewarding way to travel, and much of Europe is exceptionally well suited to two-wheeled touring. However, too many guidebooks take an overly enthusiastic and somewhat unrealistic tone—another reason why I wrote this book. Cycling is rewarding and often exciting, but like any other physical activity or form of travel, it can have its trials. While there are many advantages to cycling, it is important not to over-idealize what bicycle touring encompasses. Accept this from the start, and you will truly appreciate the unique perspective bicycle touring offers.

The key to a unique and rewarding experience is to take on a challenge and make it as easy for yourself as possible. This book will make your European bicycle tour easier.

While the book is written with a North American audience in mind, every attempt has been made by the publisher to make it equally suitable for British and other English-speaking travelers. Although the spelling adhered to is American, all information given has been carefully screened to be of maximum use to others as well.

Table of Contents

Part I – General Information

CHAPTER 1

Bicycle Touring in Europe

Bicycle touring is a good means to see and, more importantly, to experience Europe. In planning an extensive trip, I chose cycling as the best and most flexible way to combine in-depth local exploration with the ability to cover significant distances.

Cycling is an extremely personal, up-close way to travel. The energy you put into getting yourself, your bicycle, and your gear from point to point is immediately rewarded with concrete results. You are constantly greeted by new surroundings and can take pride in looking back and knowing that you met the challenge of the terrain and distance that day.

It is still possible to see Europe on a modest budget, with planning, determination, restraint—and a bicycle. Cycling is one of the few forms of transportation that is free, although it takes its toll in terms of your energy and time. If you are on a

Along the Irissh coast on the Dingle Peninsula.

tight budget, cycling is simply the most inexpensive way to see a great deal within a reasonable period of time.

Cycling also gets you into good physical condition quickly, even painlessly, if you take it slowly at the start. It brings you closer to the land you are touring, as well as its people, who have greater respect for you as a cyclist than they would as an ordinary tourist. This is particularly true in Europe, where cycling is extremely popular both for recreation and as a practical means of transportation. Sympathetic campground managers may give you a discount, and restaurants are usually happy to fill up your water bottles—sometimes with ice or juice—at no charge. Locals are glad to give you directions and will often confide a nearby point of interest to you that you might have otherwise passed by. You will come away from such experiences with more than just a quick look at the countryside, and hopefully those you meet will be left with a good impression of you as an interesting and sincere visitor.

Furthermore, cycling brings you to undiscovered corners of Europe with a quieter and perhaps more appreciative perspective. The experience of cycling from Venice to Vienna, for example, is infinitely richer than that of simply visiting those two cities connected by a quick journey by car or train. You are best prepared to absorb the character of a place through a steady approach, rather than by an abrupt arrival. By following cycling directions and maps you become well-oriented as a matter of necessity.

Cycling carries you through changing countryside and cultures in smooth transition, as opposed to high-speed shock. Especially when visiting large cities or towns, I found that I had a good sense of the layout, while many travelers I met were struggling to establish the same orientation. A short time after I arrived in a hostel in France, an American student asked me if I knew where the post office was. Another, hearing my answer, asked me how to get around town. They were impressed at my knowledge of the area and were amazed to find that I had only been in town for a few hours, just like them. Unlike them, however, I had cycled there.

As a cyclist you are totally independent. With only your own standards to meet, you can go anywhere you want to go, at any pace, via any route. If it is a rainy morning, you are free to kick back for a few hours; if the town you stopped in for lunch is particularly appealing, you can call it a day. On a hot afternoon in June I cycled five tempting miles along the Mediterranean coast before I gave in and had a swim. There is nothing to stop you from either stretching your limits or taking a break but yourself.

Many other forms of travel may frustrate you with missed opportunities—a train will not stop for its passengers to take a swim, and you cannot photograph the landscape while driving a car. Cycling eliminates having to adapt yourself to, and worry over, bus or train schedules, routes involving transfers, and, inevitably, transportation expenses. While I stuck with a fairly specific itinerary, it was great to have the flexibility provided by a bicycle whenever I learned of a new sight or area of interest. My twisting route through Northern England testifies to this.

With all the advantages of being independent comes the responsibility of being prepared. Food, shelter, entertainment, tools—everything you need—is immediately on hand in your panniers. Of course, you are also responsible for pedaling around and maintaining all your gear, but you will not find yourself stuck due to a closed youth hostel or a missed bus. When I rode from Verona to Vicenza in Italy, I found that there was no campground there—and simply cycled on to the next town. Every evening I was able to cook appetizing meals on my portable stove while other travelers made do with cold leftovers. As a cyclist, you can always pedal to a new destination or use your resources to solve any problem.

Finally, despite what you may at first think, cycling is an efficient and speedy means of travel. The pace is slow enough to let you appreciate the scenery, while easily covering 50 miles or so a day. On the border of England and Wales I met a group of Australian women traveling by car. They were astonished to see me cycling through Caernarfon the next day and again two days later on a road in southern Wales. By the end of a week we found ourselves in the same hostel in Bath. "There she is again!" one said. Hearing that encouraged me considerably at an early stage in my trip. For all the speed and convenience of a car, a bicycle proved to be at least as effective.

Bicycle touring offers great rewards if you are willing to put some effort into your travels. You will truly experience and remember Europe to a degree that few others achieve.

CHAPTER 2

Modes of Bicycle Travel

There is more than one way to travel by bicycle. You can go in a group, meet up with others along the way, or cycle alone. Here are the most important considerations that influence the way you will want to organize your tour.

Solo Travel

Traveling alone in a foreign country is one of the most educational experiences imaginable, not only in terms of culture and history, but also in what you learn about yourself. It can be difficult and lonely at times, but ultimately you will be rewarded with a great feeling of accomplishment and perhaps a newfound sense of yourself.

Solo travel brings you closer to the land and people you are visiting. Your own culture's intrusion on this contact is minimal because you have little to reinforce it against. A companion will distract your full attention by offering the security of your familiar culture in contrast to new, sometimes intimidating surroundings. This is not to say that a group of people traveling together cannot experience a foreign culture, but they do not have the focus of a solo traveler. Sometimes this immersion can be difficult, but take it as one of the challenges and rewards of touring on your own.

As a matter of necessity, you will become very good at getting by in unfamiliar surroundings. Within a few days you will pick up a useful vocabulary of a language you do not speak, or you may find yourself speaking a somewhat familiar language more naturally. It took me longer to accomplish the same once I began traveling with someone I could speak English with at any time.

You will face greater extremes in being alone than you would in the company of others. When you are tired and things are bad, you can be truly down. At these times the best thing may be to accept this low and wait for it to pass. The good times, on the other hand, are true highlights. The feeling of being entirely independent and able to overcome the challenges you face is truly meaningful.

Traveling with a friend makes facing the obstacles less trying, but it has its drawbacks as well. When traveling alone you can make your own decisions without having to compromise with others. However, group travel gives you a better sense of security as well as greater resources in terms of time, money, and collective knowledge.

I did not originally intend to set out alone, but circumstances gave me no choice—the scheduling conflicts of friends prevented them from joining me. As my departure date approached I was a bit uncomfortable with the prospect of cycling alone, but decided to take the trip in stages to see how much I could do. First, I was determined to make it through England. When I finished that portion of the trip, I set out to try cycling in France. Each stage became more and more challenging as I went from an English-speaking country where I had friends, to a country where I spoke the language haltingly and had no friends to call on, to Italy where I had no friends and could not speak the language at all. Countering these mounting challenges, however, was the familiarity with bicycle touring and the experience I gained over time. After four months, I was well used to solo touring. The experience was a good one, although at that point it was a nice change and a relief to begin cycling with a friend. Whatever your circumstances, do not let the drawbacks of solo travel stop you from taking stock of your abilities and enjoying a successful trip.

Other Cyclists

I set out to cycle Europe alone, hoping to meet other cyclists and perhaps join them for a few days if they were headed my way. Unfortunately, this never happened, but that does not rule out the possibility entirely. Even in France in June (which combined a popular place and time, or so I thought), I met only a few cyclists and then only briefly. The moral of the story is, do not bank on finding consistent cycling company.

On the other hand, I was surprised to find a large number of people cycling along the Danube. On a single day in August I saw twelve other bicycle tourists (most of them German) on their way to Budapest. One Danube campground even had prime riverfront campsites reserved for incoming cyclists due to the popularity of this area. You are not as alone as you may sometimes feel.

Fellow cyclists are the best source of information and travel tips, since they know what is important to you as a bicycle tourist. Most cyclists I met were very friendly and eager to share their experiences. After days of travel and many unfamiliar faces, it is pleasant to spend an evening sharing tea or dinner in a campground with people who can appreciate your endeavor. Even a few minutes of conversation as you pedal past someone can be refreshing, particularly if you are traveling alone. Take advantage of every opportunity you have to learn from others—if you are saved even one wrong turn or hear of an especially scenic route, it will be worth it.

Finally, there are the non-touring cyclists of Europe who generally fall into one of two categories—incredibly fast racers, who take great pleasure in speeding by your loaded bicycle, and middle-aged housewives pedaling home on their three-speeds with milk and bread in a basket. Neither is very sociable, although there are exceptions. One day in France I was steadily cycling away when five racers pulled alongside and each in turn carefully surveyed my bicycle, my panniers, and me. *"En vacances?"* one finally asked, referring, I think, to my turtle pace. This led to a halting conversation in French about where I had been and what I was doing. For this, at least, they respected me. If you are willing to give it a try, you can learn a great deal from those who are looking over their own handlebars.

Marathon Tours

Really long tours, which I refer to as marathon tours, have a special appeal. They offer an opportunity to explore a foreign country at leisure, the adventure, and the chance to see it all. This sort of trip can be very demanding and extremely rewarding, but it requires some special preparations. It can be difficult to travel for an extended period of time without some back-ups and comforts, so it is important to arrange as many of these as possible, without restricting yourself unnecessarily.

Undertaking a tour of considerable duration will put a strain on both your bicycle and you. Although there is always the unexpected, you can predict some trouble spots and plan ahead. First, there is no way to prevent the wear of parts, so you will need some replacements. You may be surprised at how quickly this occurs when you are using your bicycle all day, every day.

As a rule of thumb, I tried to have my bicycle tuned up in a shop every time I was about to leave one country for another, or after two months or so had gone by. The charge was usually a small fee or nothing at all. This kept my bicycle in dependable condition and prevented damage through wear.

My rear tire was almost worn through after 1,500 miles, and the front tire soon followed. Brake pads wear down quickly and will not grip well after a while. There are only so many times one can patch a punctured tube before a replacement is needed. Brake and derailleur cables will stretch and require adjustment. Sand clinging to the oil on a chain will eventually wear down the gears. Panniers and zippers can rip. Your clothing quickly ages with only the occasional hand wash.

You will have to replace some of these items, and it is impractical to carry them all with you. One option is to buy replacements as needed, although they may be expensive or unavailable, particularly if your bicycle is not a European model. Another possibility is to send these items ahead to a friend in Europe who can hold them indefinitely. If you can coordinate a place and time with a member of your family or a friend who is planning a trip to Europe, give him the parts before you leave.

If neither of these is possible, it is a good idea to mail a package of replacements to yourself, in care of a post office or American Express office. Wrap the package securely and address it Poste Restante, with your name and arrival date clearly shown. Choose a town with an attraction that you definitely plan to visit. For specific tools and equipment suggestions, see Chapter 3, *Equipment*.

Marathon tours can also put a great strain on your mind. Mail is a nice reminder of home on a long trip. In order to keep myself on some kind of schedule, I planned mail stops every one to two months and gave a list to my friends. This kept my tour from becoming absolutely aimless, but still left me with the flexibility of an open trip. American Express offices hold mail for their customers for six weeks at no charge (if you use their traveler's checks, this applies to you). Poste Restante letters should be held for the same period of time in a post office, but you may be charged. It is important to include a full address and postal code, and every letter should have your name and arrival date clearly marked. Correspondence will be held for you until that date, but probably no longer. A small post office branch will probably keep your mail safer than a large city office. When I arrived at the small post office in Amesbury, England, the woman behind the counter recognized my name instantly and handed over my mail.

Although your trip may be a vacation, there are times during a marathon tour that you will need a break from cycling. If you find an interesting place to stay, give yourself a week or more to relax and catch up on things like your journal or letter writing. If you are not tired of sightseeing, you can leave your bicycle in a secure place and take a mini trip. I left my bicycle in a Viennese hostel and spent three weeks visiting friends in Czechoslovakia and Poland by train, an excellent experience and a good change of pace.

Take time to think and rest to prevent one sight from blurring into the next. A marathon tour can be very demanding, particularly because you are always surrounded by the unfamiliar. My bicycle and tent proved doubly important as constants in a changing landscape. To keep motivated, give yourself the credit you deserve. Although it is impossible to see everything, there are no limitations except the ones that you impose upon yourself.

The Realities of Bicycle Touring

This section is not intended to intimidate or discourage anyone, but it would be unfair and unrealistic not to mention the disadvantages of bicycle touring. These are simple facts of the cycling life, and there is no guarantee of avoiding the discomforts they may cause.

The main drawback to cycling is that it does require a certain amount of physical effort. There are hills to get over and long distances to contend with. The simple remedy for this problem is to be in respectable physical condition. The bicycle tours in this book range from the flattest, easiest terrain possible to the most demanding. Choose one carefully according to your ability and interests.

Cycling exposes you to every condition and extreme. You cannot roll up the window if it begins to rain or turn on the air conditioning if it becomes too hot. You will be sharing the road with cars that from time to time blow exhaust fumes into your face. On the other hand, you will also be exposed to broad landscapes, cool breezes, and clean country air.

A bicycle's range and pace is limited. Unlike some other types of tours, you will not be able to visit eight countries in three days. Furthermore, a bicycle is not always practical when visiting the historic cities of Europe. Cobblestones and traffic can make cycling especially unpleasant.

You may get lost. Roads are not always marked, and there may not be anyone around to ask for directions. Again, the only person helping you is yourself. The advantages of independence come with responsibility and drawbacks.

Finally, cycling may be risky. You will be sharing public roads in a foreign country with fast cars. And there is a danger of theft to consider as well. There are times when you will leave your belongings in a tent with only a zippered door to protect them from theft. Your valuable bicycle could be damaged or stolen. In all these cases, your best protection is common sense prevention. Wear a helmet at all times and use hand signals while cycling. Keep valuables with you at all times. Ask your camping neighbors to keep an eye on your things (it may be a good idea to ask more than one so they will keep an eye on each other as well). Use a strong lock whenever you leave your bicycle unattended.

These are all possibilities that should not be ignored. Although they can never be eliminated, the discomforts and risks of cycling can be greatly minimized by thorough preparation. With a good attitude you will recognize these factors for what they are—the unavoidable inconveniences of a substantial undertaking.

If you are interested in an easy, problem-free trip, take a bus tour. For a memorable and unique experience, try bicycle touring. You will not regret your decision.

CHAPTER 3

Choosing Your Equipment

Bicycle touring is very basic in terms of the equipment required. It is possible to tour Europe on a three-speed, and some people do. Many Europeans do short weekend tours with the entire family, strapping duffel bags on the back of their bicycles. The difference comes when you are planning a more lengthy and involved tour, and then the quality and condition of your bicycle can make or break the trip.

The Bicycle

If you are going to go bicycle touring, do yourself a big favor and use a touring bicycle. These bicycles are specifically designed to perform efficiently under a variety of conditions

The dangers of cycling: Criptic warning sign at a railway crossing near Zârich in Switzerland

18

while carrying the weight of panniers, enabling you to enjoy your surroundings. Cycling takes a considerable amount of effort, and using the right equipment will greatly minimize the challenges that you encounter.

A good touring bicycle has a wide range of gears. Especially important is a third chainring, referred to as a granny gear, which makes it possible to pedal a full load up a long hill without having a coronary attack midway. The bicycle should be as light as possible—in terms of both the basic frame and any accessories.

Despite the recent popularity of mountain bikes for touring, a good touring bicycle has curved, 'drop' handlebars that allow the rider to change positions. This is extremely important, not just for improved efficiency, but also for your comfort and well- being. If you keep your hands in the same position for a long period of time with steady pressure, it is possible to cause nerve damage. I managed to do this on a long weekend ride at home. Shift your hands occasionally to avoid this potential problem. Thick foam handlebar padding can also help prevent such injuries.

Brake levers on the lower part of drop bars work directly on the brake cables for safe, quick action. Extra levers attached to the upright part of the bars do not have this direct connection and may not be as effective when your bicycle is heavily loaded or when weather conditions are poor (rain, snow). They are often called suicide levers and are not advisable for touring.

A good bicycle will also have thicker spokes to support heavier loads. This feature is not absolutely crucial, since spoke problems on a well-maintained bicycle are rare, but it is nevertheless a desirable advantage.

A well-designed, well-padded seat is also a welcome feature. A thin bicycle seat, however, can only be so comfortable no matter how well padded it is, so do not try to go too far in improving yours. During the course of a long day you may begin to get sore. The best remedy is a short break or to ride standing up for a time. A good stretch while riding is also very effective.

In the course of cycling several thousand miles in Europe, I saw a large number of people using mountain bicycles to tour. Or, I should say, I passed a large number of people on mountain bicycles. These specialized bicycles are excellent for their designed use, but are just about the last thing you should use for extensive, on-road touring. They have the gear range, but their heavy frames and components with wide, low-pressure tires, all work against you when touring on regular roads. The tires especially create so much friction that the rider must work much harder to move his bicycle. This effect will be demonstrated as you fly by sweating mountain cyclists on the road with minimum effort. The straight handlebars allow only one riding position. All this also goes against the principle that you should strive to make touring as easy as possible for yourself. Think twice before loading up your mountain bicycle.

I have just described what I think are the optimal characteristics of a bicycle to use for touring. These are only basic, sensible guidelines, and you should feel free to use any bicycle on which you feel comfortable. If you already have a bicycle that is not specifically designed for touring, but for budget reasons you cannot afford to purchase a touring bicycle, consider upgrading or modifying your present bicycle as much as possible. I wanted to be well prepared since I was facing a long trip where the bicycle's performance would be crucial, and therefore I bought a new, quality touring bicycle. I was very happy with my Miyata, but there are also many other excellent touring bicycles on the market. If you are planning a shorter trip or are visiting a region where the terrain will not be very demanding, it is not absolutely necessary to have a top-of-the-line bicycle.

Whatever bicycle you choose to use, be sure it is in safe, well-functioning condition before you leave home. Have a bicycle shop give it a thorough tune-up, and test ride it for performance and comfort. Try to do at least a short, fully loaded tour before leaving home to get to know your equipment and the feel of your bicycle.

Racks and Panniers

The money you spend on well-designed, durable panniers (bicycle bags) will be worth it. Quality equipment can last you a lifetime of touring. Depending on the length of your trip, you can use rear panniers, front panniers, or both. The most stable combination for touring is rear panniers with sleeping bag, tent, and sleeping pad secured on the rear rack, and low-rider front panniers. This combination is also preferable because you can organize your gear in several separate compartments where it will be easily accessible. Once again, if you are doing a shorter trip, you will be able to get by with a single set of panniers, either front or rear. See the Packing section for more information.

A small-capacity handlebar bag with a plastic map-viewing case is indispensable. You can keep your camera and some snacks handy and check your map whenever you need it with no hassle. A handlebar bag is also convenient to keep and carry your valuables in, when leaving the rest of your gear on your parked bicycle.

There are many reputable brands of panniers that are slightly more expensive than bags some large bicycle stores produce. They are worth the difference, due to their resistance to wear. There are also different brands of racks. Blackburn is the most reputable. Look for racks that attach securely at several points.

Tools and Accessories

The single most important piece of equipment to have when bicycle touring is a helmet. Safety should always be an important part of the planning and carrying out of your trip. A well-ventilated, well-fitting helmet will be comfortable and should be worn at all times.

Listed below are the tools and accessories that will make your trip smoother and safer. It is not necessary to have extra tools 'just in case,' only enough to help you with normal problems. Expect a flat tire or two, but do not lose sleep over potentially breaking a chainring. I carried spare tubes and spare brake/derailleur cables, but later realized they were unnecessary. Even marathon tourists do not need these additional items. There are many bicycle shops all over Europe that will be able to help you with bigger problems (see the Repairing Your Bicycle section).

- two water bottles
- pump
- tire patch kit
- extra spokes
- tire levers
- handlebar mirror
- heavy duty tape
- oil
- bicycle gloves
- wrenches that fit seat, pedals, and handlebars for shipping and readjustments

If your bicycle does not have quick-release hubs, you should take the right size tools to remove the wheels, if needed. I found a rear-view mirror to be very useful, especially in traffic where I could not safely turn to look behind me. It was also useful in judging the size and speed of passing cars that sounded like they wanted to run me down. In addition, it will help with morning routines such as combing your hair or shaving. The helmet mirrors or the type that mount to your eyeglasses are not as useful.

In the event that you do break a spoke, it is a good idea to take two or three extras of the correct length. Tape them behind your downtube. You can cause more damage than good if you attempt to replace a spoke yourself. Carry extras and have a bicycle shop fit them. If your brake or derailleur cables are old or rusty, change them before you leave home so that you will not need to carry spares.

Fenders are handy accessories as well. They keep you, your gear, and your bicycle clean. This will keep your bicycle running smoothly, and you will not have to clean your chain and gears so often.

Before I left, I was particularly worried, for no good reason, about flat tires. I got only two flat tires in seven months of bicycle touring, both on the same day in Wales. This does not guarantee that you will not have a problem, but I do not think it is necessary to carry spare tubes with you unless you want the convenience of changing a tire fast and repairing it at your leisure.

A last important thing to remember is that tire valves in Europe are Presta, rather than Schraeder, the most common type in America. Tire sizes may also differ. Be sure your pump fits your valve and consider converting both so that they may be exchanged for European parts, if needed.

Camping Gear

The cheapest and most convenient accommodations available are campgrounds, but the drawback of camping is the extra gear needed. Take the basics: a lightweight tent, sleeping pad, ground sheet, and sleeping bag. A tent with a separate fly sheet is best. An Antarctic-quality sleeping bag is not necessary. Keep everything as light as possible, without sacrificing adequate protection.

For cooking you will need a small camping stove and utensils. Bleuet stoves are very convenient and lightweight, and their fuel cartridges are easy to find throughout Europe.

Each will last about a week. Hot meals are a great comfort at the end of a long and active day and make the extra equipment worth its extra weight.

Again, if you are touring for a short time or during a warm season, use your judgment as to what you will need.

Personal

Do not take too much. Keep in mind that you will personally have to haul all that weight around. The best strategy is to take the absolute minimum and wash often. I did a little bit of washing every day and kept to the basics. If you are on a tight budget, you will probably not go anywhere that you have to dress up, which will eliminate some weight. Take something comfortable and respectable to change into for sightseeing and for the end of the day. Most churches in Europe require proper dress, not necessarily fashionable or wrinkle-free, just something that covers your arms and legs. I kept a light cotton skirt rolled up and handy.

All toiletries are readily available throughout Europe. In Eastern Europe everything is still more or less available, although the choice and quality decrease tremendously. A pair of bicycling shorts with padding sewn in are a must for anyone spending long days on a bicycle. Layering is the best way to dress and maintain a functional wardrobe. In cold conditions, a T-shirt, longsleeve shirt, sweater, and windbreaker combination will keep you warm while cycling. Make adjustments for extremely hot or cold regions.

- 2 T-shirts or tank tops
- cycling shorts
- sweatpants
- lightweight wool sweater
- shirt and shorts to change into
- 3 pairs socks
- 3 underwear
- windbreaker
- bandana or scarf
- running/cycling tights or long underwear
- longsleeve shirt
- skirt or light pants
- swimsuit
- bicycle gloves

Other items:

- medium-sized towel
- flashlight and batteries
- diary
- corkscrew
- toothbrush/comb/etc.
- first-aid kit and basic medicines
- film and camera
- lip balm and sunscreen
- plastic map case
- compass

- vitamins
- highlighter
- collapsible water container for use in campgrounds

- money belt or neck passport case
- rope (for hanging clothes or tying baguettes)
- bungee cords or straps

A youth hostel membership card is a must if you are traveling on a tight budget. Even if you are planning to camp, hostels are places to turn to in bad weather and in cities, where they are usually more favorably located than campgrounds. Some hostels are worth a stay just for their unique character. You can sleep in castles, converted churches, and manor houses. Many have rooms reserved for couples only. Hostels are not limited to students or youths (except in Bavaria and Switzerland), providing an option for all budget travelers. Day-by-day entries in each cycling tour will detail these options.

If you are under 26, an international student or youth identity card will make you eligible for discounts on some travel expenses and entry fees. Both ID cards and hostel memberships are available through CIEE (see Chapter 5, *Planning and Preparations*).

Finally, a good general guidebook will be useful. If you are planning on staying in private rooms, there are many useful guides to hotels and bed and breakfasts all over Europe. The *Let's Go* series is your best bet in a comprehensive budget guide, although they are strongly oriented toward larger tourist centers and train travel. No matter how much information it may have, however, do not bury yourself in a guidebook and forget to do your own exploring—that goes for this guidebook as well.

Packing

When packing your bike, adhere to a systematic approach. The basic strategy is to pack your panniers evenly to maintain balance. Though some things will always go in the same place, daily variations in the amount of food and other items you are carrying can make a difference. Keep tools, first aid kit, and everything you may need during the day accessible. Run a trial packing run before you leave home to avoid an untimely surprise.

In heavy rain it is very difficult to keep your belongings dry. Lining each pannier with one big bag just collects water at the bottom. Instead, wrap each piece of clothing in its own plastic bag and leave a sacrificial sock in each pannier to absorb moisture quickly, before it reaches your other belongings. A heavy duty garbage bag will protect your exposed sleeping bag. I became quite the plastic bag queen, but my things were usually dry even after days of rain.

Repairing Your Bicycle

Most likely, the worst problem you will encounter on your trip will be a flat tire. There is no need to carry bulky, specialized tools that will probably never be needed, such as headset or axle wrenches, chainring and chain tools. Even if you are doing a marathon tour you are better off saving the weight, taking the chance, and paying for a professional repair if necessary. The best protection is prevention. Keep your bicycle clean and running smoothly, and you can expect it to perform well. If by chance something does break, use some ingenuity to get to the nearest town and bicycle shop. If a local cyclist passes you he will most likely be willing and able to help. Bicycling is very popular in Europe, and small bicycle shops abound. You may have a problem getting new parts if you have a Japanese or American bicycle but the chance is slight and there will always be a way to resolve the problem. For example, a broken Japanese headset was easily replaced with Italian parts while we were in Innsbruck.

Whenever I suspected a problem with my bicycle and could not solve it, I stopped at a bicycle shop for help. After several months of touring I was especially concerned about how true my wheels were (spokes under a heavy load can bend and eventually break if not corrected). Many shopkeepers at first had no interest in helping an American cyclist who did not speak their language well. When I explained that I was alone and cycling across Europe, they seemed to have more respect for me and became very interested and helpful. I was rarely charged for a repair—from a quick trueing job to replacement bolts for those that had rattled loose from a rack. Even if you do not speak the language, you can make your undertaking clear by stating the name of your eventual destination. Be creative and you will overcome any problems that may come up.

CHAPTER 4

Accommodations and Meals

There are several options available when it comes to ways to take care of the essentials—food and shelter. If you have enough money to spend, the continent is dotted with good restaurants, hotels, and other accommodations. On the other hand, if you are on a tight budget, roadside picnics and self-cooked meals can be combined with camping or hostelling.

Camping

Besides being your least expensive option, camping is also in many ways the most convenient. Many towns run inexpensive municipal campgrounds and private operations abound, particularly in popular vacation spots. Most maps indicate campgrounds, making planning easy. As a cyclist with a compact tent you will never be turned away as you might be at a hostel or inn. Even if the campground you find yourself in is closed, it is usually possible to camp there anyway if you keep a low profile.

Camping out in Venice, Italy

Camping in Europe is not a back-to-nature experience. Your bicycle and tent will be dwarfed by huge campers in semi-permanent arrangements, wehre televisions and refrigerators are commonplace. Generally campgrounds provide hot and cold water in central toilet blocks—although you may be charged an additional fee for a hot shower. Toilet paper is not always supplied, especially in French campgrounds. The most deluxe operations have laundry facilities, small kitchens, and water taps at each site. These features are summarized in the daily tour listings, along with the rates.

Campgrounds usually charge a per person fee and a tent fee, making it more economical to travel in groups of two or more since you can split the tent fee. The price can range from as low as fifty cents to as high as ten dollars per person. Facilities will rate accordingly. As a cyclist, you may often be granted a substantial reduction if you ask nicely. If that does not work, ask for a student discount and you may get one for your persistence. It is also possible to negotiate a reduction for staying more than one night. If there is no attendant on duty when you enter the site, you may even get a free stay for the night.

You are almost always asked to leave your passport at the campground office. There are three ways to avoid this: first, campgrounds will accept a document called *Camping Carnet* instead of your passport. This may be obtained through a national camping association. I was unable to get one before I left and had to resort to alternate methods of keeping my passport. Try to pay immediately with the excuse that you will be leaving very early the next morning. You can also claim that you do not have your passport (left it at a friend's house, etc.) and offer them another ID instead. Your passport should be safe in the office, but it is more comforting to keep it with you.

The only time that a campground may not be a good option is in cities where they are often located far from the center and sights. In this case, consider a hostel or private room, but check on availability beforehand. There are notable exceptions, however, such as the convenient municipal campsites in Vienna, Munich, and Venice, where you can take advantage of budget rates and quick public transportation into the heart of the city.

Many people free camp when cycling by asking a resident's permission to camp on his property. This is usually safe and often a good way to meet the people of a country. As a solo traveler I was reluctant to free camp, however minimal the risk might have been. Camping in established sites may cost, but it assures you the convenience and comfort of showers and water at the end of a tiring day. Depending on how social you are, campgrounds sometimes provide the opportunity to meet other cyclists as well. At the same time, free is always the best option for your budget. Consider the choices and do what is best for you.

Hostels

Youth hostels are a good value but not as inexpensive as you might think. The average price is eight dollars per night, which can add up considerably over a period of time. Some offer meals at extra cost, and many hostels on the continent require you to pay for breakfast. Only members may stay at hostels, and you need to take your own sleeping gear. There is no age limit in most countries. Hostels can be crowded and even full in the summer. The vast majority of the people you meet will be Eurailers, which can become quite routine.

Hostels are best used in cities and in bad weather. The England and Wales tour is based on hostel accommodations, for example. In addition, there are many exceptional hostels that you should consider just for their unique setting or character. St. Briavel's Castle hostel in Wales was once King John's hunting lodge; the Verona hostel is a fifteenth-century villa decorated with beautiful frescoes; the Carcassonne hostel is situated within the fortress's walls next to five-star hotels. Some hostels allow you to camp on their grounds at a low rate and still use the indoor facilities (dayroom, kitchen, showers, etc.). Stop in any hostel to pick up a brief guide to that country's hostels in other cities.

Private rooms

Usually private rooms are the last option, unfortunately, for a cyclist on a budget. On many back roads and quiet streets of Europe, you will see rooms advertised. If you have no choice due to weather or a full city hostel, or if you simply need a break, talk the price down as far as you can. Even the cyclist's discount story might work. Most countries also require the legal price of a room to be posted on its door for you to see.

If you are traveling with one or more companions, splitting the cost of a room may be less expensive than a hostel, and in this case is worth your consideration. In less expensive countries such as Southern or Eastern Europe it is also possible to get a room at a low rate. The main disadvantage in each of these cases, however, is the often frustrating search for an inexpensive and available room.

Grocery Shopping

You will quickly get a feel for grocery shopping in a foreign country, from the specialties of the region to price ranges and store types. While American-style supermarkets are becoming widespread, shopping in Europe is still mostly based on small one-item shops. These often have quality goods and an astonishing selection of their specialty, but at higher prices than supermarkets. Outdoor markets often have great deals on fresh produce, although you may be expected to buy at least a kilo at a time.

The biggest problem with shopping in Europe is adjusting to local business hours. Large and small stores may close for lunch, and many stores close for the weekend—even in cities. Be aware of the local custom and be prepared. It is difficult to keep track of days while cycling, but if you are not careful you may find yourself going hungry occasionally. In England, for example, you will have to go shopping every Friday for weekend food; in Austria, on Saturday. This will weigh you down considerably but there is no avoiding it unless you can afford to eat out on weekends.

In order to keep your load as light as possible you will have to shop every day or even twice a day. At lunch, before stores begin to close, you can pick up some bread and drinks, and toward the end of the day look for a store to buy dinner and breakfast items. Keep something on hand for emergencies but do not weigh yourself down.

Eating

Although everyone has different eating habits, there are some basic formulas to keep in mind. First, since food is the fuel that enables you to power your bicycle over hills and long distances, you can expect your food intake to increase dramatically. Eat plenty of foods that will supply you with both quick energy and endurance. Well-balanced meals are also very important in keeping healthy. While it is difficult to prepare many types of food with limited resources, try to supply yourself with a little of everything. Fresh meat, for example, can be expensive and hard to prepare, but you can substitute cold cuts and pâté.

The best foods to base your diet on are compact non-perishables that you can combine with small purchases of fresh goods. Two items I found especially practical were canned pâté, in France, and dried soup mix. Pâté on a baguette with tomato and cheese makes a delicious lunch, and a few extra vegetables bought at a market added to packaged soup can make an excellent meal. I had soup for dinner nearly every day, and it never got routine because I experimented with a lot of ingredients and soup types. It is also very satisfying to have a big meal at the end of a long day. Keep a lightweight soup mix on hand for emergencies, such as those weekends when you forget to shop ahead.

Jam is cheap and available in small quantities that can last a few days without being a burden. Eggs bought by the half dozen can be hard-boiled immediately and then eaten for breakfast, at lunch in a sandwich, or at dinner in soup. Staples such as salt, pepper, tea, or coffee are good to have on hand, as is a supply of multivitamins. Powdered drink mix is very handy—water quenches your thirst but will not tickle your taste buds. Drink mixes are sometimes hard to find or are expensive in Europe—it may pay to bring some from home. Every country and region of Europe has its own distinctive breads. French bread is light and crusty, while Italian bread is floury and full of air. (I think Italian bakers should be sent to French schools.) In Austria, my favorite bread was Ankerbrot, an accurately named two-ton loaf, also available in the one-ton variety.

These are ideas that worked for me. Keep an eye out for what is available and be creative with it. One of the most enjoyable parts of a culture is its food, so be daring and experiment with new foods and combinations of your own.

CHAPTER 5

Planning and Preparation

The better prepared you are, the smoother your trip will be. Research the area you will be visiting well and have an idea of some specific things you'd like to see. Some knowledge of the language is helpful but not essential. Write to the tourist information offices of each country you will visit; addresses are included under each country's listing in Chapter 6, *Country Information*. Ask specific questions regarding cycling and any other interests you have.

Know your equipment before you leave home. If you have never cycled before, try a short local trip. If you are unable to, do not hesitate to throw yourself into bicycle touring from day one anyway. You may have a bumpy adjustment period but things will sort themselves out surprisingly well. Concentrate on routines when packing and planning to help organize yourself. I had never been touring before my first day in England, but within a few days I had the techniques well in hand and enjoyed the experience right from the start.

Although most youth hostels can enroll you on the spot, I recommend you apply for hostel membership and ID cards in advance. The Council for International Educational Exchange

Siesta time: Taking a break in Cordes, France

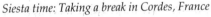

(CIEE) has a travel service that can provide you with these. The address of the main office is: CIEE, 205 East 42nd Street, New York, NY, 10017 (212/661-1414).

Pack everything a few times to be sure you are taking a reasonable amount of equipment and that your baggage attaches comfortably on the bicycle. Your panniers should not be bulging at the seams. Do not let yourself become burdened by taking along unneeded information. Photocopy the relevant pages of this and other guides and leave the rest of the book at home.

Get a box from a bicycle store for your bicycle and equipment. You will have to remove one or both wheels, the seat, and pedals, and loosen the handlebars to turn them. Be sure to also take the tools to reassemble your bicycle. Panniers and other gear can be packed into the same box. Use a sleeping bag to pad the bicycle frame. Do not put loose items directly into the box—they will be lost if the box is punctured, and airlines do not take responsibility for anything but the bicycle itself. Tape the box securely and label it. Take spare tape to the airport in case it is opened to be searched by airline personnel.

Most airlines accept bicycle-sized boxes as baggage at no extra charge. Find this out ahead of time. Many airlines actually supply official bicycle boxes at airports. This will be a handy service on your return trip. Ask at your airline's desk once you are in Europe.

If you are traveling for an extended period of time you can arrange for mail to be sent to you (see the section on Marathon Tours).

For emergencies, it is a good idea to have an extra source of money such as a credit card. Leave photocopies of your valuables at home and take travelers checks receipts and a copy of your passport to be kept separately.

Everybody has last minute doubts, when suddenly the excitement of planning is forgotten as your departure day approaches. I was worried about my flight, shipping my bicycle, arriving, buying food, finding my way around, and every possible aspect of touring. Think of the things you will see and try to convince yourself that you will have an excellent trip, and you will.

Route Planning

The tours outlined in the second part of this book will save you from having to plan a route on foreign ground. If you are striking out on your own or combining parts of these tours with other areas, however, you will have to do some extra research. With a good map and some preparation you will be able to outline an itinerary fairly quickly.

Some people prefer to travel with absolutely no plan at all. I met a Welsh cyclist who was navigating France by heading south, he said, "with the sun in my eyes." If you are restricted to a tighter schedule than 'the next couple of months,' it is a good idea to sketch out a basic route that covers an area of interest to you before you leave home. Pick a region suited to your cycling style—a compact area with many points of interest, a large undeveloped region that will require longer stretches on your bicycle, or a combination of both. A large scale map of an entire country is useful in planning and will help maintain your geographical perspective while cycling with more detailed, regional maps.

Buy a map when you arrive in the country you are visiting. This eliminates the problem of finding it from abroad and increases the available selection. A map with a scale of 1:400,000 or less is the most useful, and will include secondary roads, some local roads, and preferably a good listing of camp-grounds and other points of value to you as a cyclist. Do not get overly specific maps, since you simply do not need so much information, and they will involve much greater cost than more general ones. You will want to stay on quiet, well-kept secondary roads and avoid twisting country lanes that often do not have any signs. Basic 1 : 400,000 to 1 : 200,000 maps will guide you well without causing you unnecessary confusion on these minor roads.

Maps with symbols for vista points, prominent landmarks, and (especially) campgrounds save you the trouble of buying a separate guide. Michelin maps are available in almost every bookstore and souvenir shop in Europe. They include all these important features and are very easy to read. If these are unavailable or not detailed enough, choose a map produced by the national auto association. For example, Michelin only had a 1 : 1,000,000 scale map of Italy at the time I cycled there. The 1 : 350,000 Touring Club Italiano map was more suitable for bicycle touring.

I have included a list of suggested maps in the individual tour summaries. Often you may have to use more than one map to cover one tour. These are only recommendations based on the maps I used and may not be the best choice if you take an alternate route. The listings are intended as a sample of what is available and as basic guidelines only. There is a broad range of maps readily available throughout Europe, and you will have no problem finding those suitable for your particular tour.

With the start and end points of your trip in mind, trace a route on your map by connecting campgrounds or other accommodations with points of interest. Keep your daily goals reasonable and follow secondary roads. Use a highlighter to outline this route, and you are on your way. A front handlebar bag with a plastic map viewing case lets you check the directions without stopping to take out the map. Most people plan the day's route the previous evening or in the morning before setting out. Depending on their sizes, maps usually cost between three and five dollars.

Distances in continental Europe are measured in kilometers—and even the allegedly conservative English have recently adopted the metric system. One mile is 1.61 km. To convert kilometers to miles, multiply by 0.6 (or, more accurately, 0.62). The average day's ride in the suggested tours is about 50 miles (80 km). This is a good balance between covering large sections of countryside and having the time to sightsee in greater detail. I usually cycled 30 miles in the morning, stopped in a place of interest for a few hours at lunchtime, and quickly covered the remaining miles in the afternoon. I covered more than half the total distance by lunch so that the afternoon ride would seem shorter. This still left plenty of time to relax and sightsee in late afternoon and to later enjoy a big cooked dinner.

In areas where the sights are more concentrated, daily mileage should be lower to allow more time off the bicycle. The tours in this book include tips on many accommodations options throughout each day, leaving you the opportunity to shorten the ride if you wish. My longest cycling day was 103 miles in Wales—a big mistake that was corrected in the Northern England and Wales tour. Once I was in good cycling condition, I found up to 60 or 70 miles fairly easy but avoided covering such long distances in order to spend more time sightseeing or simply resting. Every person has a unique pace and amount of endurance, but most bicycle tourists agree that a 50-mile goal is optimal in many cases.

Bicycle touring is not just transport from point A to B; it is enjoying getting from A to B and experiencing a little of everything along the way. Do not push yourself into a strict schedule that decreases the pleasure of cycling. While you should plan a route ahead of time, remember to keep some flexibility for unplanned stops at interesting sights or for those days when you just do not feel like pedaling on. Plan ahead before crossing an international border or entering large cities—a shorter ride and earlier arrival time will help ease the transition into a new culture and simplify navigating urban areas.

If you are ever in doubt, ask a local for directions. Do not hesitate, even if you do not speak the language. Just state your destination with as good an accent as possible and look confused. You will have more success asking men for road directions than women. This is not a sexist comment but a fact. Men are usually the drivers of the family and usually more familiar with the roads and alternative routes. This is particularly valuable since you will probably want to find lesser-known secondary roads.

To save you from learning the hard way, here are some strategies to use in route planning. First, rivers and river valleys are features of the land that you can use to your advantage. Valleys usually mean smooth, gradual ascents and descents. Roads that run alongside rivers are usually fairly level and therefore save you the trouble of cycling over hill after hill. Because rivers often meander, though, these roads can be longer than a direct route but are still worth considering. The exceptions to be aware of are steep valleys and broad rivers with strong headwinds.

Following a river in its downstream direction will also work in your favor because you will be losing elevation overall and will not be steadily climbing upriver. This may not always create a noticeable difference but is a good rule of thumb.

Finally, in areas where traffic may be a problem, look for secondary roads that closely parallel highways. These are usually very direct routes where traffic is light because most drivers will choose the faster highway. Even a primary road that parallels an autobahn can be quiet for the same reason.

Alternative Activities and Transportation

For all the unique advantages of bicycle touring, it is important to recognize its limitations as well as your own. Alternative activities and means of transportation provide the opportunity to take a short break from cycling and appreciate the countryside in a different way.

The European train system is extensive and reliable. Although the cost and convenience of doing so varies widely (see the individual country listings), it is possible to combine cycling with train travel for a variety of reasons. If you have a limited amount of time but want to cover a considerable distance, you can take the train to connect distant points or to avoid difficult terrain. One cyclist I met only had three weeks to cycle in Britain and trains enabled him to spend a week each in Scotland, England, and Wales.

Trains can quickly get you from your point of arrival to the region you will be cycling. You can fly into Paris and take a train to Normandy, for example, without having to cycle that distance. Commuter trains will bring you into the center of a city so that you will not have to risk riding on a crowded road. Trains allow you to take a one-way trip as well. For example, after cycling from Vienna to Budapest, you can avoid cycling back by taking the train.

The disadvantages of train travel are a certain degree of inflexibility of routes and schedules. You will also have to pay to bring along your bicycle—another expense. Certain trains may not even accept bicycles, so you will have to wait for the next train or have your bicycle shipped as soon as possible. Even though arranging to transport your bicycle may involve these complications, the railway travel is still a safe and enjoyable means to exceed the limits of a bicycle's pace.

There are many regions that deserve a more thorough exploration than the limits of cycling allow. Put your bicycle aside, and take the time to hike some local trails. I left my bicycle with friends, locked in storage rooms in hostels, or at the baggage check at train stations. You will enjoy the change of pace and have the opportunity to observe the area from a closer and quieter perspective.

Weather Conditions

You will not always be cycling in ideal conditions. While bad weather can sometimes be a problem, it does not necessarily have to ruin your day. Do everything you can to prepare for, and where possibel avoid, bad weather by planning ahead. England in April, for example, is not a good plan. You should not, however, limit yourself to warm, sunny areas just out of fear of a chance storm since you may be missing out on a beautiful area. In unavoidable situations do what is safe and keep a positive attitude.

Rain can happen just about anywhere. If it is a brief shower, you will be able to take shelter and wait it out. This is usually the case and not a problem. The problem comes when you encounter a storm that is there to stay, which often happens in the mountains. After weeks of dry sunshine, I cycled into Austria and hit a ten-day rainy period. In this situation, you must simply persevere if you do not want to hole up indefinitely. The exercise of cycling will keep you warm, and unless the roads are actually unsafe there is no reason not to continue enjoying the ride and scenery. Those days in Austria were very wet, but still beautiful, and that region remains one of my favorites. Camping in these conditions, however, can be trying. It is not worth becoming sick in a soggy tent. If the weather gets to this point, it is better to find inexpensive indoor accommodations.

Cold weather is not ideal for cycling either. Consider indoor accommodations and be prepared. You will rarely be cold while cycling. The problem comes when you stop moving. Take breaks in sheltered areas or indoors. Dehydration can also be a problem when it is cold. Remember to drink often. Do not push your limits. After a few weeks of intense cold in the Alps, we finally took a train south to resume cycling there and did not regret the decision.

Snow should not be a problem, but remains a possibility in the mountains and in the early spring and late fall. Again, good

Signs of a hard day's work

planning is your best bet. I actually did cycle through snow during one April day in England. If you run into a chance storm as I did you should try to wait it out until the conditions improve. I was unable to stay in the hostel for an additional night, so I made a cold, twenty-mile dash to the next closest hostel. Again, do what is safest and persevere.

Headwinds can be very frustrating. They are often present along large rivers and coastlines. There is nothing you can do about a prevailing headwind except change your route or stick it out.

Extremely hot weather can be difficult to endure while cycling. A good strategy is to start early and stop before mid-day heat reaches its peak. That time can be used to sight-see or relax until it is cool enough to resume in the afternoon. You can get twice as far cycling between seven and ten in the morning than you can by cycling at noon. Do not push your limits and be aware of what your body is telling you. Drink often (fruit juices and sugar-sweetened drinks are better energy sources than water), take frequent breaks, use sunscreen, and stop if you feel ill.

Road Conditions

The quality of the roads in the various European countries varies widely. Use the most up-to-date maps available in route planning. Generally secondary roads marked in yellow on maps are well maintained and have minimal local traffic. These roads are usually but not always well-marked. Ask for directions if you are in doubt. If you do not speak the language, simply say the name of your destination or a town on the way and you will be understood. Show the person your map if it helps or use sign language, an amazingly successful method. In the rare case that you are absolutely lost and there is no one to help you out, a compass may prove useful at least to get you pointed in the right direction. Mine proved useful several times in the confusing network of isolated backroads of England and France.

Busy roads should be avoided unless you have absolutely no choice. A rear-view mirror is useful in traffic. Rather than cycling on the very edge of the road, ride a few feet in from the edge to discourage cars from trying to squeeze by. When approaching large cities you may want to take a local train into the center to avoid these roads. Regardless of traffic conditions, always signal before stopping or turning, as much out of courtesy to your cycling partner as for road safety.

Cycling in the Mountains

One of the greatest challenges of cycling is touring in the mountain regions. Although it can be extremely demanding, mountain riding is the most rewarding kind of trip. A good bicycle means a good ride. The best pedaling strategy is to stay in a low gear and spin (pedaling quickly at a low resistance). Mountains like the Alps can be tough. You may often face climbs of twenty miles or more and mountain passes several thousand feet in elevation. This is not to say it cannot be done. With some determination and the right gear anyone can succeed. Your rewards will be well worth your effort—spectacular scenery and fantastically long descents.

There are considerably fewer roads to choose from in the mountains. Take secondary roads whenever possible even though they may involve longer distances or climbs (see the section on Route Planning). Cycling through tunnels can be extremely frightening and dangerous, so avoid them if at all possible. I carried a strip of reflective band with me, which I took out before entering long, unavoidable tunnels.

Plan shorter days when cycling in mountainous regions and include frequent rest days to let your muscles recuperate. It does not take long to develop strong legs. I threw myself into mountain cycling after touring on absolutely flat terrain and adjusted within a few days. Feed yourself well and take the time to take in your surroundings. Your effort will be well rewarded. You will come away from these experiences with a strong impression of the region and a new appreciation of your capabilities.

Language

One of the interesting things about Europe is the wide variety of people and cultures in a relatively small area. Obviously it is advantageous and courteous to speak the language of your hosts. If you are unable to, it is not as big a problem as it may seem. Most Europeans speak more than one language, often including English. Ask politely if they speak English before launching into your question. Even if they do not, Europeans are usually accustomed to hearing different languages and are therefore more open to communication by other means.

Sign language is the simplest and most effective means of communication. Pointing and counting on your fingers when shopping makes your request perfectly clear, and making motions for left or right will clarify road directions.

Knowing a few key words is helpful. To get you started, 'Hello' and 'Thank you' (the two magic words) are listed with each tour in the appropriate languages. If you listen carefully you will soon pick up additional words such as numbers, left and right, where, etc. With concentration, you will usually be able to follow basic directions in a foreign tongue. I speak no Italian but was able to understand rapid directions to a youth hostel in Padua. If in doubt, follow the first part of the directions and stop to ask again. Waiting in lines can be a good educational opportunity since everyone is usually waiting for the same thing and a few key words and routines will be repeated.

Another tactic is to try a third language. For example, I found French to be useful in Italy either because some people understood it or certain words were similar enough to their Italian counterparts to be clear. A knowledge of Spanish can also help you in Italy, and German is the most common second language in Yugoslavia, Hungary, Czechoslovakia, and in certain regions of other countries.

It is best to simplify your request as much as possible. Keep to the absolute minimum so that you do not confuse the person who is trying to help you. Saying that you are sending a letter to your friend in Milwaukee who is originally from New York will not get you a stamp any quicker. Try to think of different ways to say, describe, or sign the same thing so that if you are not understood at first you can try again.

Remember that you are the foreigner, and it is your responsibility to fit in as well as you can. Smile, be courteous, and remain patient.

CHAPTER 6

Country Information

While each bicycle tour description includes specific details regarding accommodations, terrain, and sights, this section provides a brief summary of cycling conditions and general facts about each country. It can be used as a quick reference guide to get you started in planning your trip and to let you know what to expect in terms of prices, alternatives, and so on.

Austria

Although most of Austria is mountainous, there are areas such as the northeast near Vienna and along the Danube that have much gentler terrain. The exceptionally well-kept bicycle path stretching from Vienna to Passau, Germany, along the Danube offers one opportunity to visit these areas without much difficulty. This is a popular route with many sights and services geared toward cyclists. Bicycle touring through the mountains is more demanding, but absolutely worth the effort, from the green south to the stunning Salzkammergut and Tyrol regions. You will not have a wide choice of roads in mountainous areas, and it is simply impossible in some cases to take a direct route between two points. The weather can be unpredictable at high elevations, so prepare for a variety of conditions. I encountered a period of bad weather in July that made me thankful to have a wool sweater and rain gear. Late April or May to mid-October are the limits of the cycling season in this mountainous, northern country.

Prices in Austria are high but services are excellent and speedy. If you are coming from Yugoslavia or Italy this can be quite a shock. Stores are generally open every day of the week except Sunday and few close for lunch. Campgrounds are well kept and organized, and I found that most included free showers and sometimes extras such as kitchens and pools. Hostels are another good option. All include breakfast and many will give you a separate family room if one is available (even for unmarried couples). There are also private zimmer (rooms) advertised all over Austria, but most are on the expensive side.

To make an overseas telephone call, go to a post office. You can charge the call collect or pay when finished, but it is impossible to make a calling card call. The most common second language in Austria is English, making communication easier at banks, post offices, train stations, etc. Having your bicycle shipped on trains is easy, although you will be charged a fee and must remove all panniers and accessories.

For more information, contact the helpful Austrian Tourist Office at 500 Fifth Avenue, Suite 2009-2022, New York, NY 10110.

England and Wales

To an American or Australian visitor, one of the most surprising characteristics of both England and Wales is the incredible variation of terrain and local flavor. You will encounter unique accents, attitudes, and landscapes in each district and observe astonishing differences between closely neighboring areas.

English roads are well marked and numbered, and drivers are usually courteous. Remember to keep left. All roads numbered with three digits are perfect for cycling, being very quiet. Two-digit and single-digit 'A' roads are to be avoided, even if it means extra miles. One common feature of the British road system is roundabouts. The best tactic to take when riding around one of these circular thoroughfares is to hunker down and get around as fast as possible. Point your right arm into the center of the circle until you are ready to exit to prevent cars from cutting you off.

Britain has a very well developed hostel network that offers meals, private family rooms, and extra activities. All British hostels have well-equipped kitchens for your use. You can camp at many hostels for half the regular adult price and still use all the indoor facilities. Fees vary based on the quality of each hostel and your age. Hostels are a good choice for touring in Britain since the weather is frequently damp, particularly in coastal areas. There are also many campgrounds of varying quality throughout England and Wales, although some are open on a seasonable basis only. Michelin maps show the location of many campgrounds.

Shop ahead on Friday because stores are closed all weekend. Prices are generally moderate and are higher in the south than in other parts of England.

Britain is the easiest part of Europe in which to combine bicycle and train travel. With the conductor's permission (i.e., as long as he does not do anything to stop you) you can personally load your bicycle, panniers and all, into the guard's van (the only car with no seats in it, either in the middle or at the very end of the train) at no charge. Some fast inter-city trains may not accept bicycles at certain times, so check ahead.

The language spoken may still be English, but for Americans, there are a few appropriate phrases to keep in mind: first, you are *cycling* around Britain,' not *biking*. Intersections are *crossroads* and overpasses are *flyovers*. Roads are *signposted* for a particular destination. And, finally, don't ask for the restrooms, but for the *toilet* or the *loo*, to be perfectly clear.

Britain has a well-deserved reputation for rain. Summer is the best time of year to tour, although there is still no guarantee of a clear, dry ride. Nearly every hostel has a drying room, and for good reason. Try to think of the weather as a cultural experience. There is no reason to stop cycling and enjoying the countryside if it rains, unless you encounter a bad storm (see the Conditions section in Chapter 5, *Planning and Preparation*). There are exceptional periods, of course. Late in April I spent one week in Southern England, which was the hottest place in Europe at the time, beating out even Athens in temperature.

You can reach an American operator directly from any pay telephone at any time by dialing 0800-89-0011. The address of the British Tourist Authority is: 40 W. 57th Street, 3rd floor, New York, NY 10019. Britain has a good information network, with tourist offices in every city and most small towns.

France

France offers the widest cycling possibilities of any country in Europe. You can cycle flat river valleys, secluded woods, and mountains. The range of historical sights is vast, including prehistoric monuments, medieval cities, and points of interest from more recent periods. Cycling is very popular in France and as a cyclist you will have the respect of many people (even if they do not understand why you have chosen to tour rather than to race). There are many bicycle shops throughout the country.

France also has an incredible number of secondary roads that are very quiet yet well marked. If anything, you will have problems choosing a route from day to day due to the endless combinations of side roads available. For this reason, Michelin maps of France are based on a 1 : 200,000 scale, which detail landmarks (water towers, viewpoints, etc.) and campgrounds.

Camping can be extremely inexpensive, although the popularity of tourist centers such as the Riviera, other coastal areas, and the Loire Valley drive prices up. Most French campgrounds do not provide toilet paper or even modern toilets (one of the sacrifices of budget travel). Often municipal campsites are located near the town stadium (stade) and public pool complex (piscine). It is usually a safe bet to follow signs to these facilities if you are looking for the campground.

Northern France in particular can be cold and wet in early spring. You might opt for indoor accommodations if you choose to tour at this time. Late May, June, and September are the best months to tour since the weather is good and summer crowds are absent.

Shopping in France is very convenient since stores remain open on Sunday mornings. Many will close briefly for lunch but others only look closed—often the attendant is relaxing in the back and will come out when you enter. Stores do not supply bags or may charge for them. A long baguette-sized bag is a good buy because it simplifies tying the bread onto your rear rack. Baguettes are long, thin French breads of about 100 g. I was consuming so much food to keep up my energy that I soon shifted from eating a baguette at lunch to a 'pain' (200 g) and finally on to a *gros pain* (400 g). Stuff them full of goodies and enjoy.

To ship a bicycle by train you must remove all your gear and check it with a baggage handler. A fee is charged and your bicycle may take up to three days to arrive since it does not always travel on your train. One surprising exception was the high-speed TGV, which brought my bicycle from Nice to Paris at the same time I traveled. If you plan to ship your bicycle by train, check for restrictions a few days in advance to avoid frustrating delays.

You can reach an American operator by dialing 19-0011 from a pay telephone. You can reach any number in the United States from most public telephones by preceding the area code by 001. For more information on specific regions of France, contact the Government Tourist Office at 610 Fifth Avenue, New York, NY 10020-2452.

Germany

Bicycle touring is popular in Germany, with whole families taking weekend rides together. The Rhine and Mosel valleys are favored destinations, with easy riverside cycling and numerous interesting sights. Many cyclists also follow the Castle or Romantic roads, tourist routes with a central theme. Bavaria and the area around Munich offer more strenuous but rewarding bicycling in a region of beautiful mountains dotted with small towns and castles. The Black Forest in the south is another excellent destination, though also challenging. Donaueschingen in the Black Forest is the starting point of the Danube River and an excellent bicycle tour to Austria and Hungary. Many cyclists are also beginning to explore former East Germany, though facilities for travelers are not yet fully developed. The last word on road conditions is that road crews are paving away as quickly as possible.

There are well-kept campgrounds all over Germany, many providing extra facilities such as laundry and kitchens. Germany's youth hostel system is extensive and a number of castles have been converted for this use. To stay in any hostel in Bavaria, you must be under 26. Look for 'Zimmer frei' (room for rent) signs to rent a room. Germany's prices, like Austria's, are generally high. Many Germans speak English embarrassingly well. You may be frustrated by this if you are trying to practice your German, but there are times when it is helpful.

Bicycles may be shipped on night trains for a fee. It is a good idea to protect your bicycle as many Germans do by getting a carton at a bicycle shop--these fit around your bicycle's frame without requiring disassembly and still allow the wheels to rotate.

You can reach any number in the United States from most public telephones (and all private ones) in the western part of Germany by preceding the area code by 001. Calls placed during weekends and between 6 p.m and 7 a.m. weekdays are charged at a reduced rate. To reach an American operator, or to use an American telephone card, dial 0130-0010.

The address of the German National Tourist Office is 747 Third Avenue, New York, NY 10017.

Hungary

Hungary is one of the most liberal Eastern European countries and one of the easiest to travel in. For example, there is no required daily currency exchange as in other countries. Visas are no longer required for travel to Hungary.

Bring a substantial amount of cash (dollars, schillings, or deutsche marks) wherever you travel in Eastern Europe. You may at any time incur expenses for which only cash will be accepted. This is due to the poor standing of eastern currencies and the consequent need for hard cash.

The terrain along the Duna (Danube) in Hungary is very well suited to bicycle touring. Another scenic area is Lake Balaton, west of Budapest. Budapest itself is a monumental city of great historical interest. Palaces and government buildings form impressive ranks along each bank of the Duna. In similarities such as the grand scale of both Vienna and Budapest and the shape of church domes demonstrate the lasting influences of the once united Austro-Hungarian Empire.

The Danube bicycle tour is very popular, and because most cyclists ship their bicycles back to the west by train, this is an easy process. Buying your passenger ticket, on the other hand, takes time (see Vienna to Budapest tour information). Be sure to take care of this as soon as possible. Keep all your exchange receipts to show when leaving the country--while there is no required minimum amount, you must prove that you exchanged a reasonable sum legally.

While cycling in Hungary, avoid very small roads that are in bad condition and not well signed. For this reason it is not necessary to have a very detailed map. I used a 1:750,000 map in Hungary with no problem at all.

Campgrounds abound in vacation areas. Inexpensive private rooms are another option, but vacancies can be scarce at peak travel times.

Hungary: Cycling along the Danube river

Stores are closed on Sundays and services are generally good. As in Yugoslavia, you will find a sufficient number of goods, if not much variety. Products and services are incredibly inexpensive, giving your budget a chance to recover from the high cost of travel in Austria.

The Danube bike tour is very popular, and because most cyclists ship their bikes back to the west by train, this is an easy process.

Keep all your exchange receipts to show when leaving the country: while there is no required minimum amount, you may be asked to prove that you exchanged a reasonable sum legally.

Contact the Hungarian National Tourist Office for more information on tourism and travel restrictions, as well as things to see in Hungary. The address is: IBUSZ, 630 Fifth Avenue, Suite 2455, New York, NY 10111.

Ireland

Friendly people and beautiful scenery attract many travelers to Ireland. Though the weather is not always good, bicycle touring is one of the best ways to visit Ireland, a country best appreciated at a slow pace. Cycling will bring you close to the rolling green hills, quiet towns, and warm, open people of Ireland's different counties. Quiet side roads and an excellent network of tourist services will help your trip to go smoothly.

Ireland's excellent tourist offices can give you information and help reserve rooms in the countless bed and breakfast establishments all over the country. For the budget traveler, a better option is the Independent Youth Hostels of Ireland, which have little in common with the often loud, crowded, and impersonal hostels of other areas. These are usually small, friendly places run by their individual owners, each doing his or her best to provide comfortable, reasonably priced accommodations to travelers they are genuinely interested to meet. Many have private rooms and allow camping at a reduced cost with full use of kitchen and common room facilities. Campgrounds are not as conveniently located or widespread as B&Bs or hostels.

Trains connect major points throughout Ireland, though not always directly. To ship your bicycle you must pay a fee and load it onto the 'guard's van' (luggage car area) yourself. Even the smallest town in Ireland seems to have several small grocery stores open seven days a week with some variations

47

on hours as convenient to the management (some are also open late at night).

To reach an American operator from Ireland dial 1-800-55-00-00. For more information, write to the Irish Tourist Board at 590 5th Avenue, New York, NY 10036.

Italy

Italy is very mountainous, including the northern Alps and a high ridge running the length of the country. The broad Po Valley in the north, however, is absolutely flat from Milan to Venice and Trieste. Italy is one of the greatest treasure chests of Europe, with an extraordinary assemblage of artistic wonders, from Greek and Roman times up to the present day. There is no shortage of museums, historic sights, and scenery in Italy.

Despite the bad reputation of Italian drivers, you should not expect worse conditions than in any other European country. I found that even speed-demon drivers had a good deal of respect for me as a cyclist and usually gave me plenty of room.

Prices are moderate to inexpensive, and more so as you travel south. Stores are closed on Sundays and at midday. One of my favorite foods was dried tortellini, which is very convenient and makes an especially tasty, inexpensive, and easy dinner.

There are many campgrounds around Italy. Most are full of permanent residents with extensive caravan arrangements. Coastal sites are particularly popular and extremely expensive. Hostels include breakfast, but I was disappointed by the overall lack of facilities such as kitchens and common rooms. Pensions offer inexpensive rooms in every corner of Italy, an option to fall back on in cities.

Italians deserve their temperamental reputation. If you are not persistent in your request, you may never get what you want. Taking the train can truly be an ordeal, although it is theoretically possible. In one instance I was assured I could ship my bicycle from Finale Ligure, but when the time came the station manager began shouting at me in Italian for making this apparently unreasonable request. A helpful English-speaking girl shouted back and apparently won, and I eventually made it to Milan with my bicycle. In another instance, I was told by the baggage department not to ship my bicycle to Verona: "Oh, don't take the train. Ride your bicycle. It will only take a week." Be firm and good luck.

International telephone calls can be very frustrating because you must find a special telephone office. In certain areas you can sometimes reach an international operator directly from a pay telephone. The number varies, so inquire locally. For more information on cycling and sights, write to the Italian Government Tourist Office at 630 Fifth Avenue, Suite 1565, Rockefeller Center, New York, NY 10111.

Luxembourg

Luxembourg reinforced my theory that small countries are often the most interesting, especially for cyclists. Hundreds of castles, quiet woods, and endless fields are found throughout the Grand-Duchy of Luxembourg, with an excellent network of tourist services to help you enjoy them. Much of the country is very hilly, but an outstanding series of bicycle trails makes cycling a pleasure. Many of these trails are not simply a marked route along shoulders or back roads, but completely separate trails through the best of the countryside. There are trails running from the capital city of Luxembourg to Echternach, Luxembourg to Hesperange, Diekirch to Echternach and Vianden, Wiltz to Schleif, and Linger to Eischen.

French is the official language of Luxembourg, though most people use Luxembourgeois and also speak German and usually English. There are many campgrounds throughout Luxembourg (ask at any tourist office for a map guide) and ten youth hostels. Rooms for rent can be found in every major tourist town, but not always in the quiet countryside in between.

Bicycles must be checked for a fee by rail and are sent on the first train, even to other countries. Stores are open Tuesday to Saturday, except from noon to 2p.m. To reach an American operator dial 0-800-0111. Write for information to the Luxembourg National Tourist Office, 801 2nd Avenue, New York, NY 10017.

Spain

Spain is one of the most challenging countries to tour in Europe, due to a limited network of secondary roads and a lack of facilities for travelers outside the main centers of tourism, in addition to often difficult terrain. In summer, temperatures routinely top 100F, adding another difficult factor. Often cyclists must share the road with heavy traffic, as there are simply few road choices throughout the country. Outside of tourist centers, there are few hotels, hostels, or campgrounds. Though a bicycle tour in Spain can be extremely rewarding, only those with a specific interest in bicycling in this country should do so, as the difficulties involved can add up to quite a heavy load.

Where they exist, Spanish tourist offices are excellent resources. Some suggested bicycle tours have been prepared by the national tourist service, though the guides are not available at every office all the time. One of these is the El Cid route from inland mountains to Valencia--this excellent guide (practically a book in itself) provides directions, local information, and elevation charts.

Stores are closed on Sundays and during siesta times. El Corte Ingles, a megastore chain found in all major cities, is a beacon for travelers. In addition to the supermarket and general store sections, there is a currency exchange, travel agent, and information office that distributes city plans in each. Prosperity and the growing tourism industry have pushed prices sky-high, making travel in Spain, once a great destination for budget travelers, very expensive.

RENFE, the railroad service, ships bicycles without charge for passengers holding valid tickets. Despite horror stories about bicycles lost for three weeks, I nervously shipped my bicycle several times and never had a problem. Go to the Paquet Expres office to check your bicycle. Be sure to buy a passenger ticket first and show it immediately to the baggage department. It is advisable to have specific information, such as brand and color of your bicycle, written on your receipt. Bicycles only travel by night trains, arriving the next morning, except over short distances, where they may be shipped more quickly. If you can partially dismantle your bicycle and carry it on (remove the front wheel and get a bag or cover it with a plastic garbage bag), you may be able to get by with it as carry-on luggage. Since buying intercity tickets in city rail stations can involve a wait in line of several hours, it is easier to buy the same ticket in a small town or through a travel agent.

Overseas telephone calls can be made from a Telefonica office in any large city. Write to the Tourist Office of Spain at 665 5th Avenue, New York, NY 10022.

Switzerland and Liechtenstein

While Switzerland is famous for its perfect mountain scenery, the northern part of the country where the Rhine flows can be surprisingly flat. Even in the mountains, you will often have easy cycling conditions along flat lakeside or alpine valleys and only occasional mountain passes. The entire Across the Alps Tour, for example, only crosses one true mountain pass. The highest passes are in the south of Switzerland, leading to Italy. The limited number of roads in the mountains will restrict your choice of route in the Alps. Avoid cycling in Switzerland from mid-October to late April or May as conditions can be very damp and cold.

Possible touring destinations include the Rhone Valley leading to Lac Leman and Geneva in the French-speaking part of Switzerland, or down the Rhine from its source high in the Alps. This guide details a tour across the country, from Zurich to Luzern, Interlaken, Bern, Lausanne, and Basel.

The Swiss train system is almost alarmingly efficient. Every train station readily accepts bicycles and will ship them reliably and quickly, making train and bicycle travel an easy if not cheap combination. This is the perfect option for the more casual cyclist with a limited time frame. The shipping cost for a bicycle within Switzerland is 8SF. Passenger tickets are expensive (Geneva to Zurich, for example, is close to $100). On slow, local trains, bicycles cost 5SF and you load them onto a baggage car yourself. If you use the train often, look into buying a one-month half-price card at any station. It will quickly pay off.

Most stores are closed on Sundays. All Swiss services and products are exceptional but expensive. Co-op and Migros are the two main supermarket chains. English is a common second, third, or fourth language in this remarkably diverse country. However, always remember to ask first if English is spoken to be polite.

Liechtenstein is practically part of Switzerland. You can expect comparable conditions and services. The only train line entering the principality is indirect. It is easiest to use the Sargans station a few kilometers away in Switzerland for quick connections to Zurich and other points. Because of the incredibly steep slope of the Rhine Valley at this point, you should take public transportation to upper parts of Liechtenstein (there is only one road) and limit cycling to the valley floor.

Get more information for both Switzerland and Liechtenstein from the Swiss National Tourist Office, 608 Fifth Avenue, New York, NY 10020.

Yugoslavia

Yugoslavia has long been an attractive destination for budget-conscious travelers, with its rural, old-world charm and low prices. You will need a visa to enter the country, which is usually automatically granted at border crossings at no charge. My cycling experience is limited to Slovenia, the northernmost part of the country. This is the wealthiest and most western-ized province of Yugoslavia, so you can expect other regions to have less advanced conditions.

Most of Yugoslavia is rural and undeveloped. The roads are often narrow and in bad condition. Try to strike a safe medium in planning your route—avoid minor roads, as they are usually unmarked and in exceptionally bad shape, and main roads because of the heavy truck traffic. The land is very dry and mountainous as you cycle inland from the Adriatic.

This country is an interesting mix of Eastern and Western Europe. Most of Yugoslavia runs at its own slow pace. All products are readily available, but lack the choice and quality of western goods. Yugoslavia is a very popular destination for many European tourists, creating the demand for services geared toward this industry. Tourist information offices oper-ate in many cities, and there is a full range of accommodations available in frequently visited areas. Each different ethnic group in Yugoslavia speaks its own language. German is the most common foreign language because of the number of North European tourists in Yugoslavia.

More information can be obtained from the Yugoslav Na-tional Tourist Office, 630 Fifth Avenue, Suite 280, New York, NY 10111.

Due to civil strife in Yugoslavia at the time of going to press (Spring 1992), it is advisable to check on the current conditions affecting travelers when planning your trip. Call (202) 647-5225 or write to The Department of State, Citizen's Emergency Center, Room 4811, 2201 C Street NW, Washington, DC 20520-4818.

Part II – Route Descriptions

The bicycle tours described on the following pages are carefully planned routes that cover much of Europe's countryside, its varied cultures, and historic areas. Suggested accommodations and services are based on budget travel, and options are listed in order of convenience and cost. Private rooms are not detailed unless there are no other alternatives, but you can feel secure in finding these higher grade options throughout all of Europe. Recommended touring times include cycling and sightseeing days, including suggested day trips, to provide an estimate of a reasonable time in which to see the area thoroughly.

I have also listed the maps that are easily available and useful to cyclists, but these are by no means the only choices (see the section on *Route Planning* in Chapter 5). The tour is then summarized to provide an overview of the region and travel conditions. The tours have day-by-day, detailed road directions, accommodations information, and sightseeing suggestions to guide you through unfamiliar territory. I enjoyed each of these routes for their distinctive characters on my cycling tour of Europe and wish you the same success.

Dachsteingruppe, Salzkammergut, Austria

The Rhine and Mosel Valleys

A ride along the Rhine and Mosel Rivers from Switzerland to Luxembourg via the Black Forest, Alsace, and Heidelberg.

Distance: 842 km (522 miles)

Recommended touring time: 14–17 days (11 cycling days)

Terrain: mostly level though windy

Accommodations: camping or private rooms

Maps: Michelin 412 and 413 in the 1 : 400,000 series

Famous sights as well as unknown surprises await you on this easy two-week tour along two of Europe's most important and scenic rivers, the Rhine and the Mosel, from Switzerland to Germany, France, and finally Luxembourg. One of the most popular and enjoyable rides in Europe, the route takes in many distinct regions of this wine-producing area, such as the Black Forest, the Kaiserstuhl, Alsace, the castle-lined Rhine, and the lovely Mosel Valley. Much of this tour is also routed along special bicycle trails that allow you to cycle in quiet areas away from the main traffic. And because the tour follows the course of large rivers, the land is absolutely flat most of the way. The fascinating sights and easy terrain makes this an excellent tour for both first-time bicycle tourists and experienced riders.

While the tour is organized around camping accommodations, hostels and inexpensive rooms for rent abound along this popular route. Many of these establishments cater specifically to cyclists, with rooms often advertised directly along bicycle trails. There is also an excellent network of tourist services and information offices in the Rhine and Mosel valleys. Languages and dialects switch several times throughout the trip, but in general terms, German is spoken everywhere, and most people also speak English.

	German	French
Hello:	*Guten Tag* or *Grüss Gott*	*Bonjour*
Thank you:	*Danke*	*Merci*

Basel, Switzerland to Titisee, Germany
76 km (47 miles)

The tour begins in Basel, Switzerland, a stately old city on the Rhine. Basel is easily reached from any major city in Europe by train, with direct and frequent connections from Zurich, Frankfurt, Paris, and other points. The city is an excellent starting point for this tour as it lies at the crossroads of Germany, France, and Switzerland on a bend in the Rhine, historically one of the most important byways in Europe.

The closest campground is 10 km away in Reinach. A more convenient option is the youth hostel at St. Alban-Kirchrain 10. This is east of the Münsterplatz (the site of the main cathedral), just off the Rhine (it is well signed from the Kunstmuseum area). The very nice, new hostel offers private double rooms in addition to regular dorm rooms, with non-members also welcome (dorms 18 SF; private doubles only 22 SF per person; non-members add 7 SF more for either; unlimited breakfast included). If you arrive early, even in summer, you have a good chance of getting a private room, or reserve ahead (tel. 061 230572). There are usually many cyclists and families staying in this pleasant hostel.

Basel is well worth a day of relaxing and sightseeing before you begin the journey north to Luxembourg. The winding streets and Rathaus are the most interesting sights in the well-preserved old town. From the balcony behind the Münster, the view high over the Rhine is tremendous, as is the reverse view from the opposite bank. Here you can watch the waters of the river you will soon be following on its course to the North Sea.

The first day of this tour, to Titisee in the Black Forest of Germany, is the most difficult, involving the only really difficult terrain of the entire route. Though the effort is well worth it, you can save time and energy by following the shores of the Rhine directly to Freiburg. Another option is to begin the tour in Titisee by taking a train up and then enjoying a downhill ride all the way to Freiburg and the Rhine. However, the route described below takes you straight through the woods and hills of the Black Forest and offers the best perspective of that region.

To cycle to the Schwarzwald (Black Forest), cross over the Rhine to north Basel, following blue signs for Lörrach. There is a bicycle path intermittently paralleling this busy road to Riehen and Lörrach, where you will cross the border into Germany. Cycle onward for Donaueschingen, following yellow signs (in Switzerland autobahn signs are green and smaller roads are blue, while in Germany, autobahn signs are blue while everything else is yellow). Cross over railroad tracks to the right and take the first left. This will lead you to road 317 to Schopfheim (13 km from Lörrach), Todtnau, and Titisee. There are no reasonably direct secondary roads as the area north of the Rhine quickly changes to steep hills and sharp valleys with very few roads running through them. However, even on a busy summer day this road was not overcrowded or uncomfortably busy, with few trucks and a suitable shoulder. There are some bicycle paths paralleling the road, usually along the Wiese River. Unfortunately, after promising starts with clearly marked bicycling signs, many of these come to abrupt and sudden dead ends, making them worthwhile only if you are willing to take the time to explore.

Todtnau is a pretty town with a large church and shady benches, good for lunch or a quick snack before continuing to Titisee and the most difficult part of the ride, a nasty 8 km climb. From Todtnau at 658 m altitude, you cycle to Feldberg, at 1230m, before cruising downhill the rest of the way to Titisee at 850m. Approaching Titisee on the other side, you can take a shortcut to the lake by taking a left off the main road and circling around the water to the town.

Titisee is a resort town high in the Black Forest that unfortunately has made a bigger name than it should, with the result that the tiny lake's waters are crowded with rubber rafts and the little town's streets are thronged with people. At quieter moments, however, you can still appreciate the beauty of the woods and the lake. Ideally, Titisee should be used as a base for even a short hike into the forest to see the Schwarzwald up close.

There is a hostel and three campgrounds in Titisee. A short ride around the lake will bring you to each in turn. This is the only place in Europe that I was ever turned away from a full

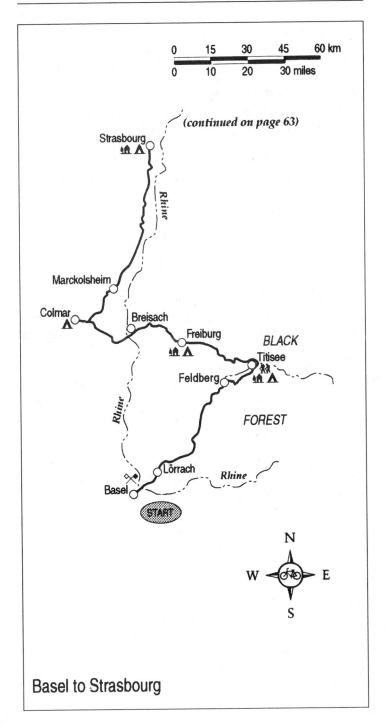

(continued on page 63)

Strasbourg

Rhine

Marckolsheim

Colmar

Breisach

Freiburg

BLACK

Titisee

Feldberg

FOREST

Rhine

Lörrach

Rhine

Basel

START

N

W ⊕ E

S

Basel to Strasbourg

campground, even having only a small tent and a bicycle. However, Camping Weiherhof, the second closest to town, lets you camp in the woods around the site when it is full and use the facilities for a fee (but if you are smart, you can do this without paying the fee). The nicest campground seems to be Sandbank, the last site across the lake from Titisee. Titisee has no large grocery stores, only several small, expensive shops. You can try two delicious specialities of the Black Forest here, Schwarzwalder Schinken, a smoked ham and, of course, Black Forest cake. There are also a few nice beer gardens in the town.

Titisee to Freiburg
31 km (19 miles)

If all bicycle touring were like this, the world would truly be a wonderful place, and automotive travel would be banned forever. It is a beautiful 31 km cruise downhill all the way from Titisee to Freiburg, an interesting university city with tremendous character. You will hardly have to touch your pedals for most the way down the Höllental ('Hell's Valley,' which it very well might be if you were coming the other way) to Freiburg.

Take road 31 to Freiburg from Titisee. This busy road has several long sections of bicycle path running alongside. For the last 10 km to Freiburg after the steep Höllental; follow the bicycle path next to the road. Cycle into the center of Kirchzarten and look for signs to Oberried. These will take you to an intersection outside town where you go straight, for Freiburg, with bicycle paths for the remainder of the trip. There are two campgrounds on the east edge of Freiburg. Follow signs to the left for Camping Mosle-Park. The second sign is misleading. Take the second left, after the railroad tracks, not the first. The second campground is slightly closer to the center of town, on the north bank of the river, but is poorly marked. There is also a hostel in the same area (Kartauserstr. 151).

The old town of Freiburg was largely rebuilt after wartime damage, with wonderful results. Tall tower gates guard the entry points and the center of the old town, the cathedral. Many of the old, balconied buildings have been restored and decorated with wall paintings. Throughout the cobblestoned pedestrian streets run clear little streams, once the town sewage system and today one of the carefully restored details that give Freiburg its unique character.

Freiburg to Colmar, France
58 km (36 miles)

This cycling day is short but full of interesting sights as you cross several distinct regions. From Freiburg on the edge of the Black Forest, pedal to the heart of the Kaiserstuhl (Emperor's Chair), a large vineyard-covered hill on the plain of the Rhine Valley and a world of its own. A downhill ride brings you to the medieval town of Breisach and across the Rhine to France and Alsace, ending in Colmar.

Cycling out of Freiburg can be a test of your route-finding skills. Unless you have a good city map, the best strategy seems to be guess and go. Head northwest out of town toward the autobahn and Gottenheim to begin. To do so find a street paralleling the direct road from the center of town to Gottenheim (it is closed to cyclists, being an artery to the autobahn). Look for signs to Lehen. Once you get past the surprisingly widespread outskirts of Freiburg and to this town, route finding is easy.

From Lehen cycle to Gottenheim and then Bötzingen. There turn left for Vogtsburg to cycle up the high ridge of the Kaiserstuhl. This is the only hard climb of the day. The effort of cycling up into the heart of the Kaiserstuhl is quickly rewarded by the close-up view of the vineyards and quiet towns of this unique area. On the Kaiserstuhl, you suddenly find yourself in a different world, far removed from the Rhine

Winetasting cellar at Bernkastel-Kues in the Mosel Valley, Germany

Valley below. This is an appreciation you cannot achieve by simply cycling around the edge of the hill.

From Vogtsburg follow signs downhill to Oberrotweil and Breisach. Approaching Breisach follow signs for *Stadtmitte* and take the second left, toward *Münster* and *Rathaus*. This will bring you to the top of the hill in the very center of the old town. Breisach offers expansive views of the Rhine below and the hills of the Black Forest in the distance, a very nice, peaceful town in which to have a break before continuing the ride. There are no stores here, only in the modern town below the south end of the hill.

The last part of the ride is in France and on a busier road for the flat 22 km to Colmar. Follow signs for Colmar and Frankreich (France) over the bridge and the Rhine to take road N415 to Colmar. There is a narrow shoulder on this road. The closest campground is on the west edge of Horbourg, 4 km east from the center of Colmar—a quicker bicycle ride than it may sound. You can leave your things at the campground, lock your bicycle in town, and explore the city on foot. Camping L'ill is clearly marked off road N415 as you near Colmar. The riverside site has a restaurant (camping 13 F per tent; 11 F per person).

Colmar is a typical Alsacian town, a curious mix of German and French elements, from architecture to language and food. The town is full of wonderful half-timbered houses overlooking flower-lined quays along the canals of 'La Petite Venise.' Ideally, one could spend an entire day just exploring the streets. If you do not have the time to do so, try to arrive early to spend as much time as possible in this beautiful town.

Colmar to Strasbourg
76 km (47 miles)

Between Colmar and Strasbourg are a number of small, pretty villages and nothing but absolutely flat terrain. The only difficulty you may encounter are the headwinds that seem to sweep up the Rhine Valley, against the direction of the current. You have the choice of several different routes to Strasbourg (thanks to the excellent network of secondary roads in France). First, you can cycle a direct route through small towns to Strasbourg, following side roads inland from the Rhine; or cycle directly along the Rhine if you are more interested in seeing the river and the barges moving along it by crossing to the German side and taking the bicycle path along the east bank. Finally, you can choose a combination of the two, by cycling through the countryside toward the Rhine, partway along the river, and then back inland toward Strasbourg. Since winds are stronger directly on the river and this section of the Rhine is not the most scenic, I would recommend the first course. The most scenic part of the Rhine is the stretch between Mainz and Koblenz. Before that point the villages of the Rhine Valley are generally more interesting than the river itself.

To see more of the countryside and villages in Alsace, take road D111 from Horbourg to Muntzenheim and follow signs to Marckolsheim. Then take D468 the remainder of the way to Strasbourg. This quiet road will lead you through a series of small towns with half-timbered houses in a more practical and down-to-earth setting than those of the manicured streets of Colmar or Strasbourg.

There is more traffic as you approach Strasbourg and merge with larger roads. Keep following yellow signs for Strasbourg. Where the road has both yellow-numbered signs and blue autoroute signs, you may still bicycle as it is only an access road for the autoroute. There are narrow but suitable shoulders all the way to the center. At a large roundabout in Illkirch, go straight for Strasbourg-centre (white signs; the 2nd exit counterclockwise). This brings you to the very center where there are separate bicycle lanes. Aim for the Cathedral's spire ahead and to the left. There are several tourist information offices in the city center that can give you a city map.

There are three campgrounds around Strasbourg; one to the east, in the direction of Kehl, Germany, and two to the south (better marked than the one to the east). To reach Camping Montagne Vert 3 km to the south, follow signs from the center of town to the suburb of that name (9 F per tent; 9 F per person). You will pass the youth hostel on the way (camping is also found at the hostel, but expensive at 33F, breakfast included).

Long the most prominent city in Alsace, Strasbourg retains its important role today as the seat of the European Parliament. You can also visit the Gothic Cathedral and château in Strasbourg. As in Colmar, there are enchanting streets of half-timbered houses and flower-lined canals, though it proves that once you have seen one pretty Alsacian city, you have not quite seen them all. Both cities, despite superficial similarities, have their own unique character and appeal. Plan on spending at least one entire day visiting this pleasant city.

Strasbourg to Baden-Baden, Germany
60 km (37 miles)

There are two options for the ride from Strasbourg to Baden-Baden that depend on your preference for the countryside on either the east or west side of the Rhine (in other words, it is fairly arbitrary). I cycled directly to Kehl and Germany from Strasbourg, but you can also choose to stay in France longer by cycling north as far as Drusenheim and crossing to Germany there (this may be the easier choice in terms of route finding). Both routes will take you through a series of small towns with few stores, so shop ahead.

To practice your French a bit longer, take road D468 north to La Wantzenau, Gambsheim, and Drusenheim, where you cross to Greffern. After Greffern cross road 36 and go straight for Rheinmünster, then Leiberstung and Sinzheim. From there it is only 8 km to the center of Baden-Baden (well marked). To go directly to Germany, cross the Pont d'Europe over the Rhine to Kehl, and follow signs for road 36 to Rastatt. There is a bicycle path alongside this busy road that begins when you leave Kehl. It will bring you to a small road marked for Bodersweier and eventually back alongside road 36 on a bicycle trail. Take a left off road 36 to Auenheim to follow secondary roads through Auenheim and Leutesheim to Rheinau, where you rejoin road 36 for 13 km until the right turn to Rheinmünster and, eventually, to Baden-Baden.

The last 6 km to Baden-Baden are along a very busy road, but there is a bicycle path along the eastbound side that leads directly to the center of town and the casino. Baden-Baden is famous for its luxurious casino patterned after Versailles. You can only get in with formal attire and a lot of money that you are ready to lose. The pretty gardens around the casino, however, are there for everyone to enjoy, and at no charge. Besides the casino and the chic town in general, Baden-Baden is also known for its therapeutic baths. You can sneak a peek at the remains of the original Roman baths through a large glass window under the present-day Friedrichsbad baths.

There are no campgrounds conveniently near Baden-Baden, forcing you to either cycle further on the same day or try to get a space in the hostel (Hardbergstr. 34, west of the center; often full in summer; family accommodations also available). The nearest campground is in Rastatt, 10 km to the north on road 3 (on the way to Heidelberg). Another option is to cycle

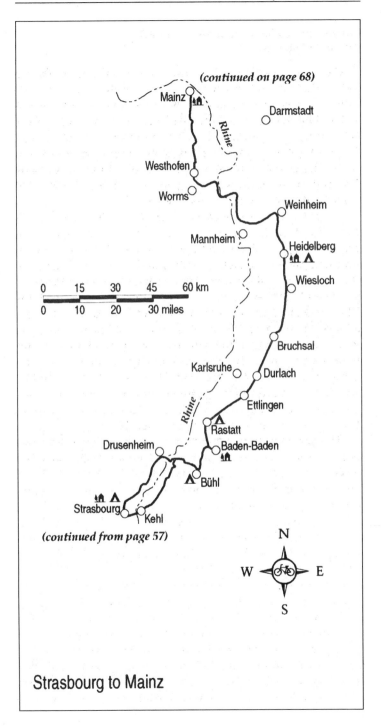

(continued on page 68)

(continued from page 57)

Strasbourg to Mainz

to one of the two more pleasant, lakeside campgrounds near Moos and Bühl, south of Baden-Baden. I left Strasbourg late, stopped at Campingplatz Adam (6 DM per tent; 8DM per person) near Moos, and cycled to Baden-Baden the next morning and on to Heidelberg the same day.

Baden-Baden to Heidelberg
92 km (58 miles)

Reverse your route back to road 3 from Baden-Baden by taking the same bicycle path west (there is only a path on the eastbound side of the main road to Baden-Baden). From there you will be able to see the sign across the road and to the right to Rastatt. I followed road 3 all the way to Heidelberg; although it is a busy road, there are good bicycle paths paralleling it the entire way (except within towns). Cycle to Ettlingen and then Durlach to stay outside the limits of urban Karlsruhe, and continue north for Weingarten, Bruchsal, Wiesloch, and Heidelberg.

Weingarten is the nicest town on this route (it is hard to go wrong with a name like that). A pretty river cuts through town, a nice place for lunch or a break. Bruchsal has a castle (schloss), but the surroundings are not as nice; a better place for a break in that town is the large central square dominated by several churches and complete with a refreshingly cool fountain.

From Bruchsal on there are more hills but nothing terrible, only annoying if you have been spoiled by the previous day's flat cycling. To gain quieter roads the last few km to Heidelberg, turn right over an overpass to the west for Sandhausen. There are signs the rest of the way in to Heidelberg, with bicycle paths all over the small city. Heidelberg stretches thinly north-south and east-west along the banks of the Neckar River and the narrow valley. The old town is on the south bank of the Neckar. On the way through town you will pass the Bahnhof where the main tourist information office is located.

Head straight through town, following signs north to Darmstadt until the large bridge over the Neckar. Turn right to cycle east along either the north or south bank (the north bank has the quieter road) in order to reach both of the campgrounds, each 6 km away (both well-signed; one on each bank, past Ziegelhausen). Camping Neckartal is on the south bank, right on the river (5DM per tent; 6DM per person). Camping Heide is nearby, on the north bank of the river. There is also a hostel (Tiergartenstr. 5, near the zoo) and rooms for rent in town.

Heidelberg is one of the top tourist destinations in Germany in the summer, so you may find its reputation as a charming university town a bit off the mark. Nevertheless, tourists or no tourists, students or no students, Heidelberg remains a captivating, lively town. The old town with its different squares, the castle ruins high above town and the Neckar, and the views from Philosophenweg across the river make this appealing city one of the most pleasant stops of this tour. Count on taking a day off to rest and enjoy the sights at leisure.

Heidelberg to Mainz
95 km (59 miles)

This long day takes you across the Rhine from Heidelberg to Worms, an old city noted for its cathedral, and on toward Mainz for a close-up look at the tiny wine-producing towns and endless vineyards of the Rhine valley. Cycle north out of Heidelberg on road 3 toward Darmstadt and Weinheim. Take this busy road (no bicycle path) 7 km until the turnoff to the left for Ladenburg and Mannheim. Follow signs to Ladenburg and from there to Heddesheim and Viernheim. In Viernheim head for the Rathaus and center, where you will pick up signs for Lorsch. These may lead you on a circuitous, somewhat illogical route around town but they will get you to the correct road, which has a good shoulder. Follow it for 8 km until the left turn for Lampertheim. This busier side road (a shortcut for many on the way to Worms) has a good bicycle path. Then head on for Worms from there. Eventually you will cycle over the Rhine and through the impressive town gate to the center of Worms.

If you are a church tourist—one that enjoys comparing the architecture and detail of every different town church—Worms will keep you very busy. Most dominant of the many important churches in Worms is the Dom St. Peter, the cathedral in the center of town. In a more secular sense, Worms is also a good place for lunch, with quiet corners in the churchyards offering some shade and a rest before the hilly ride on to Mainz. Ask at the tourist office across from the Dom for more information on the city's churches and its history.

To continue the second half of the ride, head west out of town and look for signs for *WO-Herrnsheim* and *WO-Abenheim* (in the same general direction as the soccer field that is also well-signed). Head west directly away from the Rhine on any road running just north of the Dom. WO-Herrnsheim and WO-Abenheim are suburbs of Worms. After these towns, head for Westhofen, Dittelsheim-Hessloch, and Mainz on very quiet and pretty side roads through this wine-growing region. Although the last 50 km to Mainz are very hilly, the ride goes quickly thanks to the wonderful scenery and closely spaced towns, each a mile marker bringing you closer to your destination. I found cycling through this region a pleasant surprise, not the endless ride I dreaded it might be.

Eventually you will cycle up one steep hill through Harxheim and then descend to Mainz and the Rhine, joining the main road. There is a bicycle path that begins a few km after you join the busy main road. It switches sides once but continues directly through the city. Head for *Centrum* to reach the old town and the Rhine. The hostel is in the Volkpark on the way down (above the town). The tourist office is located near the train station, a worthwhile stop for a city map that can help you leave Mainz the next day. Streets with blue nameplates parallel the Rhine and those with red signs lead to the river, a handy way to orientate yourself. Mainz has a large pedestrian area centered around the Martinsdom Cathedral and old town. The Gutenberg Museum makes an interesting stop, with an original Gutenberg Bible and other relics recounting the development of printing.

The nearest campground is across the river and to the east, about 4 km away from the old town center in Hochheim (3 DM per tent; 6 DM per person; small shop at the site). It is signposted all the way from the Theodor-Heuss bridge near the city center. Take a shortcut by following the signed walker's route to the campsite (paved all the way). Follow the road and car route to pass an Aldi supermarket (open until 6:30 p.m.) on the right on your way to the site. There is another campground on the west edge of the city (south bank) but it is very difficult to find, being poorly marked.

Mainz to Koblenz
92 km (58 miles)

Finding your way out of Mainz can be difficult and the ride to Bingen is basically without interest—from Bingen to Koblenz is where the real fun begins. This is the most impressive section of the Rhine, with castles dotting the hills and cliffs high above.

There is a good bicycle path most of the way to Koblenz and a shoulder the rest of the way. At times you can cycle directly on the river bank with unobstructed views of the vineyards and ruined towers across the valley. You will also pass many other cyclists here, one of the most popular bicycling routes in Europe. I once traveled this section of the Rhine by riverboat, and all that I have memories of are castles shooting by too fast to tell one from the next. Though you can shorten your trip by taking a ferry, cycling will undoubtedly reward you with stronger memories of the exceptional valley.

From the campground cycle back over the bridge to the south bank of the Rhine and turn right to head west out of town. Other than the color-coded streets, Mainz is not a very easily navigated city, all the roads seeming to lead to autobahns. Ask directions whenever in doubt to avoid going astray. Head (and ask) first for Budenheim and Ingelheim, towns on the way to Bingen. I cycled through an industrial zone and then found the secondary road signposted for Budenheim. Do not take the bicycle path signposted alongside this road as it quickly leads away from the road and through a bewildering series of unmarked lanes through endless garden plots.

Once in Budenheim, follow signs for Heidesheim and Ingelheim. This will finally put you safely on the direct road to Bingen (with no more possibilities of getting lost). Do not cycle into Heidesheim, only past it on the way to Ingelheim and Bingen. There are only small shops in the towns after Bingen, so if you need groceries, stop at one in Bingen. First you will enter a small town beside Bingen that has a Bingen sign, but do not be fooled. Bingen is the large town a few km further on.

Follow signs for *Stadtmitte* (not road 9) to cycle into Bingen and to the adjoining town on the north side, Bingenbrück. Go straight and cross the river Nahe. The road will soon join route 9. Watch for green bicycle path signs for *Bacharach* to the right after the long railroad tracks leading out of town. This leads you to the best bicycle path of the ride, running directly along the Rhine in a quiet area away from the main road. It lasts until Niederheimbach, where the path runs along the main road as it will do for most of the remaining distance to Koblenz. Though you may be nearer to the car traffic, excellent views of the castles and barges moving along the river continue all the way.

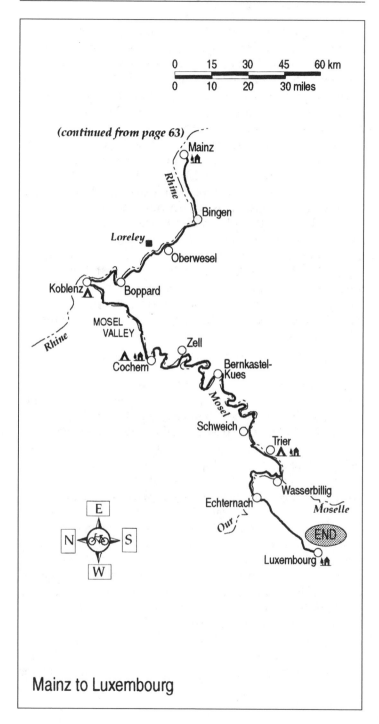

(continued from page 63)

Mainz

Rhine

Bingen

Loreley ■

Oberwesel

Koblenz ▲

Boppard

MOSEL
VALLEY

Rhine

Zell

▲ 🏠
Cochem

Bernkastel-
Kues

Mosel

Schweich

Trier
▲ 🏠

Wasserbillig

Echternach

Our

Moselle

END

Luxembourg 🏠

N · E · S · W

Mainz to Luxembourg

Take the time to detour through some of the towns on the banks of the Rhine. Bacharach is one of the nicest towns along the way, with half-timbered houses dating from the sixteenth century lining the cobblestoned streets of the walled town. Oberwesel is another nice town, dominated by the ruins of a castle. St. Goar is the most touristy town of the route, packed with busloads of people coming to videotape the too-famous Loreley cliff (which has still not budged). There are nevertheless some quiet spots in the area where you can enjoy lunch or a break away from the crowds.

Between St. Goar and Boppard the nice wide bicycle path ends for two long stretches, leaving you the option of either cycling on the side of the road or the bumpy, too-narrow-for-comfort curb. From Spay you can follow green signs for another nice bicycle path along the water. Unfortunately, there is a catch—the path is cobblestoned, then dirt, and later paved. Keep right along the water's edge unless the green signs clearly indicate otherwise. I eventually came to a dead end and then took a nice flat dirt path through the woods, keeping straight ahead (paralleling and to the east of road 9 and the train tracks). This path leads back out onto the main road a few km later.

Follow signs to Bahnhof to find the tourist office directly across from it. Central Koblenz fills the space south of where the Rhine and Mosel meet (west of the Rhine, south of the rivers' confluence). The campground is located on the north bank of the Mosel, just near the confluence point and close to the old town center. To get there, cycle straight on the road past the train station and eventually over a bridge above the Mosel. There are signs to the right on the opposite side of the bridge that lead to the campground, which has a great view of the Deutsches Eck, the confluence point of the two rivers (4 DM per tent; 4 DM per person). The only traffic you will hear is the sound of barges moving along the river at night. The hostel in Koblenz lies within the walls of the fortress on the east bank of the Rhine, directly opposite the campground and Deutsches Eck. Koblenz itself does not have many specific sights. Head to the old town for some sightseeing in the evening.

Koblenz to Traben-Trarbach
103 km (64 miles)

Turning southwest from Koblenz, you begin to cycle up the Mosel Valley, one of the most beautiful and memorable rides in Europe. This tour divides the distance from Koblenz to Trier into two long days but if you have more time to spend, stretch out the ride into three days to savor the lovely scenery. There are many riverside campgrounds and rooms for rent all along the valley, making it easy to rearrange the tour.

An excellent and thoroughly signposted bicycle trail runs all the way to Trier. The marked route comprises bicycle path, shoulders, and quiet side roads. After Cochem the bicycle signs say *Moselroute* and indicate both directions. The ride is flat or only slightly uphill all the way to Trier. Most of the small towns along the Mosel have few shops. Your best bet is to shop in Koblenz, Cochem, Zell, and Traben-Trarbach. To make the day shorter, you can also catch a ferry for part of the route (inquire at the many ferry stops on the river).

From Koblenz cycle along the north bank of the Mosel for Cochem. There is a special cycling shoulder or a separate bicycle trail all the way to Traben. Signs for the bicycle path (small green signs for Cochem) start under the north side of the bridge to the campground. If you miss them, just cycle southwest on road 416 to Cochem and you will eventually see the bicycle lane. The shoulder on the Koblenz-bound side of 416 is especially wide for use in both directions by cyclists, cleverly engineered so that you cycle against the current, the wind, and the traffic. But the ride is nice despite the road (most of the traffic goes along the southeast bank of the river), and you have an unobstructed view over the river. The bicycle path occasionally detours through small towns and short tractor trails through vineyards. In these cases the turn off the main road is very clear.

All the way to Cochem you will enjoy views of pretty riverside towns and castles. Vineyard-covered hills slope away from the river and wine tasting cellars abound (look for *Weinstube* signs for establishments that sell their house wines by the glass). Cochem is the tourist destination of the Mosel valley and is consequently a busy and crowded place. It can be difficult to enjoy the beauty of the town's architecture, castle, or site on the Mosel as a result (there is abundant accommodation in Cochem: a campground, a hostel, and many private rooms). The best thing to do there is to take a look around the old town, shop for lunch supplies, and cycle a quick 10 km to Beilstein.

Your time is much better spent in quiet and more authentic Beilstein than in the souvenir-shop and tour bus clutter of

Cochem. Beilstein is an old town on the Mosel, a tiny cluster of beautiful houses dominated by the ruins of a castle on a cliff above. There are no grocery stores. The hike up to the castle takes only about 10 minutes and affords terrific views of the Mosel, vineyards, and rooftops below. This is a great place for lunch (entrance fee 2 DM; students 1 DM).

From Cochem on, the Mosel begins a series of wild twists and bends, stretching out the actual distance you must cover to eventually reach Trier. Cycle on from Beilstein to Senheim, where you must cross back to the north bank. Senheim also has a campground. The bicycle path continues in sections. Watch for green signs to find the riverside path. Cross the river again to Neef and Bullay 10 km later for very quiet side roads, and continue on to Zell, where there is a bicycle path to Pünderich. Cross again to Reil to take a practically deserted side road the rest of the way to Traben-Trarbach.

Follow the bicycle path signs instead of the road to avoid an unnecessary climb (though the road does take you by the large, cheap Heller and Pfennig grocery store and signs for the youth hostel). There are several grocery stores and many small shops in this large twin town. The riverside Campingplatz Rissbach is 3 km away on the north bank, on the road to Kröv and Trier (expensive at 10 DM for the; 5 DM per person).

Traben-Trarbach to Trier
84 km (52 miles)

The Moselroute bicycle path continues, off and on, throughout this day. First cycle along the north bank of the Mosel from Traben to Kröv on a quiet secondary road. Then you are rejoined by the main road. Cross the river after Kinheim to Zeltingen, Graach, and Bernkastel to enjoy practically deserted, good roads along rows of grapes. Bernkastel-Kues is 23 km from Traben and is worth at least a quick stop, and even better, a long snack stop (the best kind). The towns are overrun with tourists but have nevertheless managed to retain a good deal of character. The irregular arrangement of narrow streets and leaning half-timbered houses create an appealing variation on a now common theme.

Cross to Kues and the north bank, and turn left to again ride the quieter shore of the river. There is a nice riverside bicycle path that begins under the bridge, to Lieser and beyond. After Minheim you will cross the river and rejoin road 53. Keep on the south bank for Neumagen after the main road crosses back to the north bank in Klüsserath. As you cycle through Neu-magen watch (to the right) for the Roman 'weinschiff' (wine ship) sculpture in front of the shady chapel. It is an 1800s replica of a third-century original that you can see in Trier. The sculpture serves as a reminder of the long tradition of wine production in the Mosel Valley.

You can stay on the quiet, traffic-free south bank until Thörnich, where you must cross back to the main road, but the bicycle path continues off and on. In Mehring there are signs for the ruins of a Roman villa that lie across the river if you are interested in a detour. Outside Schweich, another bicycle path leads to the town center and abandons you there. Try to find the bicycle path along the riverside; if not, ride on the main road to Trier for a few km until the Ehrang exit, where you will find a bicycle path marked *Trier-Centrum* to the left. Take this well-marked path for Trier-Centrum or *Moselroute* the entire way into the city center. It runs through industrial and resi-dential areas before finally returning to the riverbank and into town.

After passing a railroad bridge, take an underpass away from the bicycle path to gain access to the first car bridge across the Mosel. Follow signs across it to Centrum and tourist in-formation. This will lead you directly to the Porta Nigra, part of the original Roman fortifications in Trier (the oldest city in Germany, founded 15 BC). Both the information office and Karl Marx's birthplace are located immediately around the unusual stone structure. Trier is a compact city, with most points of interest located close to the Porta Nigra. The Dom and adjoining Liebfrauenkirche with its beautiful windows are two good stops. Do not forget to stop by the original Roman wine ship across the street from the Liebfrauenkirche for com-parison. A glance at the rowers' faces makes the effects of their cargo clear. A tough job, but somebody had to do it.

There are many large grocery stores in Trier. The hostel lies to the north of the first bridge into town (left as you are approaching the Porta Nigra). There are two campgrounds. Stadtcamping is conveniently located 2 km from the city center on the north bank of the Mosel, clearly marked off road 49 to Luxembourg. To get a head start on the next day's ride, head to Camping Schloss Monaise, 5 km in the same direction. The site is on the grounds of an old château, though not as en-chanting as it may sound. Ride on the bicycle paths paralleling road 49 west. As you approach Zewen the trail suddenly comes to an end. Turn left to the river and follow signs (4 DM per tent; 4 DM per person). Both riverside sites are also accessible from the bicycle path that runs directly along the riverbank, an extension of the one coming into Trier from the northeast.

Trier to Luxembourg
75 km (47 miles)

On this last day of the Rhine and Mosel tour you can take excellent bicycle paths from Trier to Echternach in Luxembourg and all the way to Luxembourg city. The ride to Echternach along the Sauer River is a worthwhile detour that will take you through more of the countryside in Luxembourg; however, you can ride directly to the capital if you are short on time (shortening the ride to 45 km /28miles). The official language of Luxembourg is French but most people speak Luxembourgeois, a confusing mix of French and German. Everyone also speaks German, and English is fairly common as well.

Take the bicycle path directly along the Mosel from Trier. It is marked *Moselroute* and *Luxembourg*. It will eventually lead you onto the shoulder of the main road and to a bridge over the Sauer River. The Luxembourg border is 13 km farther. Here you can choose to cycle either the Luxembourg or German bank of the Sauer to Echternach. I stayed on the German side because there is a marked bicycle path, the *Sauertalradweg*, for most of the distance on the east bank. This excellent, clearly posted trail begins at the German side of the bridge to Wasser, Luxembourg, running through small towns, along the river, and sometimes along the shoulder of road 418. Stay on the road past the first bridge to Echternach, 25 km from the junction of the Sauer and the Mosel, to take the second, less busy bridge across from Echternacherbruck.

A visit to the tourist office located by the Basilica (the four-towered building to your right) is a must. They will arm you with a map of the town in addition to a city map of Luxembourg city, camping information, bicycle trail routes, and anything else you need on either a local or national level. Echternach itself is fairly touristed, but still a pretty town and a good stopover before heading on to Luxembourg city. You can look around the old town and change money if necessary. The bank in the train station in Luxembourg is open on Sundays if you become stuck. Belgian and Luxembourg francs are used interchangeably in this small country.

For the final 38 km to Luxembourg, you can ride the exceptional bicycle trail from Echternach. Begin by cycling out of town on road 42 to Luxembourg. Ignore the first bicycle sign to the left (it leads back to Echternach). Continue cycling up the hill until the bicycle trail moves off the shoulder to the right and into the woods. Watch for white bicycle signs with green writing all the way to Luxembourg. This amazing trail does not simply connect a series of backroads and shoulders, it is a completely separate, well-paved path that takes you through kilometers of quiet woods and across high, open fields to the country's capital. There are only a few points from where you can even see a regular road. Though the terrain is very hilly and the open places can be very windy, one can truly appreciate the lengths to which the Luxembourgeois go to accommodate cyclists.

The trail sometimes meanders but do not worry that it is leading you astray. It quickly straightens back to a direct course. There are only a few points where one might be confused. If you find an unmarked junction, look carefully as the sign is probably just overgrown by foliage. The path splits 3 km after the *28 km to go* sign. Bear left, not right, on the road along cow barns. Later, the trail joins a backcountry road toward Gonderange for a short time but soon resumes a separate course.

After passing through a residential area, the trail emerges on the outskirts of Luxembourg at a large, modern shopping center. Cycle right, along the perimeter of the parking lot, and join the road for Luxembourg centre. I found even this main road into the capital very quiet, but there is also a sidewalk or bicycle lane if the road gets too busy. You can see the spires and guard towers of the old town as you near the city. Head for *Centre*, not for any of the other centres on the way (such as Centre Européen or Centre Concul).

The tourist information office is well marked from the road once in town. There is one in the old town on Place d'Arms and another near the train station in the Luxair office. The closest campground is 4 km away in Kockelscheuer. Follow signs toward Bettembourg from the city center to get there. The hostel in town is noisy but the location is much more convenient (in the Alzette Valley, the first gorge you cross when entering the city).

Luxembourg is one of the most fortified old cities of Europe, the 'Gibraltar of the North,' an endless chain of bastions and towers overlooking, spilling into, and even stretching through several gorges. It took some time before I noticed how the walls and towers are built right out of, into, and upon natural cliffs, how far below in the gorge the trees really stand, just how much there really is to this amazing city. Both walking tours described in a brochure from the tourist office are excellent, covering all the most interesting sights. A visit to either of the Casemates, a series of tunnels and defenses carved right into the rock, is a must. Luxembourg supported my old theory, originating in Liechtenstein, that the smaller the country, the more interesting the sights and the more time one can spend there. Give Luxembourg the time it deserves for a memorable end to this bicycle tour.

If you are not through cycling, two options are to cycle west to Paris and other points in France, or north through Belgium and Holland to Amsterdam and the North Sea. You can also explore more of the countryside in this exceptional country by following its excellent bicycle trails to other points within the country. If this is the end of your trip, there are good train connections to all points in Europe, such as Paris, Frankfurt, and Amsterdam (one way to Paris, for example, is about $60). It is very easy to ship your bicycle by train in Luxembourg. It will travel on the first available train for a fee of about $10. Luxembourg also has an international airport with bus connections to the city center.

Bavaria and the Tirol to Zürich

A four-country tour including Austria, Germany, the Principality of Liechtenstein, and Switzerland.

Distance: 657 km (407 miles)

Recommended touring time: 14–19 days (10 cycling days)

Terrain: mostly hilly, but mountainous between Munich and Liechtenstein, crossing the Arlberg Pass (1800 m). Includes option of a Brenner Pass (1400 m) day trip.

Accommodations: camping or private rooms

Maps: Michelin 413 Bayern/Baden-Wurttemberg (Germany) 1 : 400,000

Berner Oberland, in the Swiss Alps

If you do not speak German, do not panic. Use the two magic words liberally and everyone will be happy. On this tour you will cross many borders and change from schillings to German marks to Swiss francs, so estimate your expenses carefully in order to avoid excessive commission costs when exchanging money. Despite all this, however, the language, if not the accent, remains the same.

The terrain is hilly during the two-day trip from Salzburg to Munich, but you can recover from this vigorous ordeal in one of Munich's many beer halls. The historic city center is also very beautiful. From there, it is back to mountains—the Bavarian Alps to the Tirol region of Austria.

Innsbruck is a fine city to take a few days to relax before heading west for Liechtenstein. This part of the tour involves two solid days of uphill along the Inn River until you reach the Arlberg Pass, probably one of the highest you will have to cross at 1,800 meters. From the top, though, it is all downhill through Liechtenstein and to the border of Switzerland. The Rhine Valley at this point is one of the most beautiful sights in Europe. Liechtenstein, one of the few places in the world where you really can see the whole country in a day, is a place worth several, and you would do well to buy a map and climb a few mountains. Liechtenstein's capital Vaduz, however, is an appalling sight due to the mobs of obnoxious and obviously American tourists there. However, an easy ten-minute walk into the forest will take you far from the world of bus groups and cheap souvenirs. Cycle a few miles over the border to beautiful Walensee in Switzerland for a view of the Alps dropping straight down into the waters of the lake, and continue on to end the tour in Zürich. The miles covered from Salzburg to Switzerland will be hard-earned and well worth the unique perspective of the Alps you will gain.

Map 413 covers all sections of this tour with the exception of 15 km in southern Liechtenstein (the area is well signed). If you continue cycling in Switzerland, however, I suggest you buy Michelin map 427 (Switzerland 1 : 400,000) which includes all of Liechtenstein and Switzerland.

This tour may easily be broken into shorter sections with connections to alternate forms of travel readily available in the closely located cities of this area (Salzburg, Munich, Innsbruck, and Zürich). It is also easy to take a train from Innsbruck to Sargans, Switzerland (close to the Liechtenstein border), to skip the most difficult part of the tour and the Arlberg Pass.

Map 426 does not cover the German portion of this tour in detail and ends at the border of Liechtenstein. While you can consider buying a different map to include these areas, it is not absolutely necessary. The Munich area is well-signed, although a detailed map would be helpful in finding a quiet route into the city. Liechtenstein is so small (27 km long, 6 km wide) that a map is unnecessary, although the cheap map available at the tourist office can serve the dual purposes of cycling and hiking.

Hello: *Grüss Gott*
Thank you: *Danke*

Salzburg to Seebruck
53 km (33 miles)

Salzburg is a small, picturesque city tucked into a corner of Austria. Famous as the home of Mozart and site of *The Sound of Music*, Salzburg endures throngs of tourists throughout the year. The old town is terribly commercialized, although not quite spoiled. A walkway rings the crest of the mountain above Salzburg, offering good views over the city, the giant-sized chess game in the square below, and Hohensalzburg fortress above. There is a campground on the east bank of the Salzach River (Stadtcamping on Bayerhofstrasse). This site is within convenient walking distance of the city center and grocery stores. There are also three hostels and rooms for rent in Salzburg.

This ride is short, bringing you to the shores of the Chiemsee (*See* means lake), halfway to München. It shortens the following day's ride into München by avoiding having to navigate the city after an extremely long and tiring day. Head out of Salzburg east on 155 and 304 toward Freilassing and Traunstein. From the campground, cross the Salzach river on the first bridge north of the railway bridge and continue straight on this road. Crossing the Austrian-German border is a quick process—we only had to flash our passports briefly. Then watch for signs for route 20. Take the second exit for route 20 toward 304 and Traunstein. After 3 km of this busy road, turn onto 304.

Once past Traunstein, follow signs to Seebruck. This day's ride through rural areas is moderate with some long climbs. There is one campground on the east edge of Seebruck and another several kilometers farther that is right on the lake (5

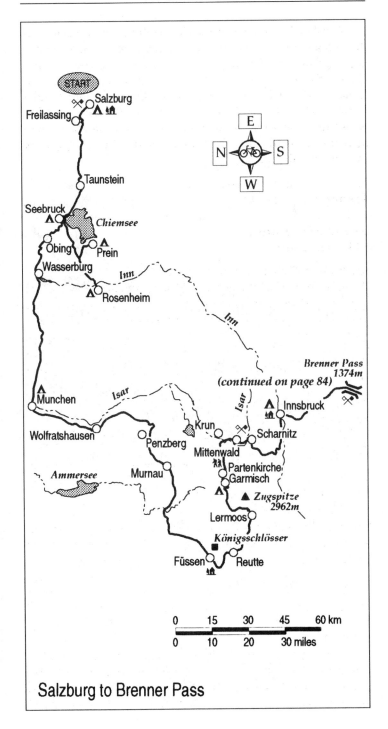

Salzburg to Brenner Pass

DM per person, 4 DM per tent, 1 DM per square meter of ground space. We were charged for 4 square meters. Showers are extra). If you want to go even farther there are also campgrounds in Prein and Rosenheim. The lake water can be chilly, but after a hot day of cycling, there is nothing more refreshing.

Seebruck to Munich
80 km (50 miles)

There are two ways into München (Munich)—direct and indirect. I chose the first since the scenery in this area is not particularly interesting, and I wanted to get into München as early as possible to get settled into the campground easily. If you are also impatient to reach München, be prepared for some uncomfortable cycling. From the campground just west of Seebruck, double back toward Seebruck and turn left onto a small quiet road to Obing, and enjoy it while you can. Once in Obing turn left and join road 304 to München and Wasserburg. This is a busy narrow road with lots of heavy trucks, not really dangerous but very unpleasant.

If you have the patience, take the longer route of a combination of side roads. Ride westward around the lake from Seebruck, heading for Endorf, then turn north onto a minor road to Halfing. From Halfing cycle west to Griesstätt, then on to Rott, crossing road 15, and to Assling, Hohenthann, Glonn, Oberpframmern, and München.

If you are on road 304, a bicycle path starts 20 km outside the city center. München itself is full of special bicycle paths separated from regular traffic. Continue paralleling the road right into the heart of the city—eventually down a few one-way streets the wrong way—until you reach Innere Wiener-strasse. Turn left and follow this curving street (it changes names a few times) until you reach the Isar River Bridge. This is the bridge over a big river, not the stream that you reach first. Do not cross this bridge. Turn left and follow the Isar southwest on a bicycle path through a riverside park. About 5 km south, cross the Isar on a pedestrian bridge. This is the ninth bridge, not counting the first one you did not cross and not the first pedestrian bridge that curves across the river at an angle near some waterfalls, but two bridges later. You can see the huge Campingplatz Thalkirchen from the bridge. Turn right and circle the campground to its entrance. This site is the best budget accommodation in München since it is convenient to the city center by bus and U-bahn (subway). Camping costs 5 DM per person, 4.50 DM per tent ($5 total per person).

Much of historic München was restored after being badly damaged in World War II. Today it is a lively center with a variety of sights and activities for the visitor to enjoy. Oktoberfest, held in September, attracts huge tourist crowds and usually drives most of the locals away from its exaggerated commercialism and gaudy events. It can still be fun, however, if you enjoy inebriated crowds. We were in München three days before Oktoberfest and there were already three thousand people staying in the campground. You can always find a patch of empty grass, but if you are interested in indoor accommodations, make reservations far in advance.

There are many churches of various styles and denominations in München, each worth a visit. The Rathaus, or town hall, is vividly decorated, and its clock tower sports model knights and musicians that fight and dance at noon. München's many beer halls, each run by a separate brewery, operate year round. However, the outdoor beer garden in Englischer Garten is your best bet as a less tourist-visited and more genuine place.

Munich to Brunnen
110 km (68 miles)

It is a long and difficult day's ride toward Füssen. Leave München on road 11 south to Wolfratshausen. To do so from the campground, go south along the river, then right where the road bends. Ride straight on this road until you reach Wolfratshausenstrasse, which runs parallel to and several blocks west of the river. Turn left on this road. Follow signs for a small road to Beuerberg in Wolfratshausen center. Continue through Beuerberg to Penzberg. We were very confused here by the lack of signs. Turn left for Stadtmitte, the town center, at the first intersection outside town. At the T-junction turn left again toward Garmisch-Partenkirchen and look for signs to Habach and Murnau. Once you join road 472 you will pass Habach and 1 km later turn left for Murnau.

In Murnau follow signs for Bad Kohlgrub and Saulgrub. Unfortunately, the 14 km to Saulgrub and the next 6 km north on road 23 toward Fussen are all uphill. (Welcome to the Bavarian Alps.) Cycle over the scenic Ammer Bridge, leave road 23, and follow signs onto road 17 to Fussen. You will pass one other campground on your way, but if possible hold out until Schwangau where you can turn right for the Brunnen campground to be closer to the area's sights. The campground is located on a lake with great views of the mountains and Neuschwanstein in the distance. Campground sites cost 8 DM per person ($4) and 6 DM per tent, but as cyclists we were only charged for half a space. Hot showers are free, and there is toilet paper—a real five-star campground. There is also a small kitchen, but you must pay to use the burners. There is another campground on the Hopfensee to the south and a hostel in Fussen if you want to be closer to the town, but not the castles. Neuschwanstein is the famous Bavarian castle built by mad King Ludwig. Visiting the building involves a strenuous hike, which I put off until the following morning.

Brunnen to Garmisch-Partenkirchen
65 km (40 miles)

Return to Schwangau from the Brunnen lakeside camp-ground. To visit Neuschwanstein follow yellow signs in town that read *Königschlösser*. Leave your bicycle at the bottom of the hill and walk up to see the building that inspired the Disneyland castle. It is a long, steep climb, but there are nice views from the top. An entrance fee is charged to view the interior. The twenty-minute hike to the bridge behind the Neuschwanstein offers the best vantage point of the castle and its surroundings.

Return to road 17 toward Fussen and turn off for Reutte on 314. Continue straight into Reutte on the secondary road that runs straight into town rather than taking indirect road 314 all the way. Back on 314 toward Fernpass you will begin a long, steady climb toward Lermoos. There is only a narrow shoulder on this road, but traffic is reasonably light and even better after the left turn for Garmisch (road 187), when everyone else takes the tunnel south. From this turnoff it is downhill or level all the way to Garmisch along the Loisach river. Road 187 be-comes 24. The campground is on your left just west of town and there is a youth hostel 4 km away on Jochstrasse in Burg-rain. Garmisch-Partenkirchen was the site of the 1936 Winter Olympics. The towns are full of beautifully painted houses and surrounded by stunning mountains, including the Zugspitze, Germany's highest mountain at 2,962 m. Garmisch-Partenkir-chen is a wonderful place to rest and explore backwoods trails on foot. Eibsee is a crystal-clear lake at the foot of the Zugspitze. Its waters perfectly reflect every rocky pinnacle of the mountains above. You can also take a rather expensive cable car ride to the Zugspitze's summit from Eibsee.

Garmisch-Partenkirchen to Innsbruck
61 km (38 miles)

Follow well-marked road 2 eastward out of town toward Innsbruck. There is a bicycle path paralleling this road between Krün and Mittenwald, where you will rejoin the main road. Cross the border at the Scharnitzpass. There is only a long steady climb and one last steep section to the border, and you will be over the pass before you realize it. 3 km past Seebruck there is suddenly a very steep, heavily-traveled descent to the Inn Valley. The *No bikes* sign halfway down the hill came a little too late for me to do anything but continue. You can take a series of side roads to avoid the hill if you wish, but these are all out of the way and the hill is not bad enough to make this worthwhile. In fact, I found it fun. You should have no trouble on the descent if you take it slowly and carefully.

At the bottom of the hill follow white signs to Innsbruck (right turn, under a ramp). Ride the well-maintained bicycle paths right into town, paralleling road 171 on the final stretch along a secondary road. The most convenient campground of the four around Innsbruck is Camping Richenau, on the south bank of the Inn (east edge of town). Follow the south bank of the Inn through town until you pick up signs directing you to this site. The charge is 60 öS ($5) per person (the showers are extra). The staff is not very attentive, however, and we enjoyed a free three-day stay at this site. From here it is a short bus or bicycle ride into the center of Innsbruck, a compact city. There are also several hostels in Innsbruck, some open only seasonally. Try the Jugendherberge Innsbruck at 147 Reichenaustrasse.

The best site in Innsbruck is the historic city center. The main square is ringed by interesting buildings, including the Goldenes Dachl, a gold-roofed balcony overlooking the street below. You can also visit the facilities used in two Winter Olympic games, such as the Bergisel ski jump. Innsbruck is a convenient and pleasant place to enjoy a rest before heading out—and up—toward Liechtenstein.

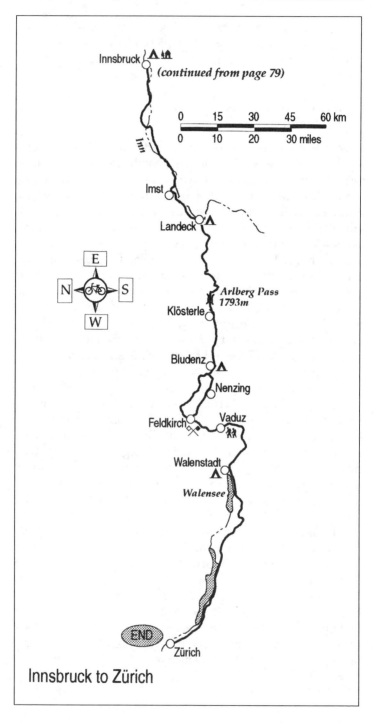

(continued from page 79)

Innsbruck

Imst

Landeck

Arlberg Pass
1793m

Klösterle

Bludenz

Nenzing

Feldkirch

Vaduz

Walenstadt

Walensee

END

Zürich

Innsbruck to Zürich

Brenner Pass day trip
74 km (46 miles)

A good unladen ride from Innsbruck is a day trip to the Brenner Pass (1,374 m). The Pass itself is not very scenic, but was important throughout history and remains so today. The 37 km uphill ride on road 182 is very scenic and there are many pretty towns along the way in which you can rest or have a snack. The climb is steady and moderate all the way from Innsbruck, with two short downhill breaks and a final steeper climb. I felt moderate headwinds at some points of the ride. This ride is especially worth the effort for the tremendous 37 km downhill cruise on the trip back. On the way you will also pass Europabruck—a huge ramp that lets the autobahn traffic do the pass the easy way. Bring your passport if you want to cross into Italy. At the edge of Innsbruck is the almost frightening ski jump (Bergisel) where there are plaques listing all the medallists of the 1964 and 1976 Olympics and great views over the city.

Innsbruck to Landeck
75 km (47 miles)

The terrain on this day is almost but not quite flat as you cycle along road 171 toward the Arlberg Pass. You will be climbing steadily and very gradually. I felt moderate headwinds all day

Austria: Goldene Dachl in the main square at Innsbruck

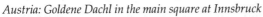

in this area. There is a steep climb into Imst with stunning mountain views all around. From Imst it is a short downhill or level ride to Landeck, a big town with two campgrounds. These are both on the western side of town, on the main road to the pass. The first is neat and small, run by a friendly woman and Gunthe the dog. It costs 115 öS ($10) for two and includes hot showers. The second is a nice, big site also on the Sanna river—a larger complex with a store and café. If you are thinking of a quick swim, the Sanna is clean and clear but shockingly cold.

Landeck to Bludenz
68 km (42 miles)

Turn right out of either campground and continue on road 171 to the Arlberg Pass. You must turn onto a side road to Flirsch, Schnann, and Pettneu before the first tunnel near the Arlberg. Say goodbye to traffic and flat riding. From Pettneu continue up the Arlberg on road 197. The first section of uphill riding under the sheltered parts of the road is the steepest, but the climb does continue for quite a distance after this curve. It is difficult, but such is the cycling life. There are nice views on the way up and also from the top. Congratulate yourself for cycling to 1,800 meters and enjoy the beautiful cruise down the other side.

Rejoin the main road at the bottom and turn right for Klosterle, just before the tunnel and a *No Bikes* sign. Follow this quiet road through Dalaas and back onto S16 until you reach another tunnel. Turn right onto the small track that goes around it. This will bring you through Innerbraz, Braz, and finally to Bludenz. The campground is above town. Walk straight through the pedestrian area that begins where the road comes to a T, then turn right and ride uphill at the western end of the pedestrian zone, following signs to Camping Bludenz 1 km away. The campground has many permanent residents and an attractive tree-lined area toward the back. Hot showers are included (120 öS for two per night). There is also another campground 2 km farther in Nüziders.

Bludenz to Vaduz, Liechtenstein
38 km (24 miles)

Hooray—you have made it all the way from Salzburg and can now enjoy an easy ride to the beautiful Rhine Valley and

Liechtenstein. From the center of Bludenz continue on road 190 to Nüziders. From here you can follow quiet side roads through the towns of Thungen, Thüringen, Schlins, and on to Feldkirch, or take a more direct route to Vaduz by crossing the autobahn to road 190 to Nenzing. Although 190 is a main road, it is very quiet due to the proximity of the autobahn. Both routes are clearly signed to Feldkirch, where you follow signs to Vaduz and CH (Switzerland). Keep in the left lane through the center of this small city to make the correct turns. There is a good deal of traffic in town but the crowded roads slow everyone down. Stick with signs to Vaduz and you will not go wrong.

Cross the Swiss-controlled border at Schannwald to enter Liechtenstein, an independent and neutral principality. Official currency is Swiss francs although austrian schillings and German marks are almost universally accepted as well. There are three campgrounds in Liechtenstein. One is in Bendern on a grassy open hill near the Rhine. Follow camping signs from the right turn in Nendeln. A nicer woodsy site 2 km south of Triesen is called Mittagspitze. Continue through Vaduz on the main road and watch for signs to the left turn. This site also has a pool. The most convenient campground is Meierhof camping—not the nicest site, but the closest to Vaduz, with easy public transport connections to upper Liechtenstein (where you probably do not want to cycle). To reach the site, turn left for Malbun and Triesenberg south of Vaduz. Hotel Meierhof is on the left near the beginning of the hill. There was a big NO CAMPING—GESCHLOSSEN (closed) sign up when we arrived, but the hotel let us stay. All campgrounds are about the same price ($5). The Triesen site has a pool in summer only. Vaduz is worth a quick look for the castle; however, it is absolutely overrun with tourists.

If you have the time, see what Liechtenstein is really about by hiking the excellent trails. Good cheap maps showing everything are available at the tourist office. The hike to Wildschloss is nice and easy, about 45 minutes walking from Vaduz and therefore well beyond the range of bus-tourists. If you have the time there are also stunning trails along the mountains in the upper valley and the ridge above the Rhine Valley. For an easy and quick bicycle trip along the valley floor, ride to Balzers for a look at its picture perfect castle. We spent a week hiking the peaks and admiring the amazing scenery in this unique and magnificently situated country. For a memorable visit, settle in and get to know Liechtenstein well.

Although this tour continues west for Zürich, you may also consider heading north to the Bodensee (Lake Constance) and the Black Forest in Germany, going on to connect with the Rhine and Mosel Valley tour from Germany to France and Luxembourg.

Vaduz to Walenstadt, Switzerland
25 km (15 miles)

This short, easy ride allows plenty of time to enjoy your last day in Liechtenstein or an afternoon on the Walensee. To stretch your time in Liechtenstein, ride south and cross the Rhine from Balzers to Trübbach to pick up the bicycle path paralleling the Rhine to Sargans (located just off the edge of map 413, where roads 13 and 3 converge). The trail does not have too many signs, but just after the river bends and you think you have gone too far, there will be a marked underpass to the right for Sargans (before the turn, you will see two small concrete bunkers along the path).

Sargans is a small town dominated by a castle perched on the hill above. It is best known for being the closest Swiss train stop to Liechtenstein. Follow blue signs for Zürich to take road 3 to Walenstadt. There are good shoulders on both sides of this quiet road and a separate bicycle path on the eastbound side. Walenstadt is 12 km down this flat road. Exit to the center of Walenstadt for a supermarket. To reach the campground, continue a short distance on road 3. *See-Camping* is clearly marked directly off road 3 (5 SF per person, 3 SF per tent— about $5 in all). This nice site is located directly on the shores of the stunning Walensee, where a rocky mountain ridge falls abruptly from two thousand meters high to the clear waters of the lake. Enjoy your first day in Switzerland either swimming or just taking in the amazing scenery from this beautiful spot.

Walenstadt to Zürich
82 km (51 miles)

The last day of this tour is a scenic and easy ride, thanks to the well-designed network of bicycle paths you may follow most of the way. Cycle west on road 3 to Zürich. After 1 km turn right onto the signed bicycle path to Murg and Weesen. This exceptional path runs along the very edge of the Walensee, allowing comfortable and quiet cycling in this scenic area. Unfortunately, the bicycle paths here are not signposted at every junction, making parts of the ride a guessing game. However, it is difficult to go wrong in the narrow, flat valley running directly west to Zürich. The yellow *Wanderweg* signs for hikers usually indicate the same route as the bicycle path, but follow red or orange bicycle markers when the two diverge as the hiking trail occasionally leads to gravel or stairs.

In Unterterzen cross over the train tracks and take the first right through an underpass signposted *See* to regain the bicycle trail. There are also two tunnels on the route but true to Swiss perfection, entirely separate tunnels are provided for pedestrians and hikers. Immediately before the first tunnel is a short, steep climb, the hardest part of the entire day. After the second tunnel follow signs for Zürich and Glarus, not Weesen (unless you want to detour around the north side of the valley floor). At the intersection with a road go straight, following blue bicycle path signs for Bilten and Niederurnen. Between Bilten and Reichenburg the bicycle path turns to gravel for a time. At the T intersection in Reichenburg turn right, then left to Siebnen on the blue signed road, N3.

I lost the bicycle path soon after and because of the lack of signs did not find it again until Richterswil on the Zürichsee. Here the trail is only a shoulder of the road. Though road 3 is not as peaceful and pleasant as the bicycle trails, it is still a

Switzerland: View of the Wallensee

reasonable route to Zürich as the shoulder is wide and traffic sparse even on the very outskirts of Zürich. Near Zürich, the mountains shrink to hills lining the long Zürichsee and cycling on the valleys floor remains flat.

Camping Seebucht, 5 km from the center of Zürich in Wollishofen, is located directly off road 3 to the right (well-marked). The nice lakeside site offers a grassy beach and good views of Zürich's varied skyline, a mixture of church spires, buildings in the old town, and modern architecture (5 SF person; 8 SF per tent). Good bus connections help you reach Zürich from the site for day trips without your bicycle. The youth hostel nearest the city is also in Wollishofen, signposted off road 3 another 1 km west. Follow these signs up the hill and turn right to find the Migros supermarket. There are also rooms for rent in Zürich.

To cycle to the center of town just continue on road 3. Zürich is a banker's city with a number of interesting sights such as the cobblestoned old town, boutique-lined Bahnhofstrasse, and long parks stretching along the lake's edge. The tourist information office is near the Bahnhof (train station) in the center of the city.

For an excellent bicycle ride through more of Switzerland, connect with the *Across the Alps* tour to Luzern, Interlaken, Bern, Lausanne, and finally Basel. Even if you do not have the time to complete the entire tour, consider cycling part of the way and then catching a train back to Zürich or your city of departure. The excellent Swiss railway system will ship your bicycle on the first train to any point in the country for 8 SF. Another good option is to cycle north to Schaffhausen and the Rheinfall, then follow the Rhine to Basel and beyond (see the *Rhine and Mosel Valleys* tour).

Zürich is the main train hub for central Europe, with easy connections to all major cities. Trains also run directly to the Zürich airport from the Bahnhof. If you are flying out of a Swiss city, look into the Fly-Luggage service that allows you to check baggage for a flight directly at a train station.

Across the Alps

Distance: 504 km (312 miles)

Recommended Touring Time:
11–13 days (8 cycling days)

Terrain: mostly along flat valleys, but also one long mountain pass and endlessly rolling hills in the southwest

Accommodations: camping or private rooms

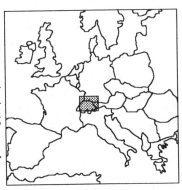

Maps: Michelin 427 (1 : 400,000)

Cycling this tour across the Alps, you will soon discover that Switzerland is not only a paradise for hikers and skiers. Beautiful mountains, quiet villages, and alpine meadows can also be appreciated from the seat of your bicycle and do not necessarily require the agony of endless uphill rides. Most of this ride 'Across the Alps' takes you along level mountain valleys

Switzerland: Village in the Engadine

and flat lakeside roads or bicycle trails, allowing you to be surrounded—and not overwhelmed—by the spectacular mountain scenery. Along this entire tour there is only one serious mountain pass to cross, and the excellent Swiss train system will give you the option to skip over the more challenging terrain if you prefer.

This tour begins in Zürich and quickly takes you to the heart of the Alps, from the city of Luzern to the spectacular Bernese Oberland, where some of the largest and most impressive mountains rise high above peaceful alpine valleys. From the capital city of Bern, the tour then heads south for Lac Léman and the French-speaking part of this multilingual country, visiting both resort cities and well-preserved, largely untouristed medieval towns. Finally, the ride swings back north to finish in the city of Basel, at the crossroads of Switzerland, France, and Germany where the Rhine turns sharply to begin its journey north to the sea.

Although the tour can be cycled in as little as eight days, you would not be doing justice either to yourself or to your fascinating host country if you did so. Take the time to appreciate the scenery, explore your own route away from the outlined path, and get an understanding of the many diverse parts of the country. Switzerland is less a single country than a collection of many distinct and unique regions. And although you may be on a bicycle trip, allow the time to slow your pace and hike some of the well-marked hiking trails that will bring you even closer to the countryside and the people.

Weather can be unpredictable and severe in the mountains. Summer and early fall are the best times to cycle this route, though there can be cold spells even then. Unfortunately, summer is also one of the peak tourist seasons, so some of the major sights may be crowded. However, the freedom of cycling allows you to escape the crowds once you have seen enough, and head for the quiet countryside. Switzerland has an excellent system of marked bicycle trails in many areas and very little car traffic in general, leaving most roads lightly traveled. This tour is based on camping, which in good summer weather is more enjoyable than any hotel. There are also hostels and inexpensive private rooms (Zimmer) for rent at all points along this route. The only drawback of a tour in Switzerland is the high cost of living, though with careful shopping and selection of accommodations you can keep your spending at a reasonable level. I was able to stay in Switzerland for between ten and fifteen dollars a day without going to extremes to do so.

I used the Michelin 1 : 400,000 map throughout Switzerland and bought more detailed maps in regions I wanted to explore more thoroughly. There are also 1 : 200,000 Michelin maps available. Another good option is the Generalkarte Schweiz, 1 : 300,000, published by Bundesamt fur Landestopographie. This excellent map covers all Switzerland with the detail of a hiking map (it also has contour lines). Finally, you can try the Kummerley and Frey 1 : 60,000 and 1 : 50,000 Velokarte series of 16 maps, which cover most of the country. These are special cycling maps that show bicycle paths and suitable tractor trails. All these are available in bookstores in Zürich and all over Switzerland (Michelin is the most readily found in the USA). Look at the incredible choice of bicycle touring books also available in these stores. There are many regional touring guides covering all Europe available, although most are written in German.

	Swiss-German	French
Hello:	*Grützie*	*Bonjour*
Thank you:	*Danke*	*Merci*

Zürich to Luzern
58 km (36 miles)

Zürich is a modern city, a banker's town having little in common with the picturesque alpine villages one imagines when thinking of Switzerland. It does, however, make an interesting and convenient starting point for this tour 'Across the Alps.' Zürich has a major airport and is the main train hub for all of Switzerland and beyond.

Bahnhofstrasse is the city's famous boutique-lined shopping street, leading from the train station to the shore of the Zürichsee, the long lake Zürich dominates. There are many pretty parks along the lake and the swimming is good. The old town is the best part of Zürich, with winding streets and cobblestones. There are expensive rooms and hotels in town. The noisy youth hostel is in Wollishofen, 5 km away on the west shore of the lake (follow signs to 114 Mutschellenstrasse). Your best bet is the pleasant lakeside campground, Camping Seebucht, directly off road 3 in Wollishofen (8 SF per tent; 5 SF per person; showers extra) in the direction of Thalwil. There is a supermarket (Migros; look for the orange sign) about 1 km away

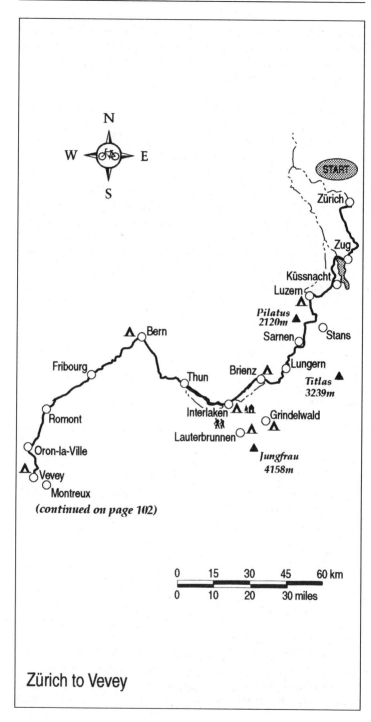

N
W E
S

START
Zürich

Zug

Küssnacht
Luzern

Pilatus
2120m

Sarnen
Stans

Bern

Fribourg

Thun
Brienz
Lungern

Titlas
3239m

Interlaken
Lauterbrunnen
Grindelwald

Romont

Oron-la-Ville

Vevey
Montreux

Jungfrau
4158m

(continued on page 102)

| 0 | 15 | 30 | 45 | 60 km |
| 0 | 10 | 20 | 30 miles |

Zürich to Vevey

in the center of Wollishofen. Follow youth hostel signs up the hill and ask. There are good bus connections into Zürich from here if you would like to go sightseeing without your bicycle.

The ride to Luzern starts with a long climb to 800m to leave the Zürichsee valley, but afterward involves mostly level lakeside cycling with some rolling hills the remainder of the way. Leave Zürich going south (take a left turn out of the campground) on road 3. Turn right 2 km after the campground, uphill toward *Adliswil* and *Kirche*. This will take you up the first ridge by the Zürichsee, down to Adliswil on the other side, and then up a much bigger ridge as you cycle to Zug. In Adliswil follow the blue signs to Zug and Luzern, which will lead you over the Adlispass, almost 800 m. It is a long and difficult climb but the road is good and traffic is light. At the Y-intersection near the top keep right for Hirschen. This road takes you over the top of the hill and on quiet side roads to Zug. Cycle through Hausen and Kappel, with downhills all the way to Baar and then flats to Zug. There are good bicycle paths paralleling this road.

Zug is a pretty town with wonderful views over the lake to the mountains in the distance. The park on the water's edge in Zug is a wonderful place for lunch. Follow signs for road 25 to get there. To resume cycling to Luzern, follow the lake's shore to the west and turn south, rejoining the road to Luzern. Follow road 4 to Cham and Holzhausern where you turn left for *Strandbad*. This will lead you over train tracks and right, to the bicycle path running south near the water's edge. The bicycle path rolls up and down hills (follow *Wanderweg* signs for *Küssnacht*) and eventually leads back to the road. This quiet road has either a shoulder or a bicycle lane at all times. The worst traffic I encountered were three horse-drawn carts in a row.

Eventually this road joins up with the larger road 2 to Luzern. Do not take the bicycle path immediately outside Küssnacht unless you want to see the center of this historic town, as it only leads you on a long detour and back onto the main road. There is a short tunnel soon after Küssnacht but it is well lit and has a separate bicycle lane. After that it is another rolling 14 km to Luzern.

Approaching Luzern, you will see the sign for the campground, Camping Lido, to the right. It is about 3 km from the center of town and located near the lake's edge but separated from it by a high wall (2 SF per tent; 4 SF per person). This is a reasonably priced campground with good facilities, including a kitchen and indoor dining/living room. There is also a hostel at 12 Sedelstrasse.

Luzern deserves a full day to see thoroughly. The city is beautifully located on the edge of a large lake and is ringed by medieval walls with guard towers. You can walk along the ramparts and climb the towers for excellent views of the city, the lake, and the surrounding mountains. The Lowendenkmal in the east part of town is a striking monument carved out of the face of a cliff. There are several supermarkets located in the squares nearby. The Kapellbrücke and Spreuerbrücke, bridges over the river, offer a different perspective on the old town, in which many buildings are beautifully decorated with intricate scenes and designs painted on the walls.

Luzern to Interlaken
60 km (37 miles)

This day is relatively short and most of the riding is on level terrain. However, the only seriously challenging climb of this tour, the Brunig Pass (1005 meters) lies between Luzern and Interlaken. This is not a big climb for the Alps, but it is nothing to sneeze at either. The climb is about 12 km long. If you are worried about the pass, you can easily ship your bicycle for 8SF from Luzern to Interlaken or to Brienz and it will arrive on the first train, allowing you to continue your ride the same day without hassle (see Switzerland in the Chapter 6, *Country Information* for information on shipping your bicycle).

If you are at Camping Lido, cycle into the center of Luzern and over the Seebrucke. Follow signs for *Horw* and road 4 all the way through Luzern. There are several junctions where it is not marked, but stay on the main traffic path and you will pick up signs again. In Horw follow signs for Stans and Sarnen. You will continue on road 4 along the lake and cross an inlet to Stansstad. Then follow signs for Sarnen, not Stans any longer. In this way you can take road 4, a mostly level road with very little traffic, all the way to Sarnen. There is one short tunnel but it is well-lit and traffic is sparse.

In Sarnen you must join the main road over the Brunig Pass to the Interlaken area. Traffic picks up but is still only inter-mittent. And unfortunately, just when you need it, there is no bicycle lane and only a small shoulder the rest of the way. The pass is a long, hard climb to 1005 m, but not too bad as passes in the Alps go. The traffic is not a problem but the road is not pleasantly quiet.

After Sarnen, cycle around the Sarnersee to Giswil, where the 12 km climb up to the Brunig Pass begins. There are steep sections of road on the way to Kaiserstuhl, then endless hairpin curves. Nowhere on the ride is there the 13% incline indicated on the Michelin map, so do not worry about that. You will get a brief break in Lungern, a downhill and a flat section, before climbing the rest of the pass and pedaling more hairpin turns. Eventually the climb becomes much more gradual the rest of the way to the top of the pass, which is in the tiny settlement of Brunig. Then your efforts are rewarded with a long, beautiful cruise down the other side. Follow blue signs for Brienz and Interlaken. It is 17 km from Brienz to Interlaken right along the shores of the Brienzersee, a mostly level ride with some rolling climbs toward the end. Head for the center (*Zentrum*) in Interlaken and look for information billboards or the tourist office.

There are several campgrounds and two hostels in town. Cycle south to the adjoining town of Matten and toward Wengen to reach Balmer's Herberge, a Eurailer-filled independent hostel on Haupstrasse. Balmer's offers both private and communal rooms, and is a great place for some conversation or company, but in general, it bears more resemblance to a college fraternity than a quiet Swiss retreat, so be forewarned. Farther along the same road to the right is the Jungfraublick campground (8 SF per tent; 8 SF per person). There are also several campgrounds on the Brienzersee, at Brienz and Ringgenberg. Around the corner from Balmer's is a Coop supermarket. There are also campgrounds in Grindelwald and Lauterbrunnen that allow you to stay closer to the mountains, but the ride from Interlaken is all uphill (I chose to use Interlaken as a base for this reason).

Interlaken is not a destination in itself, being a tourist-filled town with little of interest besides convenient transport up into the Berner Oberland with the famous peaks of the Eiger, Mönch, and Jungfrau (topping 4000 m). It is most convenient to use Interlaken as a base for day trips to the mountains, leaving your bicycle in town and taking a bus or train to reach trailheads in the Oberland. Grindelwald is a touristy town under the north face of the Eiger and a good starting point for countless hikes in the spectacular Oberland. The Lauterbrunnen valley is slightly less touristed and equally beautiful. If the prospect of a few hours' hike does not appeal to your tired legs, it is also possible to ride the many cable cars and chair lifts in the area and either walk or ride the lift back down. The unquestioned king of these pricey transport services is the train that goes to the top of the Jungfraujoch through tunnels carved through the mountain itself. The ride is said to be unforgettable, but so is the price, close to $100. Information offices in all the towns can help you pick a suitable hike or excursion.

If you are touring in the summer, try to be in the area on a Thursday or Saturday for the opportunity to see the wonderful Tellspiele, the enactment of the Wilhelm Tell play in Interlaken. The play is performed in German but you can buy an English summary. The memorable production is staged in an outdoor theater with the audience sitting in a covered amphitheater and the action taking place in a huge clearing in the woods before them. The life-sized set features an entire village with real houses, cows, sheep, and goats, and characters galloping by on horses. The play truly brings you back hundreds of years in time and, despite the language difference, clearly conveys the Tell story, an important part of Swiss folklore. Tickets are available at the tourist office. (I came late to the theater and got in free.)

Interlaken to Bern
57 km (35 miles)

From the center of Interlaken follow signs for Unterseen, Merligen, and Thun to access the secondary road on the north shore of the Thunersee (the main road is on the south shore). Before reaching the Interlaken West train station turn right, over the railroad tracks for the road leading to the north shore. In Unterseen there are two more campgrounds if you just cannot bear to leave the area, or if the 2 km covered are enough to call it a day.

Although this road parallels the lake's shore, there are many long, gradual climbs after the initially flat section. There are also two sets of several tunnels in a row. All are very short and have wide lanes, being more like underpasses than tunnels. Traffic is only sporadic on this quiet road, and the views of the craggy ridges across the south shore of the lake are incredible. Cycle through Oberhofen and on to Thun, 23 km from Interlaken. As you enter Thun, follow blue signs for Bern and road 6. This is the main road (besides the autobahn) to Bern. You will only follow it a few km.

Ignore the first (green) sign for Seftigen to the right; instead, take the second, a left turn to Seftigen about 2 km later. This will take you west of the main road and through a series of hilly villages to follow a quieter route to Switzerland's capital. Pedal through Seftigen and at the T intersection several km later, turn right for Bern and Mühlethurnen. Do not forget to turn and look back at the spectacular view of the Oberland in the distance. Cycle through Mühlethurnen, Kirchenthurnen, and Toffen. After Toffen you will merge with a larger road. Turn left for Bern. As you near Kehrsatz the road suddenly widens and there is a *no bikes* sign. Swing right to cycle through the town, and then take the bicycle path that begins when you rejoin the main road.

Keep on the marked bicycle path right into Bern. Soon after passing signs for Koniz on the edge of the city there are signs to the right for the campground. Signs will lead you directly to the large, nice site on the River Aare. There is a restaurant and shop at the campground, and they can also provide you with a city map and information (3 SF per tent; 6 SF per person; students 5 SF). The campground is 3 km from the center of town, with access via a riverside bicycle path. You can park your bicycle at one of the many bicycle racks below the old town, since there is a steep hill to the town and the streets are all cobblestoned. In addition to the campground, there is also a well-situated youth hostel on the edge of the old town on Weihergasse.

Bern is the capital of Switzerland but only the third-largest city (Zürich is the biggest, but even so its population is only 350,000). The most outstanding features of the old town are the arcaded medieval streets dotted with fountains, each decorated with a different character or symbol. The well-designed walking tour outlined by the tourist office (in the train station at the edge of the old town) will take you past each of these as well as to the clock tower, and eventually across the river to the famous bear pits. There are live bears there, reminders of the city's founding by Berchtold of Zahringen.

Bern to Vevey
90 km (56 miles)

From the center of town, follow blue signs for Fribourg. This takes you west and then south for Fribourg and road 12. I cycled the 31 km to Fribourg on this road as it was very quiet at the time I was there (Monday morning) and has a wide shoulder. You can also take side roads through Flamatt, Laupen, Bundtels, and Düdingen. There is a long, steady climb out of Bern and a few more hills on the way to Fribourg, but nothing exceptional.

At Fribourg follow signs for *centre ville* (not *vielle ville* to the right, which takes you to the same place by a longer route) and abruptly enter French-speaking Switzerland (everyone also speaks German, and most speak English as well). Fribourg is an interesting old town with medieval streets to explore and a large cathedral. Unfortunately, it is also mostly uphill. This city makes a good stopping point for lunch or a break before continuing to Vevey. It is also the best place to break this long ride into two days, though there is no campground in town, only a hostel (2 rue de l'Hôpital). For some reason, every guidebook I have seen confuses me by saying Fribourg 'is not to be confused with Freiburg im Breisgau'— which is 200 km away in Germany. How can one be confused, I wonder? But in case you are, it is an entirely different place.

Head out of Fribourg on the main road south for Bulle (road 12). There is a clearly marked right turn for Matran and Romont 3 km outside Fribourg on this road. Take this road to access quiet side roads all the way to the shores of Lac Léman. Cycle through Matran, Neyruz, and Villaz St. Pierre, following signs to Romont and Oron. Once again, the roads are full of long, steady climbs and descents through the wheat and cornfields of Fribourg Canton. There were strong head or sidewinds when I cycled this route, and several days later, when I headed back north, there were still headwinds. You are probably in for a windy ride, but the magnificent scenery more than makes up for it.

Romont is a striking town on a hill with medieval walls and towers, and completely untouristed. From there you begin the last third of the ride south by heading for Oron, 16 km away. Cycle to Oron-le-Châtel, then Oron-la-Ville, then Palézieux, Bossonnens, and finally begin the last ascent over the ridge above Lac Léman. From the top, follow blue signs for Vevey and Montreux for a beautiful zigzagging descent through steep vineyard-covered hills to the sparkling waters of the lake below.

Vevey is a small city that makes a good stopping point after a long day of cycling. From here you can appreciate the views of the lake and mountains without the hassle of dealing with a large city right away. There is a cheap campground 3 km west of town, well-marked off road 9 to Lausanne (Camping La Pichette, at the end of a long dead-end street; 2 SF per tent; 5 SF per person; students 3.5 SF). Road 9 toward Lausanne is busy but has a wide shoulder.

While the modern center of Vevey is not altogether inspiring, the long lakeside park and lovely promenade are. The pretty old town is nestled between road 9 and the promenade. You can ride your bicycle several km down the promenade (it is quite far from the campground) and enjoy views across the lake to the sharp ridges of the mountains to the south.

Vevey to Lausanne
18 km (11 miles)

This is a very short and flat ride along the lake to Lausanne. I cycled directly to Lausanne, though you can lengthen the tour if time allows, and first cycle 7 km east to Montreux and perhaps 3 km more to the château of Chillon. You can easily cover all this in a day trip, leaving your things in Vevey until you cycle back west from Montreux, a resort city famous for its music festivals. To extend your tour even more, consider cycling right around Lac Léman to Montreux, along the French side to Geneva, and then on to Lausanne. The short, direct ride to Lausanne can also be stretched into a leisurely tour of the pretty lakeside villages on the way, as many have medieval houses and towers. Cully, for example, has a lovely town center with cobblestoned streets and flower-decked buildings.

The ride to Lausanne is simple; follow road 9 westward. The road is wide enough for safety though traffic is heavy. You can detour through the towns on the way for a break from the main road. Lausanne has a hostel (1 chemin du Muguet in Ouchy), lots of rooms, and a campground located in Vidy, on the west edge of town, about 3 km from Ouchy. Ouchy is the port section of Lausanne. The city center and all its sights are on the hills above Ouchy.

To get to the campground, follow signs for *Pully-sud* and *Ouchy* as you near Lausanne. This will keep you on the lakeside road that has a bicycle lane after the center of Ouchy (where there is a pretty harbor and clock tower). Cycle in the direction of *Genève* and the autoroute signs and eventually see signs for the campground. Pass the hostel (on the right) and cycle another 1.5 km on this road, circling around one large roundabout from which point the campground is indicated. Camping de Vidy (5 SF per tent; 7 SF per person; 6 SF students)

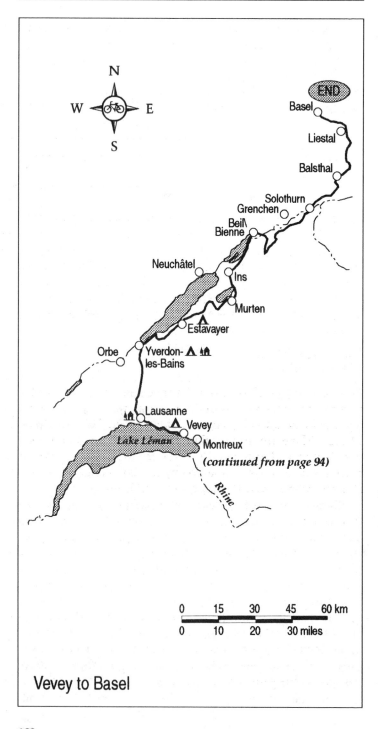

(continued from page 94)

Vevey to Basel

will be to the left, in the same direction as the office of the Olympic Committee, on the lake (but no access or views). Right next to the campground (to the east) are the extensive ruins of Roman Lousanna, with both the Forum and residential areas visible. You can cycle past these ruins when heading back through Lausanne on the way to Murten.

The campground will give you a map and an exhaustive (but still useful) *Official Guide* to Lausanne. My favorite sights were simply the old town in general and the views of the lake. There is an extensive pedestrian zone in the center of the old city, a Gothic cathedral, and a fourteenth-century château. Lausanne is called 'the Olympic city' as it houses the headquarters of the International Olympic Committee (near the campground, in fact). There is also an interesting, and free, Olympic museum on Avenue Ruchonnet near the railroad station in the city. I would highly recommend this as an inspirational stop before you cycle out of the city to Yverdon and Murten. The short movie shown there inspires exactly the stoicism and endurance you need for the long climb away from the shores of Lac Léman.

Lausanne to Murten
83 km (51 miles)

This day will take you from the mountain views across Lac Léman, through several beautifully preserved medieval towns, and finally back to German-speaking Switzerland in medieval Murten. There are many rolling hills on the way and a good possibility for a headwind. However, the expansive views over lakes and fields as well as the old towns subdividing the ride into distinct sections make the day go by quickly.

Cycle north out of Lausanne on road 5 to Yverdon. Avenue d'Echallens in Lausanne will lead you onto this road. It is all uphill the first few km but not very steep, the ridge quickly surmounted with the help of the prescribed dose of Olympic inspiration. Be careful for the trolley tracks in town. Take road 5 until Cheseaux, 8 km from Lausanne. Here you can take quiet side roads by following signs to Cossonay and Orbe. This road splits after 2 km; bear right for Boussens, Orbe, and Yverdon. You can follow this peaceful and gently rolling road through several small farming towns to Chavornay. Bavois has a castle above town and some neatly kept farmhouses, a real slice of country life in Vaud. Do not go to Orbe from Chavornay but keep straight for Yverdon. The road will soon merge with larger roads to lead you into Yverdon and the town center.

Yverdon-les-Bains is beautifully situated on the south end of Lac de Neuchâtel. The town originally developed around thermal baths and is truly unique in the array of remains from different historical periods that have been well preserved in the small city, from prehistoric standing stones to Roman baths and medieval architecture. Head for the center of town and the main square around the château. All around are beautifully restored houses and cobblestoned streets dotted with fountains. Yverdon is a great place for lunch before continuing the ride north. There is also a campground and a youth hostel if you are tempted to stay the night.

To continue the ride, take the secondary road to Estavayer-le-Lac around the south shore of the lake. To do so from the center of town, follow one of the canals to the lake and turn right. This will eventually bring you to the secondary road via several local roads. You will cycle past the lakeside campground. Immediately before the junction with the road to Estavayer there is a brown sign to the left for *Menhirs*, which will lead you down a smooth dirt path to the standing stones, arranged in rows. You can cut through the trees directly onto the bicycle path that parallels the lakeside road northeast.

There are few lake views from this road because of the marsh in the way. The bicycle path runs a level course and stops at Yvonand, but there is only moderate to light traffic on the road after that point. There is a long, tough climb after Cheyres but then a long downhill ride. Estavayer-le-Lac is another wonderfully preserved and only quietly touristed town, surrounded by medieval walls punctuated by large gateways. The streets are lined with continuous arcades a la Bern, but with a much more personal and lively appeal. There is another campground here, another temptation to cut the day short in this lovely town.

Follow signs to Grandcour from Estavayer (do not go to Payerne) to remain on side roads. Because many border cities have slightly different names in German and French, Murten (the German name) is called Morat in French. From Grandcour cycle toward Neuchâtel and Villars-le-Grand. After cycling 12 km from Estavayer, past St. Aubin, there is a large intersection. Turn right for Avenches and later left for road 1 to Bern in Avenches. This is a major road with a steady stream of cars. Cycle the last 9 km to Murten on this road.

Make the abrupt change back to German as you cycle onto the cobblestoned streets of Murten. Here is another example of an exceptionally preserved medieval town, a miniature Bern in architectural style. However, it has been invaded by tourists more than Estavayer or Yverdon, so the main street is fairly crowded. The two side streets within the town walls are very quiet (most tourists do not stray far from the main path) and allow you to appreciate the shuttered stone houses in peace. You can also walk the town ramparts.

There is a sign for the campground down to the left as you enter town. The campground, Camping Löwenberg, is actually 3 km away in Muntelier. While not a classy site, it will do. The campground is on the shores of the small Murtensee (5SF per tent; 5 SF per person). They make an effort to entertain you in the bathroom with a seemingly endless recording of such American favorites as *Yankee Doodle Dandy* and *Glory Glory Hallelujah*—in double extended version. It is enough to scare you into the woods after the third time around. The campground also has a bar and a small shop. Because of the distance, consider visiting Murten before heading out to the site. There is also a Migros market past the northeast exit of Murten's walls. There is no hostel and rooms in town are expensive.

Switzerland: Town square at Yverdon-les-bains

Murten to Härkingen
82 km (51 miles)

The scenery and terrain remain much the same on this day, with long, rolling hills and pretty rural towns along the way to Basel. There was still a headwind as I cycled this route. The first leg of the ride will take you to Biel (Bienne in French), a modern town with little of interest. Turn left out of Lowenberg campground and cycle to the intersection with a larger road. Turn left there for Ins and Neuchâtel. It is 10 km on this flat road to Ins. Cycle uphill to the town center there and watch for the right turn for Biel. After a few more up and down hills, you will cross the Aare Kanal, cycle up to Täuffelen, then downhill to Biel. First you will enter Nidau and pass the château there. Cross several sets of railroad tracks in Biel, heading for *Zentrum* and then for *Buren*. I cycled a confusing, circuitous route to the *Zentrum*, past the train station, and then to an intersection with signs for Buren. Follow this road left and straight, out of Biel. It will take you first through Orpund and 5 km later to another intersection. Turn right for Buren in order to stay on quiet roads to Solothurn.

You will enter Buren over a new, wooden covered bridge. The town is small and very pretty, with great medieval flavor. There are bear flags everywhere, a sign that you are back in Bern canton. This town makes a nice stopping point before the next 15 km to Solothurn. Follow quiet road 22 left out of Buren to ride through more farm country and long, rolling hills. Finally you will descend to the Aare river and Solothurn. Follow signs and the sight of the cathedral's dome across the river to the city center.

Solothurn is known as the most important Baroque town in Switzerland, with the cathedral as its centerpiece. Clustered around it and protected by tall walls are the buildings of the old town and a number of pleasantly cool fountains. For good reason, Solothurn is swarming with tourists, but the city's beauty is not marred even by the crowds. This is the best place along the route for a long lunch. There is a Coop supermarket outside the western gate to the old town. I was very tempted to stay in the town, but the nearest campground is 11 km (in the wrong direction) away in Grenchen and there is no hostel.

In order to make the next day's ride to Basel shorter, I cycled to the campground in Härkingen, 26 km northeast of Solothurn as there are no other campgrounds conveniently located on the direct route. There is nothing worthwhile in Härkingen except for a campground and a warehouse. Bring supplies from Solothurn. There is also a hostel in Langenbruck, at the top of the pass via road 12 to Basel.

To camp at Harkingen, follow blue signs for Olten and Basel out of Solothurn (road 5). The road has a good bicycle path next to it for the entire distance except for a stretch around Oberbipp (west of Niederbipp), where you can follow side roads through the small towns on the way and orient yourself by paralleling the main road, the railroad tracks, and the mountain ridge to your left. The ride is mostly flat all the way. In Egerkingen, 7 km after Oensingen, watch for the right turn to Härkingen. This will take you to an intersection where signs indicate Härkingen in three different directions. Turn left, cross over the autobahn, make a right over the train tracks, and the campground will be on your left by the large warehouse. There is nothing of interest here except you, since the campground is the type where people move in for the whole summer and sit around watching each other (3 SF per tent; 3 SF per person; small bar and restaurant).

Härkingen to Basel
44 km (27 miles) direct; 56 km (35 miles) indirect

From Härkingen, cycle over the ridge to the west, the last barrier separating you from Basel. There are two choices. You can either cycle the short, hard way, climbing straight over the ridge from Egerkingen to Langenbruck, gaining 800 m in 6 km, or you can retrace your route 7 km back to Oensingen and turn right for road 12 to Balsthal and Langenbruck. This involves a long, gradual climb of 10 km to an altitude of 730 m. The first choice makes the day 44 km (27 miles) long; the second takes you 56 km (35 miles) to Basel.

From the top of the ridge at 730 m in Langenbruck, it is basically downhill all the way to Basel. Cruise down through Waldenburg, Oberdorf, Hölstein, and on to Liestal. As you approach Liestal you will be obliged to turn right, off the main road, because it becomes an autobahn. So turn right and immediately left over the overpass. Follow blue signs for Liestal center and then to Pratteln. In Pratteln the secondary road ends and you must rejoin road 2. There are, however, two other big roads paralleling this one into Basel, so traffic is not too heavy.

107

Cycle on to Muttenz and then Basel-Ost. As you enter the city, keep straight for Zentrum and Bahnhof SBB (not Badischer Bahnhof). There is a bicycle path the last few km into the city center (and other bicycle lanes all over town). You will eventually arrive at the large area around Bahnhofplatz. From here the old town center is directly north (ask for directions to the Aldstadt). Turn right onto Elisabethenstrasse and then left onto Freiestrasse. This leads you to the Rathaus and Marktplatz. The main tourist office is straight ahead, along the Rhine.

While the area around Basel is heavily industrialized, the city retains a quiet and classy atmosphere. The closest campground is 10 km away in Reinach. You can get there by turning left off road 2 as you enter the city, where there is a sign for Münchenstein. A better and infinitely more convenient option is the youth hostel at St. Alban-Kirchrain 10. This is east of the Munsterplatz (the main cathedral), just off the Rhine (it is well signed from the Kunstmuseum area). This very nice, new hostel offers private double rooms in addition to regular dorm rooms, with non-members also welcome (dorms 18 SF; private doubles only 22 SF per person; non-members add 7 SF more for either; unlimited breakfast included). If you arrive early, even in summer, you have a good chance of getting a private room, or reserve ahead (tel. 061 230572). There are usually many cyclists and families staying in this pleasant hostel.

The best thing to do in Basel is to simply wander the twisting streets of the old town (many of the houses go back to the 1300s). The decorated walls of the Rathaus are also interesting. From the balcony behind the Munster, the view over the Rhine is tremendous, as is the reverse view from the other side of the river.

From Basel, you can continue cycling north along the Rhine to Germany, France, and Luxembourg with the *Rhine and Mosel Valleys* tour. Zürich is about two days away by bicycle, following the Rhine. If you are out of time, there are train connections from Basel to Zürich or other points in Europe (direct connections, for example, to Paris). If you are flying out of an airport in Switzerland, look into the Fly-Luggage service the Swiss Rail Service offers. You can check baggage, such as your bicycle, for a flight directly at the train station for a small fee.

Verona, Venice to Vienna

Incredible terrain and culture contrasts from Italy's flatlands to Yugoslavia's slow pace and Austrian mountain passes.

Distance: 848 km(527 miles)

Recommended touring time: 17–20 days (11 cycling days)

Terrain: Verona to Venice to Trieste: dead flat and easy; Trieste to Vienna: spectacular mountains followed by rolling hills south of Vienna

Accommodations: mostly camping with hostel options

Maps: Michelin 426   Austria 1 : 400,000 (partial coverage) or Hallweg Nord Italia 1 : 750,000

Mountain pass on the Austrian–Yougoslav border

109

Due to civil strife in Yugoslavia at the time of going to press (Spring 1992), it is advisable to detour that part of the route until the region has returned to peace. Cycle north from Trieste to Udine and Tarvisio in Italy. There you can cross the border directly into Austria, riding to Villach and east to resume the tour near Klagenfurt.

If you have doubts as to how far it is possible to travel and how much there is to see in a reasonable amount of time on a bicycle, consider what cycling from Verona to Vienna in three weeks includes. Verona, Padua, and Venice are all beautiful Italian cities situated in the broad, flat Po Valley. Here the often featureless landscape makes cycling easy if not as exciting as the cities' sights. Following the Adriatic coast toward Trieste may tempt you to continue south along its azure waters, but equally appealing mountain scenery lies ahead. Here the route turns inland for a taste of Yugoslavia and continues upward to the Austrian border.

Despite the higher prices and challenging cycling, Austria's well-ordered lifestyle will be welcome after the frustrations of Italian and Yugoslav bureaucracy. You can take pride in your sore muscles, having truly experienced this beautiful region under your own power—every endless climb and soaring descent. The mountains eventually subside into rolling hills on the last stretch into Vienna. This beautiful capital is dotted with monumental state buildings and public parks, and for sight-seeing on a smaller scale, the historic old town is an easy place to lose yourself in. Vienna is a city best appreciated in a few relaxed days off your bicycle, so take the time to enjoy it thoroughly.

This tour can easily be broken into two sections if mountain cycling does not appeal to you. The ride from Verona to Trieste offers flat terrain, making a good week-long trip in Italy. You can venture farther west in the Po Valley or take a train to other points in Europe from any city on the route. Michelin map #426 is an excellent guide, but only includes Austria and border areas. The Hallweg map is surprisingly detailed, despite its large scale, and is suitable for the Italian and Yugoslav parts of the trip and as an overall planning map. These and other choices are readily available in Verona and other towns along the route.

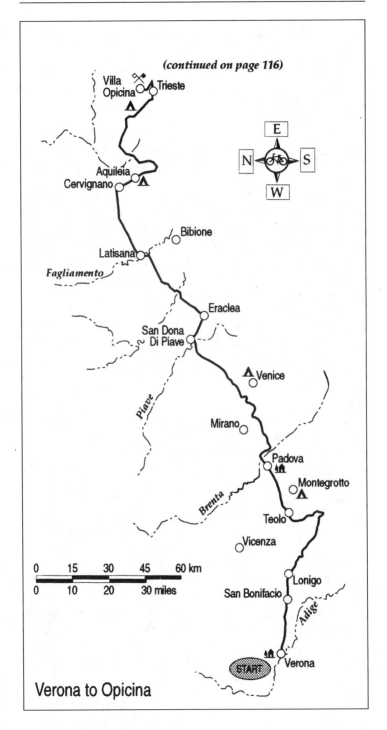

(continued on page 116)

Verona to Opicina

	Italian	Serbo-Croatian	German
Hello:	*Buon giorno*	*Dobar Dan*	*Grüss Gott*
Thank you:	*Grazie*	*Hvala*	*Danke*

Verona to Padova
87 km (54 miles)

Verona is best known as the home of Romeo and Juliet. Romantics will enjoy visiting Juliet's balcony and tomb. Others can enjoy a good laugh at these tourist traps. The famed Arena di Verona, on the other hand, promises entertainment of a more authentic kind. This two-thousand-year-old Roman arena is one of the best preserved in Europe and stages unforgettable performances during the opera festival in July and August. You do not have to be an opera lover to be impressed by the huge stagings, quality performances, and unique setting of the Arena di Verona. The arena seats twenty thousand people on original stone tiers and typically boasts a cast of hundreds, including a few dozen horses and, sometimes, elephants. *Aida* just does not get any more spectacular than this. Tickets are reasonable at about $12 and are usually available up to the day of the performance.

Verona itself is full of beautiful old buildings and public squares. The hostel, one of the best in Europe, is a newly renovated fifteenth-century villa decorated with beautiful frescoes. The management is incredibly friendly and helpful and breakfast is unlimited—two unbelievable features in an Italian hostel. Even in the crowded peak season, the staff will not turn anyone away. You can also camp on the large grounds at a fraction of the regular cost. The hostel is located to the northeast across the river from Verona's center, near the Roman Theater (15 salita Fontana del Ferro). Verona is well worth a few relaxed days and evenings at the opera before setting out for Venice.

From the Arena di Verona, follow blue signs for SS11 to Vicenza. Traffic here is constant but not too fast and generally considerate, and the road is wide enough for comfortable riding. After 24 km turn right for San Bonifacio and follow quiet roads signposted for Lonigo. From here we went ahead to Vicenza but were disappointed by the town and lack of a campground and decided to continue on to Padova (Padua). Unless you are a student of Palladian architecture, I would not recommend the detour to Vicenza.

From Lonigo, turn east to Orgiano, Sossano, Teolo, and eventually to Padova. This route skirts around Vo and Mount Berici, which would have added hills to your nice flat ride. We felt slight headwinds all day in this area, but they were not enough to interfere with our cycling.

Padova is an interesting university city with many pensions and a hostel at 30 via Aleardi. These accommodations are often full of carryovers from nearby Venice, so it is advisable to call ahead. The nearest campground is in distant Montegrotto, southwest on SS16. Padova is a nice stopover point on the way to Venice. Take the time to look around its side streets and public squares.

Padova to Venice (Fusina)
35 km (21 miles)

Cycling to Venice (Venezia) can be problematic due to the city's location in a lagoon. The most direct route to Venice is SS11, but traffic increases considerably as you near the city. Taking a series of side roads may be confusing at times but is worth the peaceful pedaling. To do so, leave Padua on road 515 toward Treviso. Get off after about 16 km. Any of the large roads going right after Vigonza will lead you to Mirano, then to Spinea. From here follow signs for Venezia and Marghera, turn toward Marghera (not Mira), and come to a large traffic circle.

At the traffic circle you can decide to take the main road directly into Venezia if you are looking for pension accommodations. In the summer three schools are put to use as dormitories, but even then a vacancy can be difficult to find. The hostel is just off Venezia on Isla Giudecca, but you cannot bring your bicycle on the ferry. Check the tourist information office on the Piazza San Marco for more details.

To reach the comfortable and well-organized campground, take the Venezia/Fusina exit off this traffic circle (just before the main Venezia exit) and follow clear signs to Camping Fusina. This is a huge, moderately priced site with a grocery store and nice views across the lagoon to Venice. Right next to the campground is a half-hourly ferry into the city. The well-priced Car supermarket in Venezia is just a few blocks to the left of the ferry landing.

Everything you have seen and heard about Venice is probably true. It is a beautiful and romantic city despite the decay and pollution. Every side street and canal has its own charm and, fortunately, the mobs of tourists tend to stay in the area around Piazza San Marco. Gondola rides are extremely expensive, but it is almost as fun to take the waterbus down the Grand Canal. Take an end seat in front and enjoy the view.

Venice to Aquileia
119 km (74 miles)

This is a long day, but the terrain is absolutely flat, and travel is fast. You can make it shorter by stopping at Bibione on the coast, but this is basically a 15 km dead end that you will have to retrace the next day. There are not many campgrounds in this area. The coastal sites are especially expensive, mosquito-laden, and full of North European caravanners.

From Fusina return to Malcontenta, turn right for Venezia, and watch for blue signs to Trieste. Follow SS14 to Trieste for 40 km to San Donà di Piave, where there is a large riverside park, a quiet place for a picnic lunch. Continue through the center of town. To get off the main road, turn right for Stretti. This turn is not signposted, so ask directions if possible. The turn will come after you pass the center of town; the main road forks, continuing either straight or right. Straight is marked *Trieste* and under it is a sign for public toilets. Instead, turn right here. If you see a Farmacia 50 m down on the right, you are on the correct road.

Several kilometers down the road a sign will welcome you to the community of Eraclea (not Eraclea itself, do not panic) and shortly after, you will pass through Stretti. Do not turn off for Eraclea or Jesolo while on this road. At the large traffic circle past Stretti, turn left for Bibione and Trieste and keep following signs for these two towns through Sindacale and Lugugnana. Rejoin the main road at Latisana and go another 28 km to Cervignano, where you will turn right, and it will be clearly signposted for Aquileia. (If you are headed for Bibione, the turn toward the coast and Bibione is clearly marked before you reach Latisana).

Aquileia is 8 km from here. As you enter the town, watch for the clearly marked left turn for Camping Aquileia, which is next to the ruins of a large Roman harbor. The campground has a pool full of Germans and is moderately priced. There is another campground farther down the main road. Aquileia has two archaeological museums and a basilica with notable mosaics, if you have the time and the energy. The harbor is the best sight—free, close, and quite interesting.

Aquileia to Opicina
50 km (31 miles)

This day's cycling will take you along tempting Adriatic waters to the large harbor city of Trieste and high above toward the Yugoslav border. There are no campgrounds immediately in Trieste, but you can spend the hot afternoon there before heading up to Opicina. You cannot obtain Yugoslavian dinars in an Italian bank, so wait until you have crossed the border to exchange money. The border bank is also open on weekends, although the grocery stores will probably be closed.

Turn right out of the campground and back to signs for Trieste. Initially, the terrain around Aquiliea is flat and boring, but you will soon turn south around the Gulf of Trieste. Follow the coast road (it is marked as such), not the industrial route. You will encounter some hills while cycling along the gorgeous Adriatic coastline, but the busy roads are very wide and comfortable, even on crowded summer days. Here there are good views of Villa Miramar, a beautiful castle on a promontory by the sea.

As you enter Trieste, you will pass a long beach, a shady park (with water fountains), and the train station on your right. Look for a sign to Opicina, Yugoslavia, and Ljubljana after the station; turn left at the first light after this sign. The road to Opicina is well marked, about 6 km of long, steady uphill cycling. Buy food in Trieste before riding up, because Opcina is a very small town, only noted as a border crossing point. Camping Obelisko is just outside of the town on your right. A final 150 m of nasty uphill climbing on the campground driveway will bring you home. The campground is moderately priced at about $4 per person. Another campground will bring you even closer to the border on the road to Ljubljana. To reach it, continue through Opicina and look for signs to Camping Europa. There is a nice viewpoint near Camping Obelisko, where you can look down over the lights of Trieste at night.

Opicina to Ljubljana
96 km (60 miles)

Now continue up the mountain (you're almost there...) to the Yugoslav border 4 km from Camping Obelisko. At the border go directly to the visa office on the left. You will get a free visa while you wait. Enter Yugoslavia and change money at the official bank (a warning: they do not accept 1,000 lira notes).

115

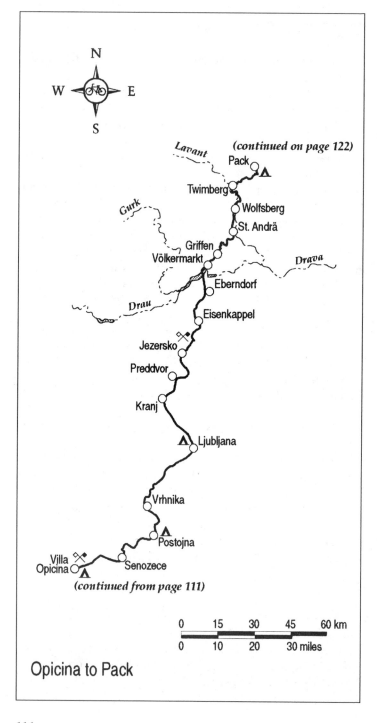

(continued on page 122)

Pack

Twimberg

Wolfsberg

St. Andrä

Griffen

Völkermarkt

Eberndorf

Eisenkappel

Jezersko

Preddvor

Kranj

Ljubljana

Vrhnika

Postojna

Villa
Opicina

Senozece

(continued from page 111)

Lavant

Gurk

Drava

Drau

| 0 | 15 | 30 | 45 | 60 km |
| 0 | 10 | 20 | 30 miles |

Opicina to Pack

Follow signs for Ljubljana on E61/70 for 20 km—this is a narrow road with lots of Yugoslav truck traffic. You will ride by beautifully forested hills, mountains, and fields. Pass through several practically non-existent towns until the intersection after Senorice, where you follow white signs to Ljubljana and Postojna (green signs are for the main highway). This quiet road will bring you through Postojna and all the way to the capital of the province of Slovenia.

Popular sights in Postojna are the natural caves with rock formations. There is also a campground near the caves if you want to call it a day. You will have a long climb soon after Postojna and then a beautifully soaring downhill coast—but watch out for sharp turns. After Vrhnika the road unfortunately degenerates to an uneven, unrepaired surface and then a jarring 8 km of cobblestones before reaching the outskirts of Ljubljana.

There is a bicycle lane into Ljubljana and clear signs for the campground, which is 5 km north of the city in the direction of the Maribor road. Cycling is not permitted in the center of the city, so we walked our bikes for a few blocks to reach the tourist information office. There are many places that offer *Tourist Information*, but most are travel agents. Ask for the national office on Titova Cesta. To reach the campground walk up the main street until you rejoin the bicycle path, and cycle the remaining 5 km. The campground is somewhat expensive

Italy: View of Venice

(about $5 a person), with an indoor pool and large, shady grounds. There is a bus stop close to the campground if you want to visit the city at night.

The scenic old town is clustered around the river Ljubljanica and dominated by a hilltop fortress. The many riverside restaurants are pleasant and are your most reasonable opportunity to eat out on this tour (three pizzas and drinks for two came to ten dollars). Life in Yugoslavia is fairly slow and low-tension, an interesting mix of East and West European lifestyles.

Ljubljana to Eberndorf
93 km (58 miles)

The ride from Ljubljana to Kranj follows a very flat valley. After Kranj, however, it is all uphill to the Austrian border. You will get a good taste of the trials and rewards of mountain touring from this point on as you enter Austria and begin to pedal toward Vienna.

Turn right out of the campground and make a left toward Sentvid. This side road takes you west to join secondary road 1 to Kranj. Go through some small towns, ignoring signs for Ljubljana, until you cross over the main highway going north; take the first left here (before a downhill to a town) and then the second right. Neither turn has a labeled destination, only an arrow. This puts you on the road to Kranj. We ignored the *no bicycles* sign.

The pretty center of Kranj makes a good lunch stop. From the town center cross the Sava River and follow signs for Preddvor and then Jezersko (located 4 km from the border). The first few kilometers of this secondary road are flat. As we cycled along, however, it was clear what was about to happen. We reached the end of the valley floor and began a 33 km uphill climb to the Austrian border.

The majority of the climb is a gradual one along a river. The road is very quiet and in good condition. Take a short break in Jezersko, where you can buy a snack with your last dinars and appreciate the beautiful view of a glacier across from the small town. The last stretch of road is nasty, with many hairpin curves and a very steep grade. Just keep at it and get your mind ready for Austria. Signs along the road indicate your elevation, for better or for worse. The border is at the top of the pass at 1,218 meters.

Show your passport to two sets of border guards, and you are on your way. Change back your extra dinars at the bank before crossing into Austria. There is a picnic table and bench just over on the Austrian side, where you can recuperate and enjoy the view.

It is all downhill from there—miles and miles of downhill—with lovely mountain scenery all around. Descend 17 fast kilometers to Eisenkappel, where you can obtain schillings and go grocery shopping. Keep cycling in the direction of Klagenfurt until 7 km after Eisenkappel, and be careful. I almost missed the right turn onto road 82 to Völkermarkt and Klopeinersee. Another 8 km into this lake-filled valley on road 82 brings you to Eberndorf. Turn left for Klopeinersee at the light just before town. There is a campground 1 km to the left from the marked turnoff just down this road, and another several kilometers farther on the Klopeinersee. The first, a veritable nudist colony, is large and well-equipped, with a pool and large grocery store. It is expensive at about $10 per person ,but we were more than ready to call it a day here despite the price.

Eberndorf to Pack
73 km(45 miles)

Return to the main road (82) for Völkermarkt, located on a hill above the valley floor. Völkermarkt (people's market) turned out to be aptly named—the day we rode through town, there was a large outdoor market complete with an oom-pah band.

Turn right for road 70 to Wolfsberg after Völkermarkt. This is a busy, hilly road with a suitable shoulder and a big climb after Griffen. At St. Andrä you can turn right toward Eitweg and then left for Wolfsberg to gain quieter roads, but at this point 70 is paralleled by the autobahn and traffic decreases. Continue through Wolfberg for Graz until Twimberg, where you will turn right for Preitenegg and Packsattel.

The cycling gets nasty again as you tackle a big, long climb of 5 km that begins after Waldenstein. After Preitenegg, the road levels out somewhat and stays high on a ridge right into Pack (Michelin shows a high point immediately before Pack, but there is no further climb).

Pack is a cluster of houses and inns with a wide view of the surrounding mountains and the raised autobahn ramp far in the valley below. There is a campground outside Pack (turn right in the center of town, and again at the first road; it is a few kilometers down) and another several kilometers farther on the main road (turn left in Hirschegg-Rein). We took a room, having spent the entire day in a downpour. Pack has only one small grocery store.

A warning: this is a long, tiring day and the mountains are prone to extremely nasty, quick-changing weather. Even in the middle of July I was soaked and cold by the end of the day. This is grueling riding but manageable. Plan on taking a rest day, either here or in Graz.

Pack to Graz
67 km(42 miles)

Continue down road 70 to Köflach and enjoy beautiful views the whole way (as you will throughout Austria). In Köflach take a left turn to Piber and Bärnbach. Piber, the site of the Lipizzaner horse stud, is 3 km down this rolling road. Turn left at the large barn as you enter Piber and follow parking signs for the Gestut. The summer tours offered are fun even if you do not speak German, offering a close-up view of the white horses and dark foals. Later in Vienna you will have the chance to see the mature, trained horses in amazing dressage performances. There are no stores in Piber.

Continue on to Bärnbach, where you will pass a wildly decorated church designed by Herr Hundertwasser. Examples of his work also appear in Vienna. Then follow signs back to road 70 and Voitsberg. Traffic picks up as you near Graz. Stay on 70 for 12 km until the left turn for Hitzendorf. Follow this road through Hitzendorf, up the last long hill of the day, and finally down into Graz.

The nearest campground is the cheap and somewhat dumpy Camping West, 4 km from the center of town. Head for the town center and keep a lookout for signs to this site. There are two other campgrounds around Graz and a hostel (Jugendgasthaus) closer to the heart of Graz on Idlhofstrasse.

Graz is a fine place to take a well-earned rest day. The toughest part of the tour is now behind you, and Vienna is only three days ahead. A walk through the Altstadt and up to the clock tower will take you past some of Graz's highlights and offers a nice view of the city, flower gardens, and the gentler terrain ahead. Although Graz certainly deserves attention, you have earned the right to call off any activities on this day and use the time to take a deserved rest.

Graz to Hartberg
64 km (40 miles)

The first part of the day is characterized by constant hills that never quite flatten into valleys, a frustrating experience. As the day goes on and you approach Hartberg, however, you will have a smoother ride.

Head northeast out of Graz on Heinrichstrasse, which becomes road 72 to Weiz. Just outside Weiz, after 28 km, continue on 72 for Birkfeld, and after another 10 km turn right for Hartberg to follow a series of well-marked side roads. Be careful to make the left turn for Hartberg and Wien (Vienna) on the uphill after Stubenberg—it is a well marked but sharp turn. There is a campground in Stubenberg if you are tempted to stop there. The last 11 km to Hartberg are on the busy road 54, a major road to Vienna, though the traffic is polite and manageable.

The campground is located directly in Hartberg, clearly marked *Herz* to the right of road 54. There are two pools next to this site. Hartberg has a small, beautifully renovated old town below the towering church, which is reminiscent of its many Yugoslavian counterparts. If you continue into Hungary you will also see more of these 'semi-onion' dome buildings, reminders of the historic relationship between these areas.

Austria: View of Salzburg

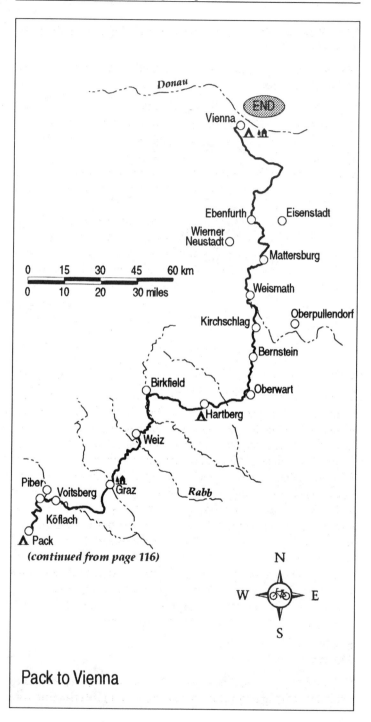

Pack to Vienna

(continued from page 116)

This section of Hartberg is especially nice for a quiet after-dinner walk.

Hartberg to Forchtenstein
84 km (52 miles)

From Hartberg it is only a two-day ride to Vienna. This cycling day will take you through quiet towns and long stretches of fields and woods. Again, you will have to suffer the frustration of continuously rolling hills. I was becoming impatient to reach Vienna at this point. Try to relax and enjoy the open scenery as you pedal steadily closer to your goal, if you start to feel the same way.

From the main road (54) turn right onto road 50 for Oberwart while still in Hartberg. This wide and quiet road runs through the woods for 15 km before rejoining a bigger road (still 50) to Oberwart, Eisenstadt, and Wien. Continue on this unpleasant stretch until you are just past Bernstein, where there is a campground. Turn left for Kirchschlag. There is a big, nasty climb here, but the views are nice and there is a picnic table at the top.

At the T-intersection turn right toward the center of Kirchslag. Look for the left turn to Oberpullendorf, Stang, and Karl. There are many intersecting minor roads here—just keep following signs for Stang, Weismath, and Wiener Neustadt. Turn right for Forchtenstein 2 km past Hochwolkersdorf. First you will pass through Forchtenstein-Rosilia. Keep going. After 5 km, more woods, and an uphill climb, descend to Forchtenstein past a twelfth-century castle.

The campground is on the road to Mattersburg, after the last stores in the center of town. Pass a parking area on the right and take the next paved road to the right, which is only signposted for 'campingplatz' from the other direction, turn around, and you will see it. Go straight through the trailer and cabin colony to the edge of the lake for the temporary campers area. This is a good site with soft ground that will not bend your stakes, and no bugs. The lake can sometimes be crowded, but it is nice for a swim, and there is a fun waterslide at one end—the kids will not mind if you join them.

Forchtenstein to Vienna
80 km (50 miles)

To avoid traffic as much as possible, much of this route traces a combination of secondary roads. Important intersections are all well-marked. Vienna can be difficult to navigate without a map—try to obtain one if your Austria map does not include a detail of the capital.

From the campground in Forchtenstein, return to the main road and turn right toward Mattersberg. In the center of town, turn left for Wiener Neustadt before the train tracks. After going under a railroad bridge 4 km later, turn right for Sigless. Pass Sigless and turn left for Wiener Neustadt and road 53 for a few kilometers until the sharp right turn in Pöttsching for Eisenstadt and Zillingtal (watch for the sign as soon as you enter Pöttsching).

Pass through Zillingtal and Steinbrunn, where you will turn left for Neufeld and Ebenfurth. Join a larger road to Wien in Ebenfurth. In Weigelsdorf, 10 km later, turn off the main road for Götzendorf. In Unterwaltersdorf keep left for Moosbrunn, Himberg, and on to Wien.

We stayed on the main road past Steinbrunn to avoid the various turn-offs and side roads, being eager to get into Wien and end another rainy day. The road was busy, but bearable. Whichever route you choose, try to enter Wien with a map. Follow signs for Wien zentrum. Traffic in the city is not bad, but finding your way to a specific destination in the large capital can be hellish.

There are several campgrounds around Vienna; the closest is Wien West. All are marked on the larger scale Vienna map included on Michelin's Austria #426 map, but are nonetheless difficult to find. The best way to find Wien West is to go to the front of Schonbrunn Palace and follow the river left (west) on the opposite bank to Huttledorf (a section of Wien). Then follow signs up Huttlebergstrasse on your right (bus route #52 comes this way—keep an eye out for the buses and stops marked 52). This is approximately 7 km from the center of Vienna, but excellent bus and U-bahn connections make the campground a very convenient place to stay at a moderate price (moderate for a campground and fantastic for Vienna, at about $5 per night). It also has a kitchen and large crowds in the summer.

There is a hostel located across the river in Huttledorf and another just a few blocks from the Ring in Vienna's center. The central hostel (on Myrthengasse) is always full in summer, but you can call ahead for reservations. The Huttledorf hostel is very large, and you can almost always get a bed there. If you are spending several days in Vienna and would like to be closer to the center, you can make hostel reservations on arrival and move from Huttledorf as soon as possible. There are also many unofficial hostels and rooms available in Vienna.

Visitors who rush through Vienna rarely appreciate its unique character. Take the time to see it well. This majestic city was the heart of the far-reaching Austro-Hungarian Empire. Most sights are located within or around the Ring, a road encircling the oldest section of Vienna. The Stephansdom is an impressive sight, even more so if you consider the war-time damage sustained and testified to by photographs just inside the main entrance of the cathedral. Mozart's one-time residence is located within the maze of streets just east of here. In contrast to these crowded quarters, the parliament building, Rathaus (City Hall), and Hofburg (Imperial Palace) command wide views of the many public parks separating them.

After a day of historic sights, the Neue Donau, a diverted section of the Danube, is a pleasant spot to swim or sunbathe. The Prater amusement park offers a fun alternative, featuring the oldest ferris wheel in the world. Vienna is also host to many famous performances, including those of the Lipizzaners in the Spanische Reitschule (Spanish Riding School) and the Wiener Sängerknaben (Boy's Choir). The Staatsoper (State Opera) is one of the best in the world, and standing-room tickets cost only $2. The opera house is built on a small, personal scale, and you will have a view as good as any orchestra seat.

Vienna's location makes it a convenient base for visiting many Eastern European countries. Czechoslovakian, Polish, and Hungarian embassies are all located in Vienna, making it easy to apply for visas. I left my bicycle in a hostel and used trains to visit these countries. If you decide to do the same, be sure to bring a large amount of cash in either Deutschmarks or dollars. You can also continue across Austria from Vienna to Salzburg and other destinations.

Vienna to Budapest

Distance: 289 km (175 miles)

Recommended touring time: 8–10 days (4 cycling days)

Terrain: riverside flats with occasional small hills

Accommodations: many campgrounds along this popular vacation area; inexpensive rooms, hostels, and camping in Budapest.

Maps: Michelin 426 (1 : 400,000) and Ravenstein Hungary (1 : 525,000)

Enjoy four incredibly relaxing cycling days along the Danube between two monumental European capitals, including the gardens and palaces of Vienna, the scenic Danube bend north of Budapest, and a close-up look at life in Hungary. This has

Budapest, Hungary: View of the city center

long been one of the most liberal and westernized Eastern European countries and one of the easiest to travel in, with relatively few restrictions. American and most other western- ers no longer need a visa to enter Hungary.

This is also a popular bicycle tour among European cyclists, so you will be pedaling along well-established routes. You will find services geared especially toward cyclists along this tour, such as the easy transportation of bicycles on trains and the occasional sympathetic campground manager willing to give you a discount. On the other hand, many roads do not permit bicycles. If you heed these signs, however, you will never make it to Budapest, so use your own judgment. Several policemen we passed while on these off-limits roads did not seem to care.

Small roads in Hungary are frequently unsigned and in terrible condition. For this reason it is a good idea to use a larger-scale map than usual and stick to bigger secondary roads. I had an inexpensive and very basic 1 : 600,000 map that I bought in Czechoslovakia.

Hungary is very inexpensive when compared to all of Western Europe and especially Austria, a welcome change. Here your budget can afford meals out and inn accommo- dations, or has a chance to recover if you stick to the camping, cooking routine. This is an excellent trip for the beginning cyclist or a great vacation for the more experienced or fit, and an educational experience for anyone interested in Eastern Europe in this transitional period. In terms of cycling and travel conditions for this part of the world, this is about as easy as it gets.

	German	Hungarian
Hello:	*Grüss Gott*	*Yanapot*
Thank you:	*Danke*	*Kusonom*

Vienna to MosonMagyaróvár
93 km (57 miles)

Vienna is the perfect starting point for a tour to Hungary. As a major city and the capital of Austria, it offers a wide variety of sights, goods, and services especially helpful as you prepare for the ride to Budapest. Maps of Hungary are available in most of the city's many bookstores. Vienna is well worth several days of sightseeing either before or after cycling this

Vienna to Budapest

route—imperial buildings, parks, and performances are just a few highlights of this beautiful city.

Cobblestoned Rennwegstrasse, which begins on a corner of Karlsplatz in Vienna, will lead you to road 10 to Budapest. Do not take A4 along the Donau. Continue on 10 for 75 km to the border crossing, where you can pass the cars and go to the head of the line (another advantage of cycling). You can change money at the official bank at the border. Moson-Magyaróvár is 13 km farther on this road. The inexpensive campground is on the main road (1) to Budapest just east of town. It is on a nice site next to a small river and has an indoor kitchen.

This is an easy, flat day of cycling. There are only a few roads crossing the border, and they are all very busy. We ignored the *no bikes* signs on road 1 in Hungary, having no choice if we wanted to reach Budapest. We passed several policemen who did not try to stop us, and we even saw a few locals cycling the same road.

MosonMagyaróvár is a modern town with little of specific interest. Most of the next few days will be the same. Take advantage of the opportunity to absorb the Hungarian lifestyle in an unobtrusive way—a far more interesting and important point of view than the conventional tourist route of 'big and famous sights.' As you approach Budapest, historic sights will be more numerous. By the time you reach the capital, you will have gained an considerable understanding of the modern culture that will serve as a firm base with which to appreciate Hungary's history.

MosonMagyaróvár to Komárom
77 km (48 miles)

Return to the main road to Budapest from the campground. After an uncomfortably busy 10 km, turn left to Kimle. Pass through Kimle and Hédervár, and in Györ follow signs for Budapest on roads 60/75/1. After about 4 km take a clearly marked left on road 10 to Komárom. This is also a no-bicycles route. You will eventually catch a glimpse of the Duna (Danube) again and will soon be cycling along its broad banks for much of the way to Budapest. There is a rest area above the Duna off road 10 that makes a nice picnic spot. Get supplies in Moson, as there are no stores in the area.

An out-of-the-way campground is located 6 km west of Komárom. You can also choose to ride on through Komárom and pick up signs for the campgrounds there. There are two, located right by a spa and pools. Camping Solair is cheap and will give you a student discount if you ask nicely. The fee includes admission to the pools. The spa is crowded with vacationing Hungarians and Germans, a fun pace to relax and people-watch. Czechoslovakia is not far across the Duna from here, but it is difficult to get a view of the river in this built-up area.

Komárom to Visegrád
79 km (49 miles)

This day's ride takes you along the Duna to one of its most scenic sections, known as the Danube Bend. Hills accent the river's twists, while historic towns line its banks. The sights become more concentrated as you approach Budapest, with towns like Esztergom, Visegrád, and Szentendre all meriting visits. The riding remains very flat as you parallel the river, and there are only a few short hills to pedal over as you enjoy wide views of this region.

Leave Komárom on the main road to Budapest. After 42 km, turn onto road 11 to Esztergom just after Tát. Esztergom is a tourist town with an impressive hill-top basilica and two campgrounds. One is in the center of town right on the river, and the second, quieter and pleasantly wooded, is on the east edge of town.

If you are not ready to call it a day in Esztergom, carry on along the Duna through Dömös to Visegrád. You will pass two campgrounds right on the Duna—both are unofficial and therefore free. The first is in Dömös. It has a water tap and toilet at the ferry landing next to the site, but no shower. The other is just east of Visegrád but is not as nice of a location. There is an official campground in Visegrád (a sign just west of Visegrád reads *camping 6 km*, but it is only 1 km). Follow signs to the right, into the center of Visegrád. The campground is easily missed—it will be on your left after you cross a small bridge. It has steaming hot showers but is not free.

King Mattias's castle, overlooking the Duna above Visegrád, is the site of a jousting tournament in July. The small church in the center of town is also interesting, and the banks of the Danube are a nice place to picnic and watch the ferries go by.

Visegrád to Budapest
40 km (25 miles)

It is a very simple ride to Budapest from this point on—just follow the signs for road 11. There is a good bicycle path paralleling the main road after Szentendre. Szentendre is a popular art center, worth a stop if you are not impatient about getting into Budapest. I was sick for several days at this point and was willing to forego the town for the comfort of being settled in Budapest at last. There is a campground near Szentendre on Pap Island.

Unfortunately, the bicycle path that follows road 11 comes to an end after a few kilometers, and you will be presented with a perplexing situation. The main road from that point does not allow bicycles, and this is one time not to ignore this fact, since it is a very crowded and narrow road. One option is to go to the small, extremely inexpensive campground located at the far side of the apartment complex across the road. Follow signs to Mini Camping to get there. There are convenient bus and commuter train connections into Budapest if you decide to make this your base.

To get to other, closer campgrounds and into Budapest itself, you will have to follow side roads along the Duna. If you head for Mini camping, the Duna will be directly in front of you. Turn right and keep as close to the river as possible. There is another stretch of bicycle path right along the Duna, but this too will end before you reach the center of the city. The other campgrounds are between the river and the main road to your right (west).

There is a hostel on a hill in Buda and private rooms scattered around the city. It is advisable to call ahead or stop at tourist information first, since vacancies can be difficult to find. IBUSZ is the official tourist agency. The main office is two blocks from the Elizabeth Bridge in Pest at Felszabadulas ter. 5.

Once you are settled, enjoy Budapest. The view from Fisherman's Bastion is especially nice, and the nearby cathedral has a decorated rooftop that resembles the one on Stephansdom in Vienna. There are many bridges spanning the river between Buda and Pest, each unique in character and in views of Parliament, the Royal Palace, and other monumental buildings that neatly line the shores. The tourist office will supply detailed information on specific sights and the history of the city.

Hydrofoils and ferries can bring you back to Vienna, but cost much more than trains. If you are taking a train, bring your bicycle to the baggage department a few hours in advance. You will have to carry your gear separately and pay a fee of about $10. Buying your ticket may involve more work. You can do so at either the IBUSZ office or the train station. Waiting in the international ticket lines can be interminably slow. Be firm with people trying to cut the line. One way of avoiding the hassle is by purchasing a ticket ahead of time in Vienna, although this can restrict your stay in Budapest if you get behind schedule.

If you have the eastern counterpart of your student or youth ID card (the IUS—International Union of Students—card), you will receive a 50% discount on the train fare. An IUS card may be obtained by presenting your western ID at an Express student travel bureau. There are two locations in Budapest: V, Semmelweis u. 4 (tel. 176634) or V, Szabadsagter. 16 (tel. 317777). The IUS ID costs about 70 Ft. ($1.50).

It is a good idea to keep all exchange receipts, as you may be asked to show them at the border to prove that you changed a reasonable amount of money legally. Do not be intimidated by these complications. Half a day lost for bureaucracy is well worth the experience of visiting Hungary.

Austria: Vienna to Salzburg

Distance: 376 km (233 miles)

Recommended touring time:
12–14 days (8 cycling days)

Terrain: along the Donau
from Vienna to Linz: easy,
level; Linz to Salzburg via
Salzkammergut:
mountainous terrain with
several long and tiring but
moderately graded climbs

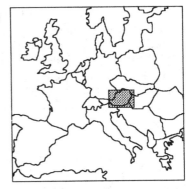

Accommodations: campgrounds and private rooms abound
along the well-traveled bicycle path; many well-situated youth
hostels, but fewer campgrounds, in the Salzkammergut

Maps: Michelin 426 Austria 1 : 400,000

This tour includes two very different Austrian cities and the
spectacular scenery in between. From the reserved capital of
the Austro-Hungarian Empire this route follows a well-designed bicycle path along the vineyard and castle lined Donau
(Danube) to one of Europe's most impressive mountain regions, the Salzkammergut. Here steep mountains fall into
beautiful lakes while picture-perfect towns squeeze in between. The trip ends in Salzburg, the birthplace—you cannot
miss it—of Mozart. This small-sized old city is well suited to a
thorough visit on foot along its pretty, though often tourist-
choked, streets.

The hills of the Salzkammergut are absolutely worth the
effort, but if you are looking for an easier ride, it is also possible
to follow the Danube as far as Passau and then follow the Inn
and Salzach rivers to Salzburg and thus enjoy less demanding
riverside terrain. I strongly recommend the lake route for its
unsurpassed scenery, however. The tour may also be easier if

done in reverse to follow the Danube downstream on the section between Linz and Vienna.

Hello: *Grüss Gott*
Thank you: *Danke*

Vienna to Krems
80 km (50 miles)

Vienna (Wien) is a beautiful city and the capital of Austria. Most sights are located within the Ring, a road encircling the central city. Sweeping vistas along parks and gardens lead to palaces, museums, and cathedrals around the city. In contrast, the maze of streets in the cluttered old town take unpredictable twists around historic buildings such as Mozart's one-time residence. It is also home to many world-famous performances, such as those of the Lipizzaners in the Spanish Riding School (Spanische Reitschule), the Boys' Choir (Wiener Sängerknaben), and the State Opera (Staatsoper). Take the time to see Vienna well before beginning the ride west along the Danube. See the Verona to Vienna tour for more information on Vienna's sights and accommodations.

There are two good ways to leave Vienna. One option is to cycle up the Donau on the Wien-Passau bicycle route, which passes through Krems. It begins near the center of Vienna on the banks of the Donau. This day's recommended route, however, climbs high through the Wienerwald (Vienna Woods), giving you a last look at Austria's capital through the large forest. If you do not mind the extra climb, this ride is worth the trouble as you will have plenty of Danube scenery later in the day and for several days to come.

Take Hernalser Haupstrasse northwest out of Vienna. Universitätstrasse, beginning on the Ring at the juncture of Dr.-Karl-Lueger-Ring and Schottenring, goes through several name changes and will eventually lead you onto this road. As you continue past Neuwallegg and Tulln, you will suddenly leave city noise behind for the quiet of the woods. The tough climb will end at the large tower on a ridge 10 km from the center of Vienna, from which point you can at last enjoy a long downhill coast.

Follow signs for Tulln until Königstetten, where you continue on to Tulbing and Judenau. At the T-junction with a larger road outside Judenau, go left for the Wien autobahn and then right, to Michelhausen. Ride another 2 km from Michel-

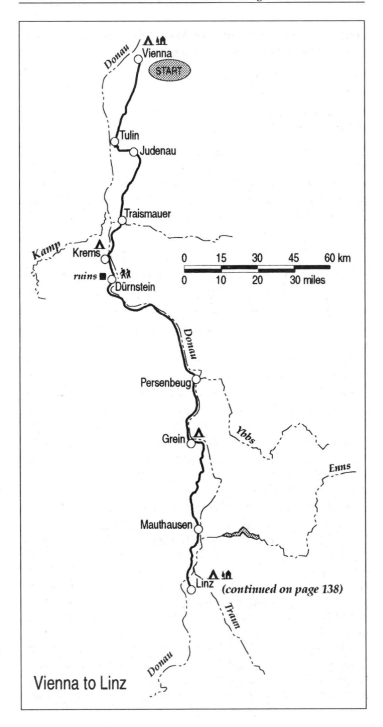

Vienna to Linz

(continued on page 138)

hausen to Mitterndorf and follow road 43 to Krems. At Trais-mauer stay with 43 to Wagram and from there, follow white signs to Krems and Hollenburg (the blue-signed SS road is definitely off-limits to bicycles). Hollenburg is a beautiful town to ride through. Just beyond it are great views of the Donau and the hilltop Wolfsberg Castle.

You will reach a stop sign and a big intersection 8 km later—go straight for Mautern. You cannot go directly into Krems on the SS road to the right. Instead, cyclists must ride 3 km on to Mautern, then cross the bridge over the Donau there. Once across, turn right onto the small road that parallels the main road to cycle into Krems. At the gas station turn right and follow the camping signs (they do not say the site's name, only that of the campground federation) to Camping Donau, a very comfortable site that is located directly on the riverbank and close to the nice town. The cost is about $4 per person, hot showers included. The thoughtful management even reserves prime riverside campsites for late arriving cyclists. There is also a campground in Zwentendorf, three quarters of the distance to Krems, if you want to make the day shorter.

Krems to Grein
80 km (50 miles)

You will follow the Donau's course on the Wien-Passau Rad-wanderweg (bicycle path) all day. The river and surrounding hills are so beautiful that you may find it difficult to ride consistently without stopping at every quiet village square and river overlook point. We could not resist and only got as far as Emmersdorf, making the following day's ride to Linz longer (101 km, 63 miles).

In Krems take the small road that parallels route 3 (on the inland side) westward to Dürnstein and St. Michael. This will lead you back past the bridge to Mautern and directly to green rectangular signs with directions for the *Radwanderweg*. The bicycle route winds a scenic course through a combination of special bicycle trails and detours on secondary roads that run through vineyards and small towns.

The ruins of a castle high above Dürnstein are worth the hike up. The site commands expansive views and an equally impressive history—King Richard the Lionheart was reputed-ly held prisoner here after the Crusades. You can lock your bicycle to the fence at the bottom of the hiking trail and walk up. The tiny town of Dürnstein is also very picturesque. The area around the church of St. Michael, 5 km later, will also tempt you to stop. There is an overlook point above the bicycle trail that makes a wonderful snack place (or lunch spot, if you are as slow as we were), with views of the river and a pretty church. You will pass more castles and churches as the ride continues toward Grein. There is a riverside campground in Emmersdorf if you, too, are ready to call it a day.

If not, continue on the Radwanderweg to Persenburg along the Donau's shores. Just before Persenburg we abandoned the trail for the main road (3) which continues right into Linz. You can also use the bicycle paths all the way to Linz, but our patience was thin on this rainy day. The last twisting stretch of the Donau into Grein is the loveliest section of the river, with wooded hills sloping to the water's edge. Grein is a small, picturesque town set on a bend of the Donau. There is a campground in town, away from the river, and another on the main road just west of Marbach, if you want to end your day there.

Grein to Linz
58 km (36 miles)

From Grein you can continue the ride by taking road 3 or the Radwanderweg into Linz. Mauthausen, 32 km west of Grein, is the site of a Nazi concentration camp. Follow signs *KZ-Mauthausen* pointing to the right, outside of town, to visit the site, 4 km away.

As you near Linz on road 3, continue over a bridge and through an ugly industrial section before reaching the core of the city. Follow signs to Zentrum and turn on Landstrasse, a cobblestoned street for pedestrians (and trams) only. If you ride north (right) on Landstrasse, you will pick up signs for the campground immediately before the bridge that continues crosses the Donau. I stayed in one of Linz's two hostels because of the rain. One is a strange arrangement within a large office building complex (Lentra 2000) across the river from the pedestrian area, and the other is 2 km west of town at Stanglhofweg 3.

Linz to Bad Ischl
102 km (63 miles)

This day involves a long but moderate and scenic ride. To leave Linz south on 139, follow signs for the Wien–Salzburg autobahn near the train station (back down Landstrasse from the

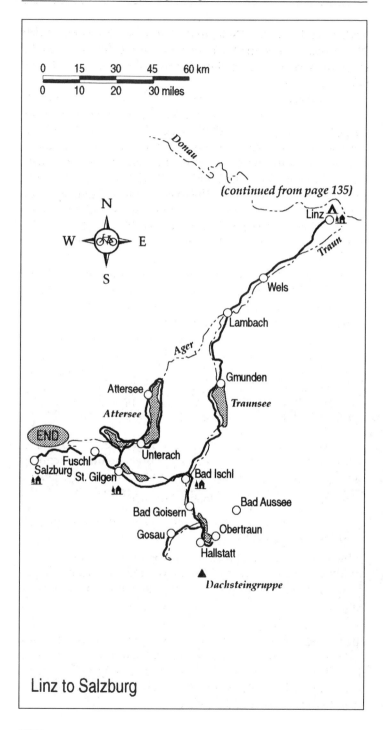

(continued from page 135)

Linz to Salzburg

bridge) and exit for Wels/road 139 soon thereafter. After 24 km watch for signs for road 1 to Wels. Continue straight through Wels, following signs for road 1 and white signs for Salzburg.

In Lambach, 16 km later, turn off for Gmunden on road 144, which will lead you right to the first of the Salzkammergut lakes, the Traunsee. The remainder of the day's route follows the course of the river Traun and the ride becomes more challenging, with more hills along the way. From Gmunden follow signs for Bad Ischl and road 145 (the road numbers change a few times). Follow the road along the Traunsee with amazing views of waterfalls, huge mountains, and the beautiful lake. The Traunsee makes an exciting introduction for the stunning scenery to come. We cycled this route in freezing rain and mist, but were still wowed by it all.

At the end of the lake, past Ebensee, continue onward and begin a gradual climb for the last 17 km to Bad Ischl. You have many options along the end of this route as to where to stay. There are campgrounds in Gmunden and Traunkirchen (halfway along the Traunsee) and hostels in Ebensee and Bad Ischl (with family rooms available in the Bad Ischl hostel).

Bad Ischl is the principal town of the Salzkammergut and makes an ideal base for two unladen day trips—a welcome idea after days of pedaling your loaded bicycle. We happily settled into the comfortable hostel to enjoy a break from camping and our heavy bicycles. The hostel that also offers family rooms is on Am Rectiensteg, a side street near the town center. There are bus connections between the towns if you really need a break, although the following day trips are fun and relatively easy to do by (unloaded) bicycle.

Salzkammergut day trip: Bad Ischl to Dachsteingruppe 66 km (41 miles) round trip

To see the pretty Halstattersee or the absolutely stunning Dachsteingruppe, leave Bad Ischl south on road 145 to Bad Aussee and Hallstatt. The road is mostly downhill or flat. A bicycle path parallels the main road and cuts through Bad Goisern, providing a quick break from the traffic, which lightens considerably after this town. Continue on 166 toward Hallstatt. You can ride directly into Hallstatt—when you near the tunnel that bypasses the town, bear left and go through town—and Obertraun on this road to see the scenic towns or to go to the cable car and ice caves.

Another option is to take the well-marked turnoff right, to Gosau and Golling. This will lead you to the Dachsteingruppe, a stunning ridge of mountains topped by a massive glacier. This involves a long steady climb from the turnoff up to the town of Gosau, from which point on you will enjoy picture-perfect views of the famous mountain ridge. From Gosau it is another easy 7 km to the Gosausee. There is one last, steep climb as you come up to the lake at the foot of the ridge. The view of rocky peaks and the glacier from the shore is unsurpassed. One peak, Hoher Dachstein, tops 3,000m in height. Bring lunch supplies for an unforgettable picnic at the lake. You can also cycle around the lake before returning to Bad Ischl by reversing your route.

I highly recommend this ride. If you want to take a day off, you can take a bus to the Gosausee, but no matter how you get there, by all means get there. You will not be disappointed. You can see Hallstatt and Obertraun by detouring on the way back to Bad Ischl or, better still, return to those scenic towns for a second day trip.

For some variation on the way back to Bad Ischl, we followed the bicycle route from Bad Goisern to Lauffen and then along the opposite bank of the Traun from the highway. This is not as level, straight, or direct as the bicycle track paralleling the main road, but it is a lot more pleasant. We did this day trip and then loaded our bicycles in Bad Ischl to finish the last 24 km to St. Gilgen on the same day.

Bad Ischl to St. Gilgen
24 km (15 miles)

From Bad Ischl return to the main road to the Traunsee (145), where you can pick up the westward continuation of this road (now 158) toward Salzburg. Signs in Bad Ischl were confusing regarding 158. It is best to remember how you originally entered and repeat the last bit of your route out. Unfortunately, 158 is a large fast road with a small shoulder and no bicycle lane. You may be able to avoid a hair-raising 600m-long tunnel just outside Bad Ischl by continuing west out of town as long as possible before joining the main road.

Since the distance was short, we stayed on unpleasant 158 all the way to St. Gilgen. It is possible to take a side road for a portion of the ride, but this is out of the way and hardly worth the trouble since you must return to 158 anyway. Just before reaching St. Gilgen at the west end of the Wolfgangsee, we switched onto a small track outside the guard rail of 158. This then widens into a road that goes more directly into town and also avoids a small climb before the St. Gilgen exit.

St. Gilgen is touristy but quaint all the same. There are many shops and a nice hostel in the town. Mozart's mother and sister once vacationed in St. Gilgen—a fact proudly advertised by a plaque on the house where they stayed. Their portraits are suspiciously reminiscent of Wolfie's own profile, which is emblazed on Mozart chocolates. Get used to this commercialization, since the next stop is Salzburg. There is also an attention-absorbing trick fountain in St. Gilgen's lakeside park.

For alternative accommodations, several campgrounds are located along the Wolfgangsee. St. Gilgen is another ideal base for a few more excursions before leaving the Salzkammergut. Cable cars and cog railways will take you to the summits of two nearby mountains for a fee. Hike back down for a change of pace. St. Wolfgang, accessible by bicycle or ferry across the lake, is a very pretty town noted for its church. You can also take another day trip to visit the other major lakes of the region by bicycle.

Salzkammergut day trip:
St. Gilgen to Mondsee and Attersee
40 km (25 miles)

For a half or full day trip from St. Gilgen, ride to the nearby Mondsee and Attersee. While the scenery is not as spectacular as that of the eastern lakes, it is nevertheless a worthwhile and enjoyable ride that rounds out your tour of all the major Salzkammergut lakes.

From St. Gilgen get back on the main road to Salzburg and immediately exit for Mondsee on 154. You will face a climb of 608m on the way, but once on the Mondsee's shores the terrain is level. Cycle around the lake on 151 toward Unterach—use the bicycle track on the right after the junction with the road to Oberwang. On the way back to St. Gilgen you will cross a thin strip of land separating the two lakes. To extend the ride, continue around the Attersee before returning to St. Gilgen by crossing back over the pass.

At first it was difficult to leave St. Gilgen, where I was so happily spending a quiet day off, but the day trip was a lot of fun once I got going. I completed this quick ride after having lunch in St. Gilgen and was back with time to spare before dinner.

St. Gilgen to Salzburg
32 km (20 miles)

Follow road 158 past Fuschlsee and cycle a few more climbs to reach Salzburg. This short ride involves several long climbs but the appeal of Salzburg will keep you pedaling strongly. At the bottom of the last hill into Salzburg there is a T-intersection; head left and follow signs for Stadtcamping (about 2 km from this junction) on Bayerhamerstrasse. This site, only a 15-minute walk from the old town and all its sights, is moderately priced at $5 per person. There are also three hostels and private rooms in Salzburg.

Salzburg is a small city overrun by tourists and Mozart-related (or completely unrelated) souvenirs, but for good reason. It is a graceful city tucked between the Salzach River and a mountain ridge. While in Salzburg try to see *The Sound of Music,* shown free-of-charge daily at every hostel (4 p.m. at the Josef-Preis-Allee Hostel), where no one will question whether you are actually a guest or not. It is great fun comparing the well-known movie scenery to the real thing.

Horsepond on Sigmundsplatz and Mirabell gardens are two particularly nice sights, and the Hohensalzburg fortress, with a modest entrance fee, commands impressive views over the city and its surroundings. Salzburg is full of alluring picnic spots, from quiet riverbanks to busy city squares and fountain-filled parks.

This tour ends in Salzburg. From this point you can continue cycling west to Münich and onward, or take a train to any city to reach an airport (there is also an international airport in Salzburg). A shorter cycling option is a trip to Berchtesgaden, about 40 km to the south, in Germany. There are two points of interest in this area—scenic lake Königssee in the midst of mountain scenery and the nearby alpine retreat built for Hitler.

The Irish Coast

The Dingle Peninsula, Ring of Kerry, and Beara Peninsula to Cork.

Distance: 389 km(242 miles)

Recommended Touring Time: 6–8 days (6 cycling days)

Terrain: rolling coastal hills

Accommodations: hostels, camping, or B&B

Maps: Michelin 405 (1 : 400,000)

Ireland has three of the most important ingredients for a great bicycle tour—lovely scenery, friendly people, and quiet country roads. This tour introduces you to one area representative of Ireland's best, the Dingle, Iveragh, and Beara Peninsulas of the southwest coast. Though ingredient number four, good weather, is not always reliable on this rugged coast, it may also be taken as a plus, providing a good excuse for a stop in a pub or to enjoy Irish hospitality in one of the many pleasant independent hostels or family-run B&Bs in this area.

Explore pretty harbor towns, singing pubs, and the Celtic history of Ireland while cycling past green fields in counties Kerry and Cork. In addition to the less-traveled Dingle and Beara Peninsulas, this tour circles the famous Ring of Kerry, including a stop at Staigue Iron Age Fort. Along the way you may also take a boat excursion to some of the isolated island monasteries off the rocky coast.

This tour is designed to be conveniently completed within the time of a short vacation. The ride consists of medium to short length cycling days (averaging 40 miles), with the entire tour comfortably covered in one week. The small towns and beautiful scenery of the peninsulas also make it easy to extend the ride to two weeks or more, by enjoying a slower pace and exploring away from the main route (tips for doing so are included in the text below). Ireland is an especially good destination for a short tour or first-time cyclists, with good facilities and services for travelers to help your trip go smoothly. Despite a conviction that something was bound to go wrong with my complicated travel plans and connections, I was always surprised at how easily my potential problems were taken care of (such as bus and train connections, finding a bicycle box, etc.) and there never was a hitch.

This tour is based on indoor accommodations as the most comfortable option in unpredictable weather. Independent hostels of the area reflect Ireland's welcoming attitude. These are small, quiet establishments that offer kitchens, living rooms, and often private rooms. Many also allow camping at a reduced cost. Unlike many official hostels elsewhere, these less institutional establishments encourage close contact with local people, their friendly proprietors being eager for you to enjoy Ireland. Even in summer, the hostels are rarely full. In addition, B&Bs abound, even in less touristed areas. The excellent network of tourist offices throughout Ireland can also call for reservations on your behalf.

A number of people I met touring in this area were using mountain bikes because they had been warned about terrible road conditions. I found this to be an exaggeration and was perfectly comfortable on my touring bicycle. This is Ireland, after all, not Africa. If you have a mountain bike, go ahead and use it, but touring bicycles or standard ten-speeds are also sufficient for this short tour.

Tralee to Dingle
32 miles (51 km)

The starting point for this ride is Tralee, a town on the edge of the Dingle Peninsula. For this tour it is most convenient to fly in and out of Shannon International Airport, though to include a visit to Dublin, it is possible to fly in to Shannon and out of Dublin at little or no extra cost. The CIE desk at the Shannon airport has bus and train information; there are frequent buses to Tralee via Limerick (change required) and less frequent direct connections (3 hours; about $15). Keep your bicycle in a box for the bus trip. You can also reach Tralee by train from Dublin. If you have any difficulties with your bicycle, head for the bicycle shop located just a few blocks from the train station (also the bus stop) in Tralee.

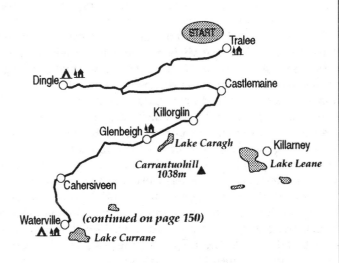

(continued on page 150)

Tralee to Waterville

The independent hostel in town (Droumtacker, off Listowel Road) attracts many cyclists, and the friendly owner allows camping on the front lawn. To get there from the train station, turn right to cycle away from town on the main road north. At a large crossroad in 2 miles, turn right (uphill) on a road marked with an arrow to the hostel, which is a quarter mile up, on the left. The hostel commands excellent views over the ocean and the Dingle Peninsula (£3.5 dorms; £2.5,camping).

To begin the ride to Dingle, head southwest, following signs for *Dingle N86*. My Michelin map had entirely different numbers for all these roads, making it more reliable to navigate by destination. The quiet and mostly level road runs right along Tralee Bay. After 10 miles, the road splits. I went right for the road signed *Conor Pass*, which winds 20 miles to Dingle. It is a quieter and more scenic route, but requires a long haul over the 500-meter high Conor Pass. Though not too high, the road gets steep and windy, and the climb is tough, particularly so for the first day of a tour. It is worth the effort, however, for the tremendous views of Brandon Bay and the ocean the pass offers. Brandon Bay is the point from which St. Brendan set sail for his voyage west, possibly to the New World, in a curragh (a boat made with leather). To avoid the pass, take the road to the left, continuing on N86 to Dingle (22 miles) via gentler terrain.

Dingle is a pretty town on the waters of Dingle Bay, full of pubs and B&Bs. Most of the pubs have live music every weekend and some weekdays. A good place to stay is the independent O'Sullivans West Lodge Hostel, which offers both indoor dorm-style rooms and camping in a large field in the back (£3 rooms; £2 camping). Follow signs to the west edge of town, past the docks. Dingle also makes a good base for exploring the westernmost tip of the peninsula. If you arrive early and still have the energy to do so, cycle 5 miles west to Ventry with its pretty harbor, and 5 miles more to Slea Head, a scenic point overlooking the Blasket Islands. There are boat excursions to these rocky islands (ask in Dingle). Fungi the Dolphin seems to be the unrivaled star of Dingle, but he is hard to spot among the fishing boats of the harbor.

Dingle to Glenbeigh
42 miles (68 km)

The day is fairly easy with many gradual climbs and long downhill cruises. The ride directly along the coast can be very windy, particularly near Inch and the ride west from Milltown to Glenbeigh. Start by cycling east out of Dingle, following signs for Tralee (not back over the Conor Pass, but on the main route along the water). In 11 miles make a right turn onto an even smaller road for Inch and Killarney, which will keep you heading east along Dingle Bay. Shortly after the turnoff from the Tralee road, take another right at the yield sign to continue for Inch. Inch Strand (5 miles later) is a long, wide beach that could be a nice stopping point in good weather (in bad weather, head for tea and scones in a nearby café).

Continue east until you reach Castlemaine, 12 miles farther, and turn right toward Killarney. Continue to bear right toward Cahersiveen and Killorglin through town. In Milltown 2 miles later, follow the *heavy traffic* and *Cahersiveen* sign right; this road curves left past the church. Then ride straight to rejoin the direct road west along the bay. Killorglin, 4 miles later, is another 8 miles from Glenbeigh. There are B&Bs along the road for the entire ride from Dingle, and many are centered in Killorglin and Glenbeigh.

The Hillside Hostel on the left side of the road in Glenbeigh has private two-person rooms for £4 per person (shower 50p extra; no camping). The friendly manager eagerly points out that Glenbeigh's beach was named the Cleanest and Safest Beach in Europe, though as one disappointed German cyclist noted, clean and safe is not necessarily stunning. Even so, it does offer non-life-threatening views across the water to the hills and shoreline cycled earlier in the day.

Glenbeigh to Waterville
27 miles (43 km)

The Ring of Kerry is a route of 100 miles encircling the Iveragh Peninsula. Killarney is the standard starting point for excursions around the Ring, but the town has been largely spoiled by the waves of tour buses that sweep through. It may be worth a detour to cycle around Lough Leane and Killarney National Park, but otherwise keep along the coastline, the real star of County Kerry's attractions. A short and rather easy ride along the northern part of the Ring of Kerry brings you to the small town of Waterville. Beware of tour buses on the narrow roads of the Ring, though traffic here is only slightly heavier than the quiet roads of Dingle and Beara.

From Glenbeigh continue on the main road west to Cahersiveen, 17 miles away. The road broadens after a few miles, with nice views of the Dingle Peninsula and Blasket Islands across Kell's Bay. This cliffside road runs by one of the most dramatic parts of the Ring of Kerry. After turning inland and passing through the (almost non-existent) town of Kell, there is a long, gradual climb and then a beautiful downhill cruise toward Cahersiveen. Ride up a few more hills into town, where you will find many grocery stores and shops. From here, only 10 miles remain for the ride to Waterville. On the way you will see signs for the ferry to Valencia Island, another good detour or stopping point.

Waterville is a small town situated on a particularly beautiful bay (in Ireland, each bay seems better than the last). There are several B&Bs as well as two hostels and a campground. The Waterville Leisure Center hostel in an old stone mansion lies on the north edge of town. The other hostel, Peter's Place, is right in the middle of town and probably a better option. There is also a Club Med on the south edge of town for those who really want to relax.

Other than enjoying the views from the beach in Waterville or holing up indoors, you can hop back on your bicycle for a trip to St. Finan's Bay on the edge of the peninsula. The nearest departure point for ferries to the abandoned monastic settlement perched on the Skellig Rocks is Ballinskelligs, west of Waterville. Boats also leave from Derrynane, to the south.

Waterville to Kenmare
39 miles (63 km)

This day's ride is full of wide views of the Beara Peninsula (weather permitting) and many long, gradual ups and downs. Leave Waterville heading south to continue your counter-clockwise ride along the Ring of Kerry. The road soon begins the long climb up the Coomakesta Pass (300 m). The entire climb is not steep though very long. At the top is a pull-out point that looks over Sheehan's Point and across the wide Kenmare River to Beara.

As a reward for the climb, enjoy the very long downhill cruise to Caherdaniel. The entire road has good views and there are a few convenient lookout points from where you may stop and appreciate the scenery. Again, be careful for the tour buses that make very wide turns. Most circle the Ring counter-clockwise. There is an option of a side trip from the main road in Castlecove, cycling up to Staigue Fort. The fort is clearly signposted to the left (inland) in this town. It is 2.5 miles away. Modest in size, the Iron Age fort is a walled ring on the rocky landscape with good views back to the bay. The detour is only worthwhile if you are interested in seeing the fort close-up and have a skewed enough sense of humor to enjoy the rough ride up a one-lane road; otherwise ride directly on to Sneem and try to catch a glimpse of the fort from a distance.

Sneem, sometime winner of the 'Tidy Town' award of Ireland, is a good place for lunch or a quick break. Unfortunately the distinction has brought on the plague of bus tourism, and souvenir shops now dot the pleasant town (luckily, though, Irish souvenirs are mainly sweaters and blankets, not tacky trinkets). There are several grocery stores and a bakery in town.

The ride from Sneem to Kenmare (17 miles) consists of more of the same terrain, long and gradual slopes. At the junction outside town, turn right to cycle to the center. For the pleasant, centrally located independent hostel, look for the right turn up Henry Street. Failte Hostel is at the top of the street (£4.5). The town is dotted with B&Bs, and there is another hostel on Main Street.

Kenmare is a very nice, large town at the end of the bay separating the Iveragh and Beara peninsulas. Each house is painted a different color, a useful navigational aid for late-night drinkers. A short walk will take you to the stone circle on the edge of town; an even shorter one brings you to one of Kenmare's many pubs.

Kenmare to Bantry
45 miles (72 km)

Cycle up Henry Street in the direction marked Bantry and Glengarriff to get started on the ride across the Beara Peninsula to Bantry. After a short distance, cross over a bridge and make a decision. You may choose to ride directly south to Glengarriff, cutting off most of the Beara Peninsula. Although this route avoids a difficult climb, there are two tunnels on the way. Traffic is moderate to light and many cyclists use the tunnel, so you should have no problems. In this case, follow the main road to Glengarriff (17 miles) and Bantry (28 miles).

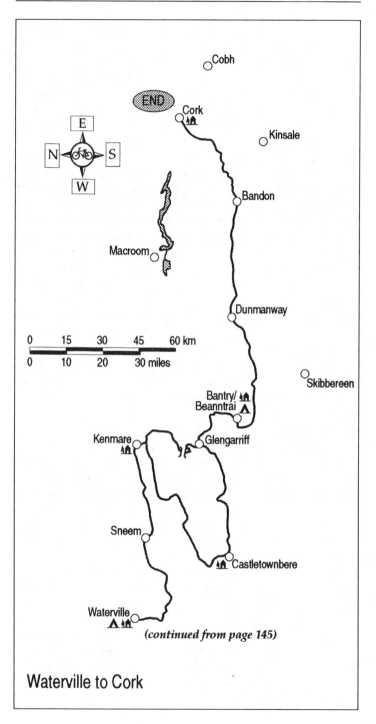

(continued from page 145)

Waterville to Cork

After cycling in Italy, I swore off tunnels, and therefore decided to take the longer, harder route over the Healy Pass. This takes you halfway down the Beara Peninsula and up to 330m. By this road it is 45 miles to Bantry, most of the ride strenuous. To make this ride, turn right after the bridge and follow signs for the Healy Pass all the way. First you will cycle to the top of one rocky bluff overlooking the bay, then descend, and climb again to the upper pass on a long, gradual incline. The road is sometimes gravelly but generally in good condition. This ride offers unparalleled views of the inlet and Glanmore Lake far below and also gives you a chance to cycle right into the coastal mountains that until now could only be seen from a distance. From the top there are good views of the serpentine road descending to Adrigole. Unfortunately, once you reach the south coast of the peninsula to turn east for Glengarriff, there can be very strong headwinds.

A final option is to circle the entire peninsula, a trip few tourists take and consequently one of the quietest, most undisturbed routes to follow. There are independent hostels in Ballydonegan and Castletownbere.

Glengarriff is a small but tidy town with a nice harbor, an independent hostel, and a number of B&Bs. Cycle around the harbor and continue on to Bantry, 11 miles away. This ride has more downhill sections and far less wind than the exposed south coast of Beara. The road winds around many small towns before finally bringing you in to Bantry.

Bantry is a large town overlooking Bantry Bay. Ask for directions to the independent hotel on Bishop Lucey Place, uphill off Glengarriff Road (to the right as you cycle into town; no signs). This is a small hostel with a nice yard and traditional Celtic designs painted on the walls. There is a tourist information office in the center, many B&Bs, and a campground northeast of town. The interesting town is a good place to spend your last evening along the Irish coast before turning inland the next day to Cork.

Bantry to Cork
57 miles (92 km)

As this tour is designed to be completed in a short time, it ends with a direct ride into Cork, a rather long and unexciting ride. If you have more time, however, the ride south to Skibbereen and Kinsale, then to Cork, is more interesting and scenic.

151

To cycle directly from Bantry to Cork, circle the harbor and head southwest out of town, following signs for the main road, N71, to Cork. This road was a source of major confusion to me, as two different maps seem to show the roads differently. I planned to take N71 and soon turn off onto R586 to Cork via Dunmanway and Bandon, but it seems R586 does not exist and N71 is the direct road to Cork. Ignore whatever numbers may be on your map and navigate by town names. Therefore:

Cycle out of Bantry on N71 to Cork and pass an Opel dealer and gas station on your right, 3 miles outside of town. Soon after road 591 from Durrus merges with your road, come to another intersection with a right turn (downhill) for the road to Ballydehob and the coastal route (the road sign at that junction was turned in the wrong direction when I cycled by). Unless you plan to take that detour to the coast, bear left to continue on the same road. You will reach Drimoleague 8 miles later; after 8 more miles you will reach Dunmanway (Ireland's 'Tidy Town' in 1982); and another 18 miles will bring you to Bandon. The road is wide and well paved and traffic is not heavy, although sometimes it is alarmingly fast. The biggest problem you may face is the possible headwind. There are many long, gradual uphills and, it seems, fewer downhills. Dunmanway and Bandon make good stopping points as the ⅓ and ⅔ markers of the ride. Bandon has a small park convenient for a picnic.

To take quieter roads the last 19 miles to Cork, look for signs to Macroom to the left upon entering Bandon. Pass an empty lot and a row of trees, then find the sign pointing left and cycle up the hill. Bear right for Cork 2 miles later, leaving the road to Macroom. In Cross Barry there are two intersections. Go straight through the first (for Cork) and left up the steep hill at the next for *Cork 11 miles* (not the one saying *Cork 13 miles*, which leads to the main road). While these secondary roads are well paved in sections, they are very hilly, with several more sharp climbs along the way.

Ride through Waterfall and begin the last 5 miles to Cork. The road merges with a larger one and goes straight into town. You can choose from a number of B&Bs and two hostels in Cork. Follow signs for the center of town, taking a left at the first roundabout. Watch for the small brown hostel sign that will lead you to both the large, official hostel and the small Campus House hostel a few houses away. Closer to the train and bus station is Sheila's Cork Tourist Hostel on Wellington

Road and York Place. To get to this airy, newly renovated hostel, cycle to the very center of town (St. Patrick Street) and cross St. Patrick's Bridge. Straight up the steep hill and to the right is Wellington Road. Use caution, as traffic in Cork is heavy.

Cork is an excellent end point for a tour because of the many options it affords: ferries to England, Wales, and France; trains to Dublin and other points in Ireland (including Limerick and connections to Shannon); or the option to continue cycling east. There is also an airport in Cork.

Note on Dublin: If you are flying out of Dublin, take the train from Cork; your bicycle will be shipped on the same train (£26 per person; £6 per bicycle; time, 3 hours). The train comes to Heuston Station at the west edge of the city. I managed to hit the jackpot in Dublin; hopefully you can do the same to ease your transit through this city. We managed to convince the Airport Express bus driver waiting at Heuston to give us a ride to the center of the city and the Busaras station. Conveniently located just one block from this bus stop is Isaac's Independent Hostel on Frenchman's Lane, complete with bar and bench-filled courtyard (dorm and private rooms, from £5). Even more conveniently located next to Isaac's is a bicycle shop where you can get a box to pack your bicycle.

When you are ready to leave Dublin, catch the Airport Express bus at Busaras. Officially, bicycles are not allowed but some drivers will allow you to bring one on and keep it in the aisle. A bicycle in a box is always allowed. All airlines at Dublin airport are basically run by Aer Lingus, which distributes plastic bags in which to ship bicycles (no boxes at the airport).

Northern England and Wales

Distance: 1160 km (721 miles)

Recommended touring time:
21–26 days (18 cycling days)

Terrain: rolling hills with
challenging mountainous
stretches

Accommodations: hostels

Maps: Michelin 402 and 403 in
the 1 : 400,000 series

Britain is an ideal touring destination for many reasons. Besides the convenience of using a familiar language and taking advantage of a good network of hostels and Bed and Breakfast lodgings, the large number of closely concentrated sights makes cycling one of the best ways to travel in this area.

England: Taking a walk in the Lake District

This tour winds through much of northern England and Wales, visiting areas of spectacular natural beauty and distinct character. Many tourists—cyclists and others—tend to stay in London and the south. In doing so they are truly limiting themselves and missing some of the most beautiful and interesting parts of Britain. This unique tour offers a thorough and memorable experience of the distinct regions, local flavors, and natural wonders of the national parks of Northern England and Wales.

From Hadrian's Wall and Northumberland National Park, cycle through two of Britain's favorite regions, the mountainous Lake District and the pastoral Yorkshire Dales. Then cycle south to Sherwood Forest or choose to go directly to the Peak District National Park before cycling toward northern Wales. The challenges of cycling the harsh terrain of this country are rewarded by views of the mountains of Snowdonia and a castle-lined coast. Turn south through the Wye Valley and return to England, finishing the tour in historic Bath.

This tour is based on hostel accommodations, the most practical and inexpensive option for cyclists touring soggy Britain. All hostels along this route have kitchens, common rooms, and drying rooms in addition to offering prepared meals at an extra cost. Most have separate family accommodations and rooms for couples as well. A complete list of hostels and their facilities is available by mail from the Youth Hostel Federation in London and at any of the hostels. The best thing about these hostels is the variety and unique character of each. You can sleep in castles, converted churches, commercial buildings, and manor houses.

For private lodgings, Bed and Breakfast accommodations are also widely available in each area this tour visits. Individual establishments are not listed here simply because there are so many. The tourist office in each town can direct you to locals B&Bs, where advance reservations are not a must. There are many useful guides to country inns available in the US and Europe if you wish to organize your stays beforehand. Campgrounds dot the route as well. Most are marked on Michelin maps.

A note on the weather: England and Wales have reputations for bad weather and constant rain. Although many of these reports are exaggerated, the weather *is* unpredictable. The first weather report I heard in England, for example,

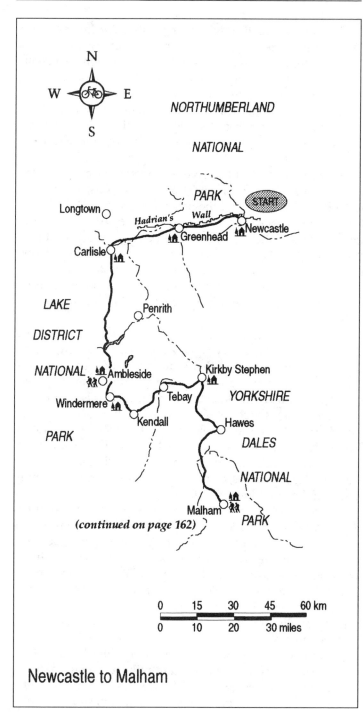

NORTHUMBERLAND

NATIONAL

PARK

START

Longtown

Hadrian's Wall

Newcastle

Greenhead

Carlisle

LAKE

DISTRICT

Penrith

NATIONAL

Ambleside

Kirkby Stephen

YORKSHIRE

Windermere

Tebay

Kendall

Hawes

PARK

DALES

NATIONAL

Malham

(continued on page 162)

PARK

| 0 | 15 | 30 | 45 | 60 km |
| 0 | 10 | 20 | | 30 miles |

Newcastle to Malham

(continued on page 162)

forecast a 'chance of snow, chance of rain, possible hail, and partly sunny.' For the most part, however, you can expect overcast skies and occasional light, steady drizzles. You will appreciate warm, dry accommodations at the end of the day, but these conditions will not prevent you from enjoying the scenery and a day on your bicycle. The key to a comfortable trip is preparation. Bring clothing for all conditions.

This is a long tour, covering considerable sections of England and Wales in a challenging three-week trip. For a shorter excursion, the Newcastle to Chester segment can be covered in two weeks, or the southern section of the Welsh tour can be combined with part of the Trans-Channel Connection tour to cover more of southern England in a week-long trip. Remember to always keep left while cycling around Britain.

Note: This tour is designed to take in the best sights along the most sensible cycling routes. Parts of this tour have been altered from the exact route I followed while researching in order to reflect these interests. One of the advantages of pre-researched tours is that they have made and corrected the mistakes for you. Most notably, the route through northern and central Wales has been adjusted. Under the appropriate daily instructions I have noted the actual route I took if it differs and the reasons for any changes in order to help you know what to expect so that you will enjoy a smooth trip.

Newcastle to Greenhead
40 miles (64 km)

Newcastle-upon-Tyne is a city of manageable size that makes a convenient starting point for this tour. Frequent trains leave London's King's Cross Station for Newcastle. Bicycles can be brought on only certain trains so check ahead or be prepared to wait. There is no extra charge to ship a bicycle. The hostel in Newcastle is located at 107 Jesmond Road. Ask at the station for directions. You will not need much time in Newcastle as there are few points of particular sight-seeing interest in this modern city.

In leaving Newcastle it is best to ask instructions several times to avoid getting lost. Follow West Road A69 to Throckley, in the same direction as Carlisle. Traffic is moderately heavy but this road is wide enough to allow comfortable cycling. Ride up one big, long hill west of Newcastle. During this ride you will encounter several roundabouts. To an

American cyclist, these may be awkward to navigate at first. Take up all the room you need, and let the motorists know you want to be treated with respect. To prevent cars from cutting you off, stay near the middle of your lane until just before you have reached your exit.

Cycle around one of these roundabouts in Throckley and follow signs to Heddon where B6318 starts. Heddon is a lovely town of tidy stone houses—a perfect introduction to cycling in England. B6318 is called the Old Military Road because it follows Hadrian's Wall. You will pass a section of the Wall in Heddon. It was built almost two thousand years ago to protect Roman-controlled Britain from northern tribes that were never subjugated. You will ride along the wall all day. Many sections are still incredibly well preserved, although at some points it is difficult to distinguish the historic barrier from the maze of other stone walls along the road. On the horizon north of the Wall is Northumberland National Park, a region of stark slopes and dry fields.

Cycle over long, rolling hills to Chollerford—up, down, up, down. Pass Harlow Hill and continue on a mile-long downhill into Chollerford. This is a typical Northumbrian town, all stone and very small. Bring lunch supplies from Newcastle or buy a sandwich at the pub in George's Hotel, which has a warm, comforting fireplace. There are no stores in Chollerford.

The last 18 miles on B6318 from Chollerford to Greenhead give you a chance to see the sentry posts dotting Hadrian's Wall up close. At Brocolitia Fort you can walk around the ruins in solitude. Judging from all the warning signs posted in the parking lot there, car theft is apparently rampant, possibly due to disillusioned cyclists. Halfway to Greenhead is Housesteads Fort, one of the largest and best excavated sites along the wall. The fort is worth the entry fee charged.

To make this day shorter, you can stop at the hostel in Once Brewed, two miles past this fort. One of the organized activities at this hostel is an excavation of the Roman remains. If you stay to dig for one week, the hostel will give you free lodgings.

After a few more hilly rolls, cruise down a 1-in-7 hill into Greenhead. The hostel, a converted church, is located on a side road to the right near the middle of this small town. It offers a variety of snacks and prepared meals for a fee. You can also get your own supplies at the nearby store and prepare dinner in the hostel's well-equipped kitchen. Having completed your first day, relax and rest well in this comfortable hostel.

Greenhead to Carlisle
22 miles (35.4 km)

This short ride will let you recover from the previous day and allows you plenty of time to see Carlisle. Luckily, the hills along this ride are smaller, more gradual, and fewer in number than those behind you.

Take route B6318 from Greenhead. When the road runs out after Walton, turn right toward Longtown and take the first left toward Irthington. These are all small towns separated by large fields of curious sheep. After Irthington turn right onto B6264. Traffic picks up at this point but never becomes heavy.

The hostel in Carlisle, Etterby House, is located about a mile from the center of town in Etterby. You can ask for instructions and buy food at the huge indoor marketplace in town. There is also a helpful tourist office in the town center. Carlisle has a castle, but as with everything even slightly historic in Britain, an entry fee is charged. If you plan to visit many historic sights, it may pay to buy a National Historic Trust membership, available at Carlisle Castle. This will earn you discounts and free admission to many sites throughout Britain.

The cathedral in Carlisle is fantastic, a treasure chest of religious and military objects. A blue, star-painted ceiling and stained glass windows rise above countless banners from various army regiments. Some are so old they are hanging by a thread. There is an interesting, and free, museum between the church and the fortress that has many Roman artifacts including weapons, remains of leather tents, and stones proudly carved by the builders of Hadrian's Wall: 'we of the third cohort dedicate this wall....'

Carlisle to Ambleside
38 miles (61 km)

Although the distance from Carlisle to Ambleside is short, the 1,500-foot Kirkstone Pass divides the two towns. For Britain, this is pretty big. However, most of the ride covers almost level or only slightly hilly ground.

Take A6 toward Penrith a few miles out of Carlisle, until the roundabout just after the BP station. Take the roundabout almost 360 degrees to the last exit toward Dalston. Then turn left onto the third big road, not including farmer's lanes, immediately in front of a white public house (pub). This puts you on what is locally known as the Penrith Back road. After a few miles, pass the Crown Inn. I was misdirected and ended up riding into Dalston, then back out to the correct road, so follow signs closely. Cycle to Greystoke and cross road A66 after Penruddock. Turn right on A66 and then immediately left toward Hutton. This is the correct road. It winds through hills and valleys and is clearly marked all the way to Windermere. There is a great descent on a narrow, winding, walled lane from Penruddock into Motherby. This is what England is all about. Neat stone houses show no change after hundreds of years, walls stretch in all directions, and sheep are everywhere. One house near Barrow is built directly into the ruins of a castle.

One mile from Pooley Bridge, follow signs to Ullswater and take the lakeside road to the right instead of left to Pooley Bridge. This will take you along the first of the Lake District lakes, Ullswater. Ride along the water's edge on A592, with spectacular views of snowcapped mountains around the lake. The road is narrow and so are the cars, but there is still a bit too much traffic for peaceful cycling.

Nine miles after Ullswater you will reach the Kirkstone Pass. *Danger!* reads the sign, but this is really an overstatement. It should more accurately read 'Sweat! Groan! Pedal!' Keep plugging away around the curves of the road to the top, at 1,500 feet. The grade over the first mile is a hefty 20%. It lessens to 13% after that until a final rise of 20% again near the top.

There are amazing Lake District views all the way to and at the top. Conveniently enough, there is also a pub at the top of the pass, so reward yourself for a job well done. Wordsworth was moved to write the following about the view from the Kirkstone Pass:

Who comes not hither ne'er shall know,
How beautiful the world below

You may be sweating and groaning on the way up, but you too will agree that the effort is well worth it. After oohing and ahhing at the top, cruise down the other side into Ambleside. Watch out for the little reflective UFOs embedded in the road.

The Lake District has the highest concentration of hostels in England. The most convenient hostels along this route are in Ambleside (at Waterhead) and near Windermere, in Troutbeck (High Cross, Bridge Lane). Ambleside is a smaller town than the tourist town of Windermere. Both sit on Lake Windermere. There are B&B's everywhere.

Wordsworth and Beatrice Potter are just two of the many famous authors who lived in this beautiful area. A walk over the hills of the Lake District will quickly show you where they found the inspiration for their works. Settle in and take a day or two off from cycling in the Lake District. The area is best appreciated on foot, with hundreds of well-marked, frequently traveled footpaths to choose from. The views are incredible, sweeping over beautiful lakes and peaks, including Scafell Pike—the highest mountain in England. One very nice walk is that from Ambleside to Rydal Waters and Grasmere, Wordsworth's home. There are also frequent bus connections between towns, giving you the option of enjoying longer, one-way walks and returning to Ambleside by bus.

Ambleside to Kirkby Stephen
55 miles (89 km)

This is a long and hilly day, crossing from the Lake District to the edge of the Yorkshire Dales. To shorten the ride, take A591 south four miles, through Windermere to Bowness. In Bowness there is a ferry (about $5 per person with bicycle) to the south corner of the lake and the uninteresting town of Lakeside.

Otherwise, you can ride overland from Ambleside. Cycle west on A593 but then turn south toward Hawkshead. Take the left fork one mile later and cycle into Hawkshead. From this town continue south along the eastern shore of a small lake on B5285 to Sawrey. Parallel Windermere's shores as you cycle south, hitting one very steep incline along the way. Then cycle on to Lakeside and Newby Bridge.

Take A590 south and then north (it curves in a U shape) to Kendal. The road is crowded and only has a small shoulder at first, although it widens after a few miles. The grounds of Sizergh castle on the way to Kendal are free and open to the public, making a nice spot for a quick break. After Kendal take road A685 northeast. Here the hills begin again—up, down. The road winds and eventually brings you to the top of the ridge that you saw from the bottom. It is slow, hard going, but scenic. I managed these long climbs by resigning myself to the boredom of pedaling uphill in lowest gear. Happily, you can

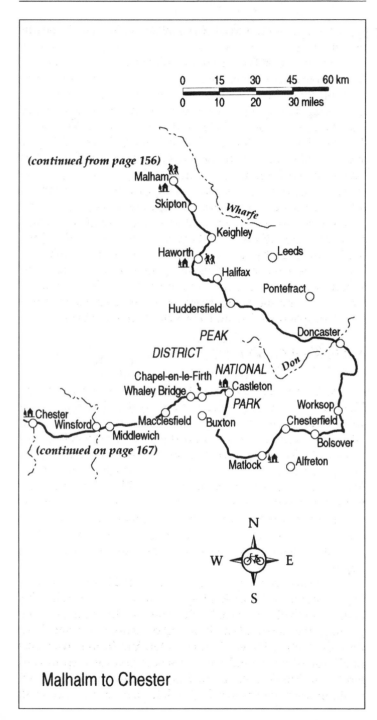

(continued from page 156)

Malham

Skipton

Keighley

Haworth

Halifax

Leeds

Pontefract

Huddersfield

PEAK

DISTRICT

NATIONAL

Doncaster

Don

Wharfe

Chapel-en-le-Firth

Whaley Bridge

Castleton

PARK

Worksop

Chester

Winsford

Macclesfield

Buxton

Chesterfield

Middlewich

Bolsover

(continued on page 167)

Matlock

Alfreton

N

W   E

S

Malhalm to Chester

enjoy a long downhill coast after that as A685 parallels the M6 for a time.

Continue on A685 to Tebay, an uninspiring town. Leave the A road here and follow a series of pretty side roads. Take B6260 to Orton, then B6261 to Kelleth and eventually back onto A685 for the last few miles to Kirkby Stephen. There are several Stonehenge-type stone circles and cairns in the hills around this area. You may spot a site in the distance. I tried cycling to one but failed because there was only an extremely muddy lane leading to the site.

There are a few more climbs on the way to Kirkby Stephen. Kirkby translates into 'place where the church is,' and the hostel here is in fact a converted church, located in the center of town. A sign informs you that it was originally a 'Primitive Methodist' church—use your imagination to figure that one out. The hostel is a memorable one. While the bedrooms are in a modern addition, the common room is in the main body of the church, and the dining room seats are pews. There is also a well-supplied kitchen and a bicycle shed in the back.

Kirkby Stephen to Malham
41 miles (66 km)

I remember this day as perhaps the most serene and lovely ride I had throughout all of England and Wales. The route takes you through the Yorkshire Dales, where dry, yellow-green hills are dotted by sheep and lined with a spidery network of stone walls. The terrain is mostly level down the lengths of the sweeping valleys. After a few miles, you reach the end of one valley, climb up, and drop into the next. The scenery is spectacular at the top of these rises, as you look at the land behind and the valley to come. This area is a national park. While there are towns within it, no new buildings can be added and no present houses altered in a way that disturbs the characteristic appearance of the Dales.

From Kirkby Stephen, cycle south on B6259 south to Nateby, passing the ruins of Pendragon's castle on your right. This is supposedly the home of Merlin's father, although the sheep grazing over the rubble make it a bit difficult to imagine. Turn right on A684 to Hawes 11 miles later, and from Hawes take B6255 for 10 miles until the fork where you turn left toward Horton in Ribblesdale. From Horton follow B6479 to Stainforth. In Stainforth watch for the left turn onto a very small road to Malham. You will hit a steep hill right away and have a lonely but striking ride to Malham.

There is a hostel in Malham. Ask in town for directions. Malham is a tiny town of stone houses and a grocery store. Most hostel guests are hikers, as the Pennine Way passes through the town. For some time off your bicycle, walk a section of this famous trail. The path cuts directly across private fields, offering a close-up view of Yorkshire's landscape.

Malham to Keighley
25 miles (40 km)

You will leave the Yorkshire Dales in this ride south to Haworth, home town of the Bronte sisters. This brings you to a more densely populated area with more traffic than the Dales, but still many hills. Continue south from Malham to Kirkby Malham, Airton, and Gargrave. Turn left in Gargrave toward Skipton and Keighley on A65. Follow this busy road until Steeton. Exit here and turn left at the first traffic light to follow signs for Halifax through the center of town. Past Keighley, ride toward Haworth. A65 is an uncomfortably busy road with a tiny shoulder.

Haworth (pronounced Hah-wuf) is a dark stone town, home of the Bronte sisters and the bleak moors that inspired their stories. You can visit their house or take a short hike across the moors to get a good feel for the area. There is a 'Bronte walk' that takes you on a short, easy hike. It begins at the top of the hill near the Bronte house.

At this point in the tour you have several options. Because of the proximity of several urban centers, cycling south through the area can be problematic. I chose to take a train from Keighley into, through Leeds, and on to Knottingley, in order to continue cycling to Sherwood Forest. Combining train and bicycle travel in England is very simple, so do not hesitate to use this option. Train connections are frequent and easy, and your bicycle will travel for free. You can stay at the Haworth hostel (Longlands Drive, Lees Lane) and take the trains the next day.

However, if you are determined to cycle a continuous line, head south to Halifax, Huddersfield, and Doncaster to pick up the route to Sherwood Forest. You can also choose to go directly to Alfretown in the Peak District to leave out the Sherwood Forest ride (see below). For full information on trains and the best routes to take, go to the Haworth tourist office, near the Bronte home.

Knottingley to Sherwood Forest
41 miles (66 km)

Knottingley is a town to the southeast of Leeds, near Pontrefract and its racetrack. This is the starting point for the 40-mile ride to Sherwood Forest. It is only fair to say that Sherwood Forest is not the most exciting sight on this tour and that the ride to Edwinstowe is not of any great scenic value. A further problem is that there are no hostels in the area. You will have to camp or go to a B&B in Edwinstowe. Much of the actual forest in Sherwood Forest has been cleared for pasture land or dried out by a reduced watertable. The forest Visitor's Centre, while fun, offers only a mixed collection of scattered facts of the Robin Hood story. A good example of this is the 'Major Oak,' the highlight of the Centre. Tourist information boards colorfully describe Robin Hood and his merry cohorts meeting under this tree, and then go cheerfully on to prove that this could not possibly have been the actual meeting place. The theme of the Centre seems to be that it is all in good fun, anyway. With a good imagination and the will to try something different, the trip to Sherwood Forest can be pleasantly diverting.

If, on the other hand, you are not a die-hard Robin Hood fan and are more impatient to move on toward Wales, I would recommend traveling directly to Alfreton, near Matlock in the Peak District. To do so, give to the already rich and take a Britrail train from Leeds to Alfreton, or cycle a more direct course from Knottingley to Doncaster and Bolsover.

To ride to Sherwood Forest, turn right on A645 east from the Knottingley train station. At the sign for *Cribbing Stubbs 2*, turn right over the railroad tracks on Womersley road. Follow signs for A638 and Bawtry through Doncaster. After you cross over the M18, turn right to Rossington and B6463 to Blyth and then continue south on B6045 to Worksop. The roads around Worksop are confusing and make for messy route finding. Ask directions and head to B6034, which runs through Sherwood Forest (apparently the B6005 on the Michelin map is a typo or there has been a change). Then follow signs to the Sherwood Forest Visitor's Centre outside of Edwinstowe.

At the Visitor's Centre, you can take a short hike to the Major Oak and spend time in the exhibit buildings. There are no hostels in the area, the nearest being 30 miles away in Matlock. There is an overpriced campground nearby (about $5 per person). From the Visitor's Centre go through Edwinstowe and follow signs to the right. You can also get a B&B in Edwinstowe. Ask at the Visitor's Centre for the nearest one.

Sherwood Forest to Youlgreave
43 miles (69 km)

From Edwinstowe, take A616 and A632 west to Bolsover. (For a shortcut from the campground, take A60 north to Warsop and Cuckney on the A616.) These roads have a considerable amount of traffic,but there are no alternate B roads going west. You can visit the castle in busy Bolsover for a quick break before pedaling on to Chesterfield and continuing on A632 to Matlock. Soon after Chesterfield you will begin to encounter long hills. Black Hill on A632 is particularly nasty, but offers great views as you enter the Peak District, where the hills grow higher, sharper, and darker.

There is a dramatically situated castle high above Matlock. It is best appreciated from down in the town itself. I sweated my way to the top of the hill, only to find the ruins closed to the public, a children's zoo open, and a two-pound entry fee. This was not quite what I had in mind.

Cycle north from Matlock on the A6 to Rowsley and Buxton for a short distance. Turn off to the left toward the Carriage Museum and take the next major left to gain quieter but still hilly roads to Winster. From this small town, take B5056 north to Youlgreave. There are several megalithic monuments in the area, and the turnoff for Setton Moon stone circle is marked from B5056. The sign reads '2 miles,' but it is actually much farther. Bear left at the quarry on the top of the hill to get there and then ask for directions. The site is out on the moors. Hills? Moors? I went about 5 miles before heading back to Youlgreave, discouraged.

Continue on B5056 and turn left for Youlgreave. The hostel is past the church on the left in a tall, narrow building that was once a grocery store. This is a fun hostel, with nice managers and rooms named after items once stored there. I stayed in *Ladies' Underwear*.

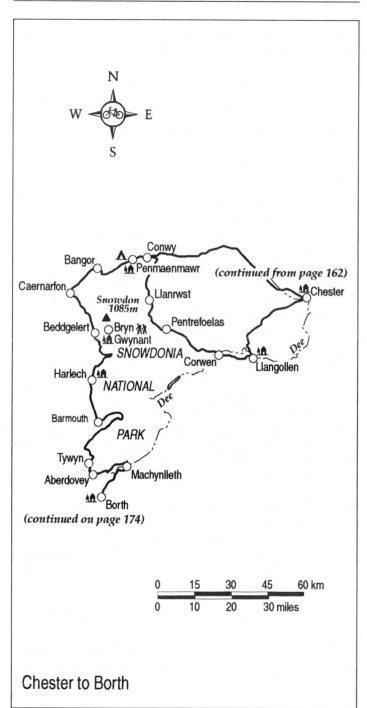

N
W ← → E
S

Conwy
Bangor
Penmaenmawr
Caernarfon
(continued from page 162)
Chester
Snowdon
1085m
Llanrwst
Beddgelert
Bryn
Gwynant
Pentrefoelas
SNOWDONIA
Harlech
Corwen
NATIONAL
Dee
Barmouth
Dee
PARK
Llangollen
Tywyn
Aberdovey
Machynlleth
Borth
(continued on page 174)

| 0 | 15 | 30 | 45 | 60 km |
| 0 | 10 | 20 | 30 miles |

Chester to Borth

Youlgreave to Castleton
20 miles (32 km)

On this day you will cycle deeper into the Peak District and see more of the distinct mountains that this region is named for. I awoke to a snowstorm and cycled a frigid 20 miles to Castleton since the Youlgreave hostel was closing for the day. You can look forward to a short, scenic ride as long as the weather is good.

Ride west out of Youlgreave and bear right at the second junction (unmarked) to ride up past the fields toward Monyash. Bear right to Monyash at the next T-junction outlined by stone walls. After Taddington go left on A6 toward Buxton and turn left where it is marked *Priestecliffe*. Follow this road straight down to the bottom of the hill and turn right on B6049 for Bradwell. There is another hostel 2 miles from Tideswell on this road.

After Tideswell keep heading for Bradwell, from which point you will pick up signs for Castleton. On the way, pass the Britrail station in Hope. I stayed one day in Castleton, then took a train from Hope to Manchester and Macclesfield to visit a friend and wait out the snow.

Castleton is a pretty town set in one of the most beautiful parts of the Peak District. The stone buildings, views, and comfortable hostel will revive you from the effort spent on all those hills. There is, of course, a castle on a hill above town. The admission fee is collected at the bottom. The hostel also has a day room in which to seek shelter during the daytime lockout period.

Castleton to Chester
62 miles (100 km)

Since there are no hostels between Castleton and Chester, you will be forced to do a long 62-mile ride from the Peak District across Cheshire to Chester. While the first part of the ride is hilly, the terrain from Macclesfield to Chester is unchallenging. One way to shorten the ride is to cycle to Macclesfield to stay in a B&B and continue cycling to Chester the next day.

Cycle west out of Castleton on A625 to Chapel-en-le-Firth. There is a small side road from Chapel to Whaley Bridge, where you join A5002 for ten miles to Macclesfield, on the western edge of the Peak District. Follow signs through this small city to Siddington and Holmes Chapel via roads B5392 and A535. Take busy road A54 2.5 miles to Middlewich and continue on to Winsford. After Winsford, cross the line into Crewe-Nantwich Borough, then cross out again within 5 miles to avoid going into Crewe. It is very easy to get lost for lack of signposts in this area. First follow signs to Wettenhall, then turn off. The route directions in this area are so confusing that it is best to ask a local. Do not feel shy about stopping at someone's house or at a farm if there is no one in sight. When I did this everyone I met was very friendly and helpful. Ask for Eaton, from where B5152 leads to Tiverton, Huxley, and Rowton. In Rowton, join busy A41 into Chester.

You can stop in the medieval town right away or cycle straight to the hostel on Hough Green and return later. To get to the hostel, ride past the horse racetrack and turn right at the first large traffic circle for Hough Green Street. The hostel is in a large, aging white house one mile from town on the right side of the street.

Chester has a fascinating history, from Roman fort to medieval trade center. There is a Roman amphitheater within the medieval walls and half-timbered houses clutter many of Chester's streets where musicians often perform. On race days you can watch the horses compete from the street above the track.

Chester to Llangollen
28 miles (45 km)

From Chester, I cycled directly west along the coast to Conwy via roads A548 and A55. That I lived to tell the tale and continue cycling still surprises me (and that's only a slight exaggeration…). I do not recommend that you do the same as traffic is uncomfortable to downright dangerous, route finding is frustrating, and the coast is not visible from the road anyway.

While the overland route to Llangollen and then Conwy is hilly and longer than the direct, coastal ride, it is much safer and more enjoyable, and includes more Welsh countryside. I regretted missing Llangollen, known for its pretty town and impressive castle hostel.

From the hostel in Chester follow Saltney road (A549) to Saltney, Broughton, and Pen-y-ffordd (Pen). Welcome to Wales, where every every *d*, *h*, and *l* seems to be doubled and names are bigger than towns themselves. Llangollen is pronounced Hlan-goh-lan. From Pen take A5104 southwest to Leeswood and Treuddyn. 11 miles past Pen turn left onto A542 south to Llangollen. Steel yourself for the 345-meter Horseshoe Pass on the last 8-miles into town.

The castle hostel 1.5 miles from town was given a million-pound facelift in 1989 and is by all accounts magnificent. Llangollen is also home to Dinas Bras (castle) and an international music festival in July. Be sure to have reservations if you plan to be in town at this time. Ask at the tourist office in town for more information on Llangollen and Welsh history.

Llangollen to Penmaenmawr
51 miles (82 km)

From Llangollen the road runs west to the edge of Snowdonia National Park before turning north for the coast and Conwy. The ride is very challenging as you pedal through northern Wales's hilly countryside. The striking scenery will keep you motivated, however, as you ride toward the coast and the first of Edward I's three Welsh castles.

Ride 25 miles east on the A5 to Pentrefoelas. This road can be very busy, but the only alternative is an endless series of B roads that mainly run north to south and not east to west. Try to set out early to beat any traffic. You can take a quick breather by detouring onto B5437 7 miles east of Llangollen and returning to the A5 at Corwen. A5 follows rivers so it is more level than many minor roads in the area.

From Pentrefoelas turn right for B5113 to Nebo and Llanrwst in the scenic Vale of Conwy. Your ride will be quieter and easier from here to the coast. In Llanrwst cross the river and turn north (right) on B5106 to Trefriw, Dolgarrow, Tal-y-Bont, and finally to Conwy.

Conwy is a town typical of the Welsh coast, with a mystical castle and foggy, boat-filled harbor. You can walk along the castle's walls around the entire town and explore the pretty waterfront where the smallest house in Britain is located. Coastal conditions are ever changing, constantly altering Conwy's appearance. I cycled into the town in a murky downpour when the castle's towers and ships' masts were half-hidden in mist. Half an hour later I was marvelling at the bright, sun-drenched town and clear blue sky. When the clouds rolled back in they choked out the sun, leaving only individual shafts of light to point out sections of the walls and stone buildings. In the end, I left for Penmaenmawr in a heavy downpour.

The last few miles of coastal road A55 to Penmaenmawr, known locally as 'Pen,' are very busy and unsettling. The best thing to do is cycle on sidewalks for the last three miles to the Pen hostel. The hostel is a rustic, one-story building to the right of the road. To reach it you will have to go left to gain access to an overpass. It is a comfortable if simple hostel with spectacular views of the coast. Camping is permitted on hostel grounds.

If your budget permits it, another option is to stay in a B&B in Conwy, where there are several, and retrace your route down the Vale of Conwy the next day, and then turn west for Caernarfon. This eliminates the difficulty and stress of cycling along the coast but adds miles to the ride.

Penmaenmawr to Bryn Gwynant
36 miles (58 km)

From Pen resume the slow ride on the sidewalks of A55 another 9 miles past Aber to Llandegai, near Bangor. Stay patient and do not risk riding the road if it is busy. As you approach Bangor, follow signs that read *Caernarfon—Alternative Tourist Route*. Take B4366 and breath a sigh of relief as you pedal this quiet side route to Caernarfon. You have finished the most uncomfortable section of riding of the entire tour. Enjoy the tranquility and magnificent views of Mount Snowdon as you cycle past deep green fields and woods.

Caernarfon's major site is its castle, built by Edward I and site of the investitures of the Princes of Wales. The town and harbor will make you delay your departure even more. I spent the greater part of the day holed up in a warm pub, waiting out another rainstorm.

Begin the second half of the day's ride back to Snowdonia by taking B4085 out of town to Waunfawr and Beddgelert. This leads past the Roman fort of Segovium on the outskirts of Caernarfon, a small site easily visited in a short time—and no admission fee. It is another 16 miles to Bryn Gwynant and the hostel there. Luckily the roads to Bryn Gwynant wind a level course between and not over the mountains of Snowdonia, making this a fairly quick and easy ride. In Beddgelert turn left onto A498 to Bryn Gwynant. The hostel is a large, stone manor house located to the right above the shores of Llyn (Lake)

Gwynant with wonderful views of snow-capped Mount Snowdon and its neighbors. The management will happily supply you with information on local hiking trails, from short hikes to the climb up Snowdon itself. Half-price camping on the hostel's grounds is also available.

Bryn Gwynant to Harlech
20 miles (32 km)

This is a well-deserved, short ride out of Snowdonia back to the coast, allowing for a morning hike or a full, lazy afternoon enjoying Harlech's views. Return to Beddgelert on A498 and then turn left (south) on A4085 to Garreg and Penrhyndeudraeth. Michelin maps indicate a mountain pass on this road but there is very little climbing to be done since the pass cuts an almost flat path between two mountains. Cross the bridge into Pen and turn onto A496 to Harlech. You will get your first glimpse of Harlech castle from this road.

There are two choices for the last few miles into Harlech. The A road (A496) nearer the coast is flatter, more crowded, and involves a final steep climb into Harlech. The inland B road (B4573) covers the distance in a long, gradual climb with less traffic to contend with.

Incredible views and the availability of a comfortable hostel convinced me to end my day earlier than I had planned, in Harlech. From the castle and any of the rocky outcrops around town you can take in the gorgeous blue coastline, the green and purplish mountains of Snowdonia, and the hills of the Lleyn Peninsula stretching westward. Sea level was once as high as the cliff's top, below the castle. The hostel is located on a rise near the center of town. Ask in town for directions.

Harlech to Borth
50 miles (80 km)

Now that you are well rested, head south on a quiet ride to Borth. From this point specific sights are farther apart as you cycle through the Welsh countryside. The terrain is smoother but still hilly on these next few days back to England. After one day in Harlech I set out directly for Glascwm, having misjudged the distance. It turned out to be 103 miles. Needless to say, I do not recommend this route. I have therefore recommended a stop in Borth on the way south. Beware of simply eyeballing the next day's distance. My mistake was caused by not carefully measuring the route, which crossed from the area represented by one map to another.

Continue on A496 from Harlech to Barmouth, where you can cross a bridge across Barmouth Bay. It is a train bridge but there is a pedestrian walkway next to it. The inlet is beautiful though windy, with views of Cader Idris to the east. From Fairbourne on the south side of the inlet, cycle southwest to Llwyngwril, Tywyn, and Aberdovey on A493. Circle around another inlet to Machynlleth and turn south on A487 to Eglwysfach. Three miles after this town, turn right on B4353 to Borth, a small coastal town with a hostel. (Note: This hostel was closed some time in 1991; check ahead to make sure it will be open at the time of your trip.)

Borth to Glascwm
58 miles (93 km)

From Borth cycle to Aberystwyth on B4572. This is a hilly road with a very steep climb, but then a long downhill coast into Aberystwyth, home of the University College of Wales and the Welsh National Library.

Head east out of the city on A4120 and cycle 12 miles to Devil's Bridge. Ask for directions in Aberystwyth, where the roads can be confusing because so many converge in one place. Continue eastward over the hills on B4574 from Devil's Bridge

Harlech Castle in northern Wales

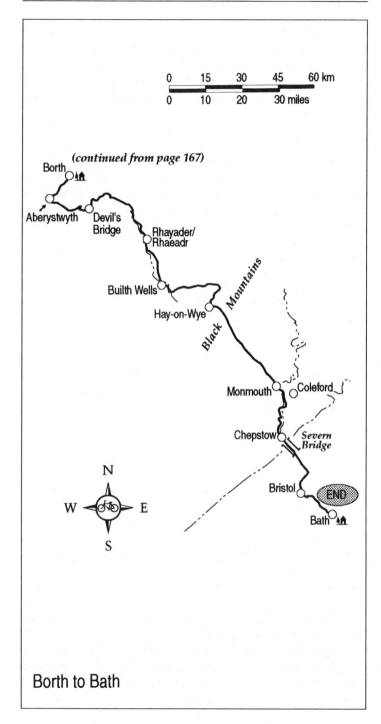

(continued from page 167)

Borth

Aberystwyth

Devil's Bridge

Rhayader/Rhaeadr

Builth Wells

Hay-on-Wye

Black Mountains

Monmouth

Coleford

Chepstow

Severn Bridge

Bristol

END

Bath

N

W E

S

Borth to Bath

to Rhayader. From here turn south on A470 toward Builth Wells and then left for Disserth 8 miles later at Newbridge on Wye. This peaceful back road will take you past the town of Hundred House to Glascwm. Keep your eyes open for signs in this little-traveled area and you will have no trouble getting to the tiny town of Glascwm.

In Glascwm you will get to experience an original-type youth hostel. Officially, it is a simple grade hostel, located on the right of the main street through town. There are no showers, although there is running water. All other facilities are good enough to keep you happy after a long day on your bicycle. There are two long bunkhouses, kitchen facilities, couches, and a cozy fireplace. The warden lives a block away. Instructions to his house are printed on the hostel door. He will assign you a bunk and collect the modest fee of about $4. There are no stores in Glascwm so be sure to get supplies in Rhayader or another town on the way. If all this is too primitive for you, there is a pub with rooms for rent in Newbridge on Wye.

Glascwm to St. Briavel's
51 miles (82 km)

This day's ride will take you from the center of rural Wales to the Wye Valley and St. Briavel's. Bid the Glascwm hostel goodbye and head to Bryngwyn, continuing on the same road you used to enter Glascwm. Keep right and follow signs to Bryngwyn and Rhosgh until you see signs for Hay-on-Wye. At Clyro cross the A438 to go to Hay-on-Wye. This is a wonderful town with possibly the highest concentration of bookshops per block in all Britain. It is a very pleasant place to take a morning break before continuing toward Monmouth.

There are two choices in cycling south of Hay: through the Golden Valley or over the Black Mountains. This is an easy choice to make. Take the road going uphill directly across from the BP station in Hay. Bear left at the top, following signs for Peterchurch. This leads you to B4352 and two miles later, to a right turn for Peterchurch and B4348. B4348 winds along the pretty Golden Valley. If you look to the west you will see the ridge of the Black Mountains. After Vowchurch follow B4347 to Monmouth. Do not take any turnoffs from the main road despite what the signposts may say—I discovered that two were reversed. If in doubt, ask for directions.

There is a large Gateway supermarket in Monmouth. Go over the bridge and follow signs to A466, which runs along the Wye River. This is a very scenic road although there is no shoulder and moderate to heavy traffic. Turn left 3 miles later onto B4231 to Coleford and Newland. Unfortunately, the last few miles to St. Briavel's are all uphill and poorly signposted. After Newland, pedal to Clearwell. Turn right at the first Y-junction after this town, and then left at the next Y-junction. One hundred yards later turn right for Lindney. St. Briavel's is signposted as being 2 miles from this point.

The hostel in St. Briavel's is a renovated castle, complete with moat and drawbridge. This can be your well-deserved resting place after the previous night in Glascwm. The castle was once King John's hunting lodge, and his bedroom is now used as the common room. It is a very popular hostel, and for this reason it is best to make reservations a day or two in advance. There are B&B's in town if you find yourself crowded out.

The area around St. Briavel's is also very nice. This is a great place to put your bicycle away for a day or two . Besides seeing the castle and the town, you can go down to the Wye Valley and hike a few miles of the Wye Valley walk. This is a section of Offa's Dyke Path, a long-distance hiking trail that follows the course of a one-time barrier between England and Wales.

St. Briavel's to Bath
40 miles (64 km)

When you are ready to leave the castle and St. Briavel's, continue down B4228 toward Chepstow. You can drop down into the valley and take A466 to visit the ruins of Tintern Abbey, but this route will put you on a far busier road with a long uphill pedal as you head south.

From Chepstow, cycle for the Severn Bridge and Bristol. The road joins the huge M4 just before the bridge, but there is a bicycle path alongside this highway. It begins at the round-about where A466 meets the M4. Follow the bicycle path onto the bridge where there is a wide, separate lane for bicycles and maintenance vehicles only. The views from the bridge are impressive, and the experience is exciting. It is not often that you can cycle over such a large bridge and enjoy your own lane.

Once on the south side of the bridge, and now in England, cross to the east side of the M4 to the Aust Service Station. There is a pedestrian overpass for this purpose. Follow *way out* signs from the station to pick up signs for B4461 to Alveston and calmer cycling. At the first stop sign and intersection in Alveston go straight. When the road comes to a T, turn right, then left where A38 is signposted. Take A38 for less than a mile until Rudgeway where you turn left on B4059. As you approach Yate on this road, take A432 toward Bristol for ¼ mile, then turn off to the right for Westerleigh, opposite the Swan pub. In Westerleigh ask for Puckleschurch and Wick, since there are no signs. In Puckleschurch turn left after the school and the sign for children playing. Turn right at the T-junction at the bottom of the hill and take the first left, which is signposted *Wick 3 miles*. In Wick, carry on straight through town until you intersect A420. Turn left to Chippenham. At the top of the long hill turn right toward Bath (6 miles).

The hostel in Bath is located across the valley on Bathwick Hill in the direction of the American Museum. Ask for directions in the center of town and watch for YHA signs on the left, more than half a mile up the hill (all the cyclists in the hostel were complaining about this one). The hostel is a beautiful Italian-style villa with a bicycle shed and a large, comfortable common room.

Bath is full of interesting sights and makes a great finale to this tour of England and Wales. Besides the Roman and Georgian Baths, you can visit luxurious town house complexes, such as the Circus and Royal Crescent, built in the eighteenth century. The cathedral in the center of town is also very interesting, with angels climbing up and falling down a ladder carved along its facade. Ask about the free walking tours of Bath at the tourist office or the hostel. Guides are proud residents of the city who colorfully describe the lush Georgian lifestyle and other aspects of the city's history.

England, France: Trans-Channel Connection

Distance: 402 km (250 miles), of which 156 km (97 miles) in England, 247 km (153 miles) in France

recommended touring time: 7–9 days (5 cycling days)

Terrain: fairly easy, with rolling hills throughout

Accommodations: camping and hostels or Bed and Breakfasts

Maps: Michelin 403 in 1 : 400,000 series (England), Michelin 59 and 54 in 1 : 200,000 series (France)

The Trans-Channel route covers two countries, two cultures, and an overview of history from prehistoric to modern times in a simple one-week tour. This is an ideal ride for beginning cyclists and for those who wish to experience some real variety over a limited amount of time.

Bath, the starting point of this tour, offers a good introduction to the mixture of sights that lie ahead, with its Roman Baths, Gothic Abbey, and Georgian town houses. Cycling south to Salisbury will take you even further back in time, past hillside chalk drawings and low, rolling hills to Stonehenge. Salisbury itself boasts an interesting town center and a cathedral with the tallest spire in England.

Cycle south from Salisbury through the New Forest and see the ponies named for this region. From the historic seaport of Portsmouth, cross the English Channel to Brittany and St. Malo, a walled pirate town. Finally, turn east to visit the island monastery of Mont St. Michel and the Normandy beaches before finishing the tour in Bayeux.

This short tour is based on campground and hostel accommodations. However, Bed and Breakfasts abound along the route in both England and France if you prefer private lodging. Mid-June to early September are the best times to cycle this tour and enjoy clear weather, since the English Channel area can be wet and cold at other times of year.

Buy a ticket for the Channel ferry from Portsmouth to St. Malo beforehand ($30–50). The easiest place to do so is the Sealink office in Victoria station in London. If seats are sold out you can buy an even less expensive 'no seat' ticket and bunk out in the ship's hallway during the overnight passage. You will not need reservations or a ticket for your bicycle—it travels free.

Bath and Bayeux offer frequent train connections to London and Paris. It is also possible to extend your ride by taking a train from Bayeux to Dinan and joining the Brittany to Loire Valley tour there. Remember that in France there is an extra charge and wait of up to three days for shipping a bicycle by train.

Hello: *Bonjour*
Thank you: *Merci*

Bath to Salisbury
47 miles (76 km)

Bath is an interesting city with a mixture of historic sights. The tourist office in the center of town offers enjoyable and free walking tours of Bath that are well worth a few hours one morning. The hostel in Bath is located in an Italian villa in Bathwick Hill, on the way to the American Museum. It is more than half a mile up the hill, on the left.

When you are ready to leave Bath and begin the ride south, cycle to the top of Bathwick Hill toward Claverton and the American Museum. Cycle down A36 for 3 miles until the right turn onto B3108 to Winsley and Bradford-on-Avon. In Bradford, turn onto A368 south through Trowbridge. After Trowbridge and just before Westbury, turn left for Bratton (B3098). From this road you will see the White Horse chalk drawing on a hillside. You can climb directly up to it, although this large-scale figure is best appreciated from a distance.

Continue on B3098 to Edington and Erlestoke. Then turn south across Salisbury Plain on A360 to Shrewton and Amesbury. This area is well named, being broad and mostly feature-

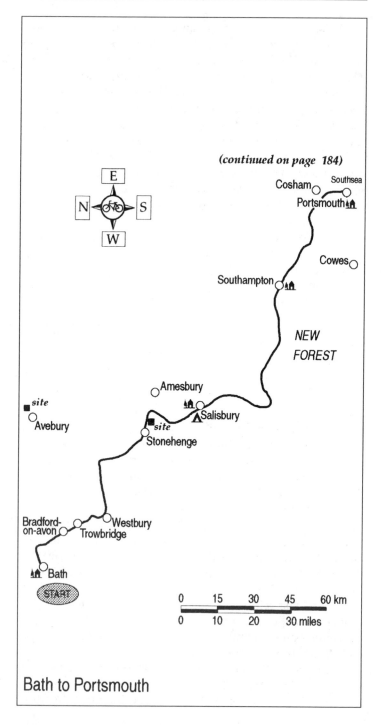

(continued on page 184)

Bath to Portsmouth

less. Military exercises are conducted nearby—keep an eye out for 'Tank Crossing' signs along this road. As you near Stonehenge and Amesbury, traffic picks up considerably. Use caution and expect an uncomfortable ride for a few miles.

Stonehenge will be to your right, but the entrance is to the left. Many tour groups advertise their customers 'unraveling the secrets of Stonehenge.' I do not see how this can be done from an air-conditioned bus, but then it is just as hard to do from a bicycle. You will have to settle for just wondering. While nobody likes the throngs of tourists or the hefty entrance fee, almost everyone agrees that Stonehenge is not to be missed. You can see it well enough from outside the fence, but paying to enter will get you closer to appreciate the tremendous size of the stones. The days of walking under and touching the stones are unfortunately long gone. For a similar, less tourist traveled site, consider detouring or making a day trip from Salisbury to Avebury, 25 miles to the north. There, another collection of megaliths encircles much of the present-day town.

After Stonehenge, join A303 east to Amesbury. This is a very busy road with heavy truck and tourist traffic. It is best to cycle on the grass track alongside the right of the road. Get off the sidewalk at the first road to the right after the junction of A360 and A303. This is the back road to Middle Woodford and on to Salisbury along the River Avon. This River Avon is not the same as many other rivers with the same name in England. *avon* actually means river, but the Romans misunderstood, thinking locals were telling them individual names of the rivers when asked. Hence the profusion of River Avons (River River, when translated) in England.

Salisbury is a small cathedral city with a large market square and a well-situated hostel. It is located on the opposite side of town, past the market. There are magnificent cedar trees on the hostel's quiet grounds, where camping is allowed for half-price. Salisbury Cathedral boasts Britain's tallest spire and a lovely, quiet cloister.

Salisbury to Portsmouth
50 miles (80 km)

There are hostels and B&Bs in both Southampton and Portsmouth, so you can cycle the distance in two days if you wish. The least complicated method, however, is to cycle directly from Salisbury to the ferry in Portsmouth and not bother with accommodations at all. Since the ferry leaves in the evening (usually 8 p.m.), you will have time to ride to Portsmouth and find the ferry landing with hours to spare. The ride is fairly level and easy, although roads between Southampton and Portsmouth can be crowded. The Southampton hostel is at 461 Winchester Road in Bassett; the Portsmouth hostel is in Wymering Manor in Cosham.

Follow A36 south out of Salisbury. About one mile from town, take the first road to the right, signposted for Alderbury, and keep right for Downton. At the first stop sign in Downton turn left up a gradual hill for Redlynch. Cycle straight through Redlynch (do not turn left and go downhill) to join B3080 across the moors of New Forest. Continue straight on B3078 to Cadnam and then take the busier A336 to Totton.

New Forest is not all forest and it is not even very new. William the Conqueror had it planted as his personal hunting ground in the eleventh century. Some of the New Forest Ponies you see across the scrubby moors and along the road are still wild. This is a beautiful area to cycle through before entering the suburban tangle near Southampton.

From Totton follow signs for Southampton. The road will be very busy. Stay on A3025 to Bursledon, which lies near the coast (do not ride into Southampton center). After Bursledon join A27 to Portsmouth. This is a main road, but some of the traffic is diverted onto the motorway that parallels it. A27 is also lined with sidewalks, which you should ride on if the traffic is too heavy for safe cycling. There are no alternate routes to Portsmouth since this city is a virtual dead end against the English Channel. Continue on A27 through Sarlsbury, Titchfield, and Portchester.

After Portchester there are several roundabouts with roads heading south to the port area. Find A204 to Southsea. This road goes through residential and commercial areas and is paralleled by a motorway that takes much of the traffic. Head for the southwest corner of Southsea, a section of Portsmouth, and the historic dockyard. Signs to the dockyard are inconsistent and difficult to follow at times—ask for directions several times along the way.

The Sealink (and other lines) Ferry dock is north of the historic port. It is advisable to ask directions and find your ferry as soon as you reach Portsmouth to avoid a last-minute rush in the evening. You can then spend a few hours visiting the historic ships before returning to the ferry landing. There is an information center in the port area that can direct you to the ferry landing and give you information on the historic ships.

The *Victory* and the remains of the *Mary Rose* are two of the many ships in the historic dockyard. Each charges a separate admission fee, but entrance to the overall area is free. There are plenty of benches where you can enjoy a last picnic meal in England before heading back to the ferry and France.

Channel Crossing

When boarding the ferry, get in line with the cars. Bicycles may go to the front of the line but must then wait for a signal to board, and are then left together in one section of the massive car hold. There were more than fifty bicycles on the ferry I took in late May. There is not much you can do about the safety of your belongings since passengers are not permitted to remain in the hold once the ship sets sail. Lock your bicycle, take all your valuables and sleeping bag, and head for the upper decks. Keep external accessories such as water bottle and pump out of sight in your panniers. If you have a no seat ticket, try to find a quiet hallway or place on deck to spend the night.

St. Malo to Mont St. Michel
56 km (35 miles)

St. Malo's beautiful harbor and intriguing offshore islands will clear your bleary eyes after an early arrival in France. Head for the walled Vieille Ville (Old Town) from the ferry landing. There is a tourist information office outside Port (gate) St. Vincent that will provide you with a city map and directions to the hostel on Ave. du Pere Umbricht, outside the Old Town. Head over to the hostel or find a B&B as early after arrival as possible. Get to the hostel before the 10 a.m. lockout, or you will have to wait until 5 p.m.

Once settled, walk around the walled city. What was once a busy pirate's haven is now a thriving tourist resort, and with good reason. You can explore the twisting streets for hours and climb the ramparts for views of the sea. In summer there are many street musicians in St. Malo, adding to its lively atmosphere. There are also many stores in the city where you can buy maps of Brittany and Normandy for the upcoming ride, as well as several banks at which to change your money.

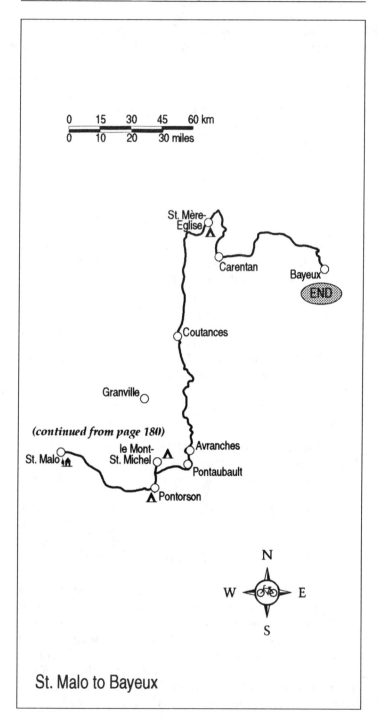

0   15   30   45   60 km
0   10   20   30 miles

St. Mère-
Eglise

Carentan

Bayeux

END

Coutances

Granville

(continued from page 180)

le Mont-
St. Michel

Avranches

St. Malo

Pontaubault

Pontorson

N

W   E

S

St. Malo to Bayeux

Take some time off in St. Malo to recover from the overnight trip and the change to a new country and language. I found my first few days in France trying and the first day of biking and route finding frustrating. Try not to rush yourself. The best antidote for culture shock is to head directly to a boulangerie (bakery) and a crèmerie (dairy store), and then take your supplies to a scenic point for a bread-and-cheese fest. Throw in a little wine and the shock will quickly subside.

From St. Malo, try heading southeast for la Gouerniere. I say try because the maze of roads in the area is difficult to navigate. I ended up taking D155 toward St. Meloir and then turned south on D76 to la Gouesniere. There are sideroads that run more directly to this town, but I could not find them.

I threw in the towel and cycled a direct route to Pontorson via roads D4 and N176. The secondary roads in the area were poorly marked and made my first day of navigating very frustrating. None of the sideroads runs directly west to east, so following them adds miles to the trip. While D4 and N176 are marked red on Michelin maps, traffic is not very bad

France: You are entering Normandy.

although it can get busy. If you are determined to try small roads, take D80 from Dol de Bretagne to St. Broladre and then D797 to Pontorson.

Pontorson is a large town that has a very inexpensive campground near the river. You can use this as your base and cycle to the monastery of Mont St. Michel after unloading. However, the higher-priced campgrounds directly across the bay from Mont St. Michel are worth the expense for their prime location and views, especially of the floodlit monastery at night. Staying here will also shorten the next day's ride to St. Mere Eglise. There are B&Bs in Pontorson and a hostel in Avranches.

Mont St. Michel is an incredible sight in spite of the throngs of tourists choking its narrow streets. The monastery was built over hundreds of years on its protected offshore island. If you visit the monastery during a full moon, you will be able to see the extreme tides for which the bay is known. Old prints show galloping horses trying in vain to outrun the surge. You can spend hours walking the streets of the complex. Best of all is to find a quiet corner and look out over the bay in solitude.

Mont St. Michel to St. Mère Eglise
112 km (70 miles)

This is a very long cycling day that will take you farther from Brittany into the heart of Normandy and the region of the D-Day landings of 1944. The day can easily be divided into two by stopping at the campground in Coutances, 64 km (40 miles) from Mont St. Michel, and then cycling on to St. Mère Eglise the next day (48 km, 30 miles). Seventy miles is a long distance but it can be covered fairly easily by cycling steadily all day. Since there are few specific sights in this stretch of Normandy, I cycled the entire distance at once.

There are many hills along this route, but many level sections as well. The Norman scenery is very pretty and will keep you pleasantly occupied during the quiet ride north. From Mont St. Michel, cycle east on D75 to Pontaubault. This road offers beautiful views of the monastery across the fields. Then head north to Avranches on N175. This road is very busy, so turn off to the left to follow a wide loop through le Val St. Père before joining D104 around Avranches.

Start heading for Granville on D973, but turn right onto D105 to la Planche and Lolif soon after. Here you can relax and enjoy the quiet backroads that make France perfect for bicycle touring. At la Croix du Gros Chene, take D41 to les Chanbres and then D231 to la Haye Pesnel. From there, take D35 to Folligny, le Loreur, Cerences, and la France, where the road number changes to D235 all the way to Coutances.

Continue pedaling north from Coutances. Join D971 for 6 km until la Houssaye, where you turn left on D535 to Périers. Turn west on D900 for a short distance before abandoning it for D24 to the right. D24 runs due north through St. Jores to Pont l'Abbe, bringing you within 10 km of St. Mère Eglise. There is a campground about 7 km before this town, but you should hold out until you reach a much better site in St. Mère Eglise itself. There are several grocery stores in town, as well as the usual collection of boulangeries and charcuteries.

St. Mere Eglise was one of the first towns in Normandy to be liberated by the Allies. Paratroopers landed in the town on the night of June 5,1944 (the day before the marine landing). One man's parachute caught on the church's tower. He survived by playing dead, but went deaf from the constant ringing of the church bells that were signaling the liberation effort. In addition to all the conventional monuments around town, there is also a parachute, complete with a dummy GI suspended from the church in honor of that night. It is enough to make you look twice.

St. Mère Eglise to Bayeux
79 km (48 miles)

This is a long cycling day, but there are so many points of interest along the way that you will be constantly motivated to pedal onward. Bring lunch supplies to enjoy a picnic at one of the stops.

From St. Mère Eglise, cycle to Utah Beach by taking D15 north through Ravenoville to Ravenoville-Plage on the coast. Turn right for the 10 km ride along the first of the famous D-Day beaches. There are several cemeteries and monuments along the way, including a map of each ship's position for the landing that conveys an idea of how extensive the operation was. After la Madeleine, cycle inland on D913 to Ste. Marie, Vierville, and St. Come.

From St. Come you have no choice but to join the bustling, narrow N113 to Carentan and Isigny sur Mer. Be especially careful when trucks pass you going in the opposite direction because they can seriously destabilize your bicycle if you are not ready for the gust of air they send over. Trucks that overtake you can also be frightening because they tend to slowly drag you in. Both of these effects, however, can be counteracted by concentrating and pedaling smoothly.

After Osmanville you can breathe a sigh of relief and turn north onto D514 to Grandcamp-Maisy and Pointe du Hoc. This is on Omaha Beach, the most difficult landing point. Concrete bunkers and barbed wire have been left in their original places and information boards describe the landing in detail. Visiting the remarkably preserved site of Pointe du Hoc made me feel as if the landings occurred just five years ago, not fifty.

Ride back to D514 to St. Laurent, site of the American cemetery. It is a strikingly beautiful and sobering spot overlooking the beaches far below. Then continue along D514 for the final 20 km to Bayeux. At Port-en-Bessin, turn south onto D6. These are both marked red on the Michelin map, but are lightly traveled roads. Keep an eye out for signs to the campground in Bayeux. It is a large, tidy site located on the outside edge of town.

While in Bayeux, visit the cathedral, which combines Romanesque and Gothic architecture in one building. Of course, you should not skip the Bayeux Tapestry, housed in a seminary near the cathedral (follow clearly posted walking tour signs). There is an excellent exhibit that helps you understand the story of William the Conqueror's invasion of Britain that is depicted on the linen.

From the SNCF train station (gare) in Bayeux you can catch a train to any point in France. I continued cycling by taking a train to Dinan and riding the Brittany and Loire Valley tour. Keep in mind, however, that there will be an extra fee for shipping your bicycle and a wait of up to three days to receive it (in my case it took two days). All panniers must be removed from the bicycle, and it will be loaded for you. When purchasing a ticket ask for the directions to the baggage area (it is to the left of the ticket window in Bayeux).

France: Brittany and the Loire Valley

Medieval towns, megaliths, and the Loire Valley châteaux

Distance: 709 km (440 miles)

Recommended Touring Time: 10–12 days (9 cycling days)

Terrain: moderate to easy; some gradual hills; mostly level riverside riding

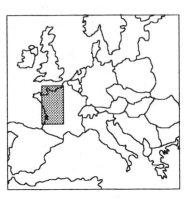

Accommodations: camping, hostel options

Maps: Michelin 230, 232, 64 in the 1 : 200,000 series

This ride combines two of the most popular regions of France into a moderate ten-day tour. It begins in St. Malo, a stone-walled pirate's port on the English Channel. From here it is a

France: Chambord in the Loire Valley

quick ride to Dinan, one of the best-preserved medieval towns in Europe. As your ride continues south through deep forests to the Atlantic coast and Carnac, you will discover another side of Brittany. Prehistoric stone alignments stretch for miles along this scenic coastal area, impressive monuments erected for unknown purposes.

The hilly, wide expanses of Brittany will open into the Loire Valley, where you will enjoy mostly level, riverside cycling while visiting the celebrated châteaux. Cycling is perhaps the best way to visit the Loire Valley, since distances between sights are short and the terrain is undemanding. The rewards are what bicycle touring is all about—pleasant rides and the flexibility to visit any number of impressive sights at your own pace. Campgrounds and tourist services abound in this historic region, making unstructured bicycle travel even easier.

If you have seen one château, you have not seen them all; this tour visits Ussé, known as the Sleeping Beauty castle; Villandry, famous for its gardens; Chenonceaux, one of the most beautiful châteaux that is actually built over the river; and Chambord, the most flamboyant. In addition, there are a number of lesser-known châteaux included in the ride that merit quiet visits on a more manageable scale. Instead of trying to see every inch of every château, it is wiser to keep your visits short to enjoy the overall flavor of each. Otherwise you may remember no more than a blur of towers and wrought iron gates. A quiet picnic lunch of French bread and pastries will do more for your appreciation of the area than guided tours of every château.

Because these are popular vacation areas, it is advisable to time your tour to avoid the height of tourist season (particularly August). However, there is a such an array of sights, services, and meandering back roads that you can enjoy the Brittany to Loire route at any time of the year. The tour ends at Bracieux, near Chambord château, with easily available train connections from Blois and the option to continue south on the Provence tour. The starting point, St. Malo, can also be reached by train or by the Trans-Channel ferry from England.

Hello: *Bonjour*
Thank You: *Merci*

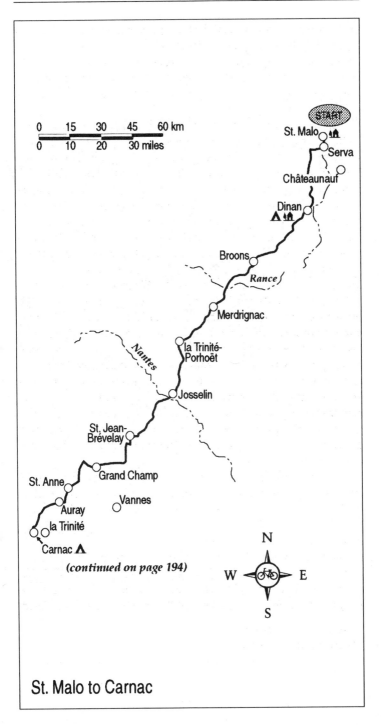

St. Malo to Carnac

(continued on page 194)

St. Malo to Dinan
35 km (22 miles)

Once a pirate's port, St. Malo is an exciting point of entry into France. The town is encircled by imposing walls and full of twisting streets and granite houses. The atmosphere is authentic and catchy—every offshore island seems to hide buried treasure or long-lost wrecks. There are hotels within the walls and a youth hostel a short distance away (Auberge de Jeunesse, 31 av. du Pere Umbricht). Michelin maps for Brittany and all of France are available in St. Malo's many shops.

Leaving St. Malo can be troublesome. Head south for St. Servain sur Mer and N137 to Châteauneuf. Just after St. Servain, N137 becomes a four-lane road; turn right (west) toward La Richardais when the road widens and follow a secondary road that roughly parallels N137 toward St. Jaran. After Les Gastines road D117 bends in the direction of St. Sullac. Follow D7 until the intersection with D366 at La Ville es Nonais; turn right, and cross over the Rance River. From Les Landes take D61 to St. Samson. Cross D57 and continue on toward Dinan (do not take D57; it will lead you onto nasty road D766). At the T-junction 2 km later turn left and then right onto D12 and into Dinan.

There are several campgrounds clearly marked from the center of Dinan. Châteaubriand municipal camping is fairly close to the center of town. There is also a hostel in a secluded spot by the river that offers camping sites in a nicer setting, although a bit farther from the center.

Dinan is one of the best and most completely preserved medieval towns in Europe, with steep streets and half-timbered houses snaking to the river's edge. The bridge high over the Rance offers a great view of the whole town in its picturesque setting. Much of the Château de Duchesse Anne in the upper part of town is open to the public at no charge. I took advantage of this to explore the building, including the eerie crypt and ramparts. It is also possible to sneak into several of the towers guarding the entrance to town to gain a better vantage point over the medieval streets. If you are facing the river, look for the door to the left under the tower on rue de Petit Fort.

Dinan to Josselin
103 km (64 miles)

From the center of Dinan, between the market square and train station, head southwest toward St. Esprit and road D793 to Broons and Merdrignac. The turn onto D793 can be tricky because it is marked ahead of time and not at the juncture itself. Watch for signs carefully to make a left turn toward Broons. D793 is a good, smooth road with very little traffic. This is a fairly easy day's ride on a quiet road passing through several deep, dark forests.

Continue on D793 through Merdrignac and on to the small town of La Trinité Porhoët. This is a logical lunch stop, although the town is of little interest. From La Trinité continue south on D793 the last 17 km to Josselin. Josselin is a scenic town complete with a riverside château, a hilltop basilica, and a campground.

Josselin to Carnac
70 km (43 miles)

From the castle in Josselin cross the river and go up a very steep hill, heading south. Take D126, a very minor road toward Plumelec. After 4 km, turn right on D123 to Guehenno and then take D778 8 km to St. Jean-Brevelay. Continue on D778 toward Vannes. This road passes several dolmens and menhirs (on the right). Turn off at tiny Morbouleau (10 km from St. Jean) for road D133 west to Locqueltas and Grand Champ. Pass through Grand Champ and turn left on D133 to Plumerget and then D17 south from there. It is another 6 km to St. Anne, the site of a famous abbey. After St. Anne continue on D17 south to Auray. The last two kilometers into this small city are on busy route N165, but the shoulder on this road is very wide.

Go across town to D768 southwest to Carnac. This is a primary road to a popular area, but the shoulder makes it safe for cycling. Turn left after 8 km to Carnac on D119, a quieter and more direct route to the coast. You can head into the town and stop at the tourist information office by following signs for *Carnac-ville*. Carnac-plage is the rocky beach area outside the town. This area is packed chock full of campgrounds ("*Il est plein de campings!*" I was told by an enthusiastic local). Many have menhirs right in their grounds. Those nearest to the town and beach are ridiculously overpriced; the others are just

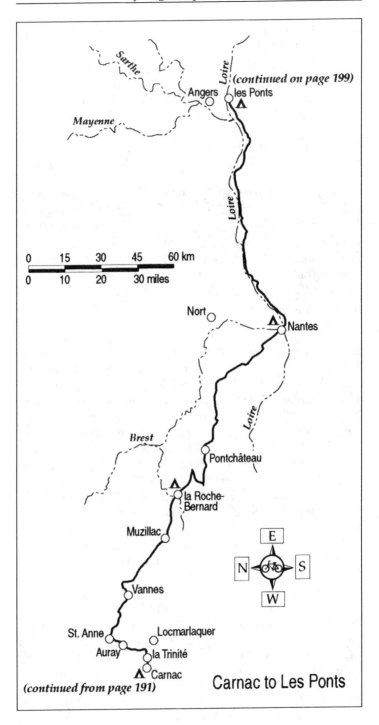

(continued on page 199)

Sarthe

Loire

Angers   les Ponts

Mayenne

Loire

0   15   30   45   60 km

0   10   20   30 miles

Nort   Nantes

Loire

Brest

Pontchâteau

la Roche-Bernard

Muzillac

E

N   S

W

Vannes

St. Anne   Locmarlaquer

Auray   la Trinité

Carnac

(continued from page 191)

Carnac to Les Ponts

overpriced. However, there is a good chance of being granted a cyclist's discount.

The whole area makes shameless use of the puzzling stone alignments it is known for. You can stay at Camping Obelix or Dolmen and shop at the Supermarche des Druides, which sports a billboard of the comic character Getafix happily pushing a shopping cart. I received a discount at Camping Obelix (about $7 with the discount). The tea and conversation offered by a friendly English family 'next door' helped me to pass an enjoyable evening in this area.

Les Alignments are parallel rows of stones that run on for more than a mile, occasionally interrupted by dolmens (stones arranged in a hut fashion). Although there is no arrangement of Stonehenge-like complexity here, the stones are just as impressive for their sheer numbers and tenacious procession across the fields of Carnac.

Carnac to La Roche Bernard
88 km (55 miles)

The alignments are particularly appealing early in the morning, when they take on a pink color. You can actually cycle between the stone rows along the length of the complex. Early morning, before the tourists come out, is also the best time to have the stones to yourself.

When you are ready to move on, take D186 along the coast to La Trinité, a cute town with a nice harbor. Traffic is no problem on these 'red' but still secondary roads. As you cross the bridge in La Trinité you will join road D781, which is busy with tourists but wide enough for safe cycling. This road will take you south on a 10 km round trip toward Locmariaquer to see more megaliths. In contrast to the Menec lines, the Merchant's table and Grand Menhir are impressive due to their great size. The Grand Menhir was once 60 feet tall and now rests broken in four pieces. Whether it broke while being built or after being erected is a matter of speculation. These two sights are fenced off and require an admission fee, but you can see them fairly well from outside if you need to watch your budget. There is another, smaller dolmen nearby that is free and virtually unvisited, Dolmen de la Mere Lun. As you leave the Grand Menhir and head back north on D781, watch for signs to the left.

When you are ready to leave the megaliths, retrace your route north and continue to Auray on D28. Turn east and pedal back by taking N165 and turning left for D17 north and St. Anne. Just off the main road, in Pluneret, follow D135 east to Meriadec and then D19 and D779 to Vannes. Here traffic picks up again as you cycle through the city and on to N165 in the direction of Nantes. This road is always comfortable, as you ride through quiet sections of Vannes. Pedal N165 for 3 km until you reach the turnoff for Theix. N165 is a main road, but the shoulder is very wide and your ride will be smooth if not particularly scenic or quiet. There are a few extended, gradual inclines on N165, but nothing overwhelming.

At Theix you can switch onto good quiet side roads. Take D7 east to Berric. Just outside Berric turn right onto D140 to Lauzach, where you will turn left and follow an unnumbered road to Bourgerei and Noyal Muzillac. There is a short, steep climb before Noyal, but generally the day's ride continues to be fairly level and easy.

After Noyal Muzillac follow the main road right toward Muzillac, then keep left for Marzan. You will reach the Vilaine River 2 km after Marzan There is a nice view of Roche-Bernard as you pedal across the bridge over the Vilaine. The pretty town curves its way down a steep slope to the river, where there is a pleasant campground ($3 per person). The only disadvantage of the site is the climb back up through town the next day. Despite the uphill climb, a walk through Roche-Bernard makes a nice afternoon activity. I indulged myself at the boulangerie and spent the evening taking shelter under a slide in the campsite's playground while it was raining. May in northern France proved to be much like April in England. Thoughts of the upcoming Loire Valley sights were enough, however, to keep me in good spirits.

La Roche Bernard to Nantes
75 km (47 miles)

Cycle back up through the center of town and take N165 for 4 km south until the right turn on D4 to Marongle, where you pick up D33 east to Pontchâteau. At Pontchâteau, cycle on toward Nantes on D16 (do not go to 'centre ville'), then follow signs for Campbon, Nort sur Edre, and Fay de Bretagne. From Fay turn southeast on D81 (not due south on D15 to le Temple) and merge into D281, which then merges with D42. This will bring you straight into Nantes, the largest city on this tour so far, but luckily very easily navigated. The campground in Nantes is close to the horse track (hippodrome), which is marked as an oval on Michelin maps. You will pick up signs for both the campground and the hippodrome from D42.

Nantes is a city with a series of wide, tree-lined boulevards, making a short bicycle trip into the center of town easy. The best sight is the château, which sits in its own enclave, its walls holding out the modern world. Weeping willows droop into the castle's moat, making this a great place to relax and get excited about the Loire ride. It is also free. The nearby Jardin des Plantes is 'très jolie' as well, making it a nice picnic site. You can obtain specific directions to the center from the campground.

Nantes to Les Ponts de Cé
96 km (60 miles)

The area known as the Loire Valley actually includes the Loire, Indre, and Cher rivers. This will be your first day on the Loire. It is exciting to cycle the river's banks and anticipate the sights to come. However, this day will not bring you to any glorious châteaux as yet, so keep patient and enjoy the pleasant river scenery.

From camping Nantes turn left (make a U-turn after turning right out of the campground because it is one-way), following signs for Angers. This puts you on the main highway to Angers, which has an excellent, separate bicycle path on either side. Exit at St. Luce; turn left at the T-intersection past warehouses (not all the Loire is châteaux) and to the center of St. Luce. Then follow signs to Thovare where you cross the Loire, and then turn left to follow quiet riverside road 751 all day. The first few kilometers are dead flat. As you ride on, the terrain becomes more hilly. Towns line hills above the river, which means you can expect a climb up to each but a descent afterward. This is enjoyable, relaxing cycling. Take D751 as far as Murs-Erigne or les Ponts de Cé on the south bank of the Loire. Both have campgrounds and are more practical stopping points than Angers.

I cycled right into Angers and regretted it. Angers is a loud and dirty city. It is not the place to be on a bicycle since it is crowded and uncomfortable (unlike Nantes, where wide boulevards make up for the city's size). The château is possibly worth a look but its many towers are now greatly reduced from their original proportions, and it is surrounded by throngs of traffic. If this were the only château around it might be worth the trouble and risk, but it is not, so do not bother unless you are determined to see each and every château. Angers is simply not worth the threat to life, limb, and peace of mind. This is also true of other major Loire cities such as Tours and Orleans—unless you have a specific reason to venture into them, it is better as a cyclist to avoid them.

Les Ponts de Cé to Ussé
83 km (51 miles)

Cross back to the south bank of the Loire and head for D751 to Saumur by first cycling 3 km on D132 along the riverbank to avoid larger roads. It is a pleasant though hilly ride past small towns. There are several dolmens just outside and to the northwest of Gennes. In Gennes I followed signs to the Gallo-Roman amphitheater, but it is difficult to get in or even to get an outside glance. Tickets are available at the museum in town if you are really determined to see it. Continue on to Saumur, where a hilltop château commands sweeping views of the Loire. The panorama from the grounds next to the château are especially impressive, making this another nice picnic spot.

From Saumur you can cycle directly to Chinon along the river via routes D947 and 751, or take a detour away from the river to visit the twelfth-century abbey in Fontevraud. To do so take D145 through the forest of Fontevraud to reach the abbey where Richard the Lionheart and other English royalty were buried (their bones were removed during the French Revolution, however). In either case, cycle onward to Chinon on main road 751. This is a safe road with surprisingly mild traffic.

Chinon is a very pleasant town with streets of medieval houses and a château above. It also has a very attractive campground right on the river opposite the center of town. There is another tempting campground on the river between Montsoreau and Chinon, although it is not particularly convenient to any sights. If you are ready to cycle a bit farther, head west from Chinon on D751 toward Azay and Tours. Turn to the left for D16 north to Huismes and Ussé. In Huismes turn right on D7 to follow the Loire again to Ussé. There is an inexpensive, plain campground on the east edge of town, a quick ride away from the château.

This fifteenth-century château is known as the Sleeping Beauty Castle because of its fairy-tale look. Its towers and walls are floodlit at night, providing strong inspiration for a pleasant

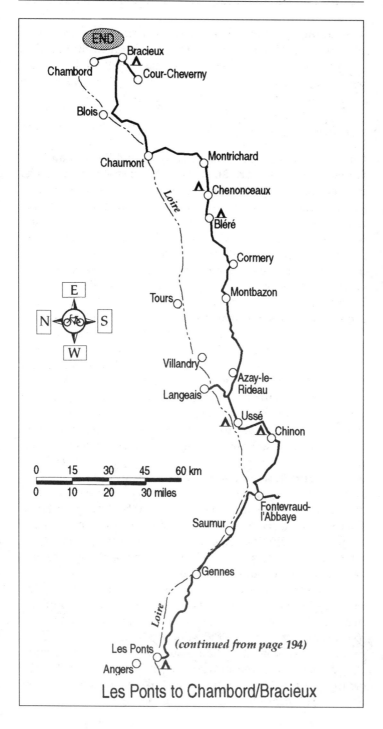

END

Bracieux

Chambord

Cour-Cheverny

Blois

Chaumont

Montrichard

Loire

Chenonceaux

Bléré

Cormery

Montbazon

E

N   S

W

Tours

Villandry

Azay-le-Rideau

Langeais

Ussé

Chinon

0   15   30   45   60 km

0   10   20   30 miles

Fontevraud-l'Abbaye

Saumur

Gennes

Loire

(continued from page 194)

Les Ponts

Angers

Les Ponts to Chambord/Bracieux

after-dinner walk or bicycle ride. The road heading north from the château offers the best outside view of the building.

Ussé to Chenonceaux
87 km (54 miles)

This ride takes you through more typical Loire scenery and to several more châteaux. The riding is level to slightly hilly. Take the road leading directly away from the château (north) and turn right at the T-junction to follow the Loire to Langeais. Cross the old-fashioned suspension bridge for a quick look at the château in Langeais, one of the best defended châteaux. Double back out and cross the bridge again when you are ready to leave. Continue along the river for 6 km until the right turn where you rejoin D7 briefly. This will take you to Villandry, which is known for its perfectly manicured gardens, although you will have to pay to see them. For budget-minded cyclists, riding up the hill behind the château will do you no good in terms of a free peek.

After Villandry, it is a moderate 8 km ride to Azay-le-Rideau, with just one big climb. From the château at Villandry, double back 4 km west on D7 and turn left on D39, riding up a steep rise after Moulinet. The town at Azay is a bit of a tourist trap, but nice. Every souvenir shop here sells the full Michelin map series so you can buy ahead. The château is nearly invisible from outside because of the tall walls surrounding it, so you will have to pay to get in for a look. The grounds close for two hours at midday so you might have to find another picnic spot. The view of this pretty château on the river Indre is well worth the admission fee.

Go east from Azay on D84 for a nice, slightly hilly ride along the Indre toward Chenonceaux. At Sache you will pass another small château. D84 becomes D17 and crosses the Indre. Begin winding steadily along the river to Montbazon, after which you switch onto D250 to Veigne along the south bank, avoiding the busier D17 on the north bank. At Cormery cross the bridge to Truyes and take D45 to Athee. Thankfully, the terrain from the Indre overland to the Cher is one long plateau so it is easy, level cycling for the most part.

You can avoid N76 after Athee by taking minor roads to Bono and Grandlay and then on to Bléré. Cycle to the center of Bléré and take the bridge over the Cher. Signs for the campground and stade (stadium) take you to this bridge. Follow D40, clearly marked to Chenonceaux.

The municipal campground in Chenonceaux is accessible from the château parking lot and is very cheap, although trains periodically rush by in the night. This château is one of the prettiest in the Loire, sitting picture-perfect on a row of arches spanning the Cher. It was built during the sixteenth century by Henry II for his mistress Diane de Poitiers. Justice prevailed—after Henry's death, his 'mourning' widow happily booted Diane out. You will have to pay to get into the grounds and château, which is totally hidden from the road. This is one of the few châteaux where you are permitted to wander at your own pace without a guide. Two of the most interesting features of the building are the broken arch vaulting in the hallway and the long gallery that served as an escape route from occupied France on one side of the river to free France on the other during World War II.

Chenonceau to Chambord (Bracieux)
72 km (45 miles)

Cycling and sightseeing in this part of France is absolutely effortless—the days are long and full of river scenery and historic sights. To leave Chenonceau for another day of chateau-hopping, follow the river and D176/D40 toward Montrichard. Turn off at Chissay on D27. This road winds through large tracts of farmland with little else in sight. There are several unmarked forks, but continue on the main road. It is pretty easy to judge the correct route with a close eye for landmarks and your map. Aim for the white tower, marked as a blue circle on Michelin maps.

Ride into Chaumont, where an impressive Renaissance château overlooks the Beuvron River. You will pass the iron gates as you enter town. To continue, follow D751 to Cande-sur-Beuvron and turn right for les Montils just after passing the bridge over the Beuvron River (do not cross the bridge). From Les Montils cycle on to Seur, a pretty town, and then to Chitenay. These towns are all very well marked. After Chitenay follow signs for Cormeray. At the intersection with D956 go almost straight across to the unmarked minor road (if you turn right and head for Cormeray, you have gone too far), which goes right to Cheverny. The ride along the Beuvron is quite scenic. Once you get away from the riverbanks the ride is still not too hilly. The terrain is a level plateau of long fields rather than rolling hills.

The château in Cheverny is more of a stately home than a castle. You will get a good look at the building through the driveway as you enter town. There is also a small park in Cheverny where you can take a shaded break from cycling. Continue on to Bracieux where the campground is on the north edge of town on the way to Chambord. Leave your gear here and cycle a few kilometers more to this château, one of the most ornate and famous in the Loire area. There are very few services available at the château. Stock up on picnic supplies before you head out. Ride through the Parc de Chambord forest, where king François I often hunted. The grounds of this flamboyant château are open to the public at no charge, but there is a fee to visit the interior of the building. One interesting feature is the double helix staircase designed by Leonardo da Vinci. Outside you can pass the remainder of the day on the château's lawn. I spent several hours drawing, picnicking, and simply relaxing on the grass across from the château's canal before cycling back to Bracieux for dinner.

The campground in Bracieux has lots of gnats, but is moderately priced ($3) and the closest to Chambord. It is a big and popular site, close to town. This tour ends in Bracieux, but you can continue cycling south toward the Dordogne Valley on the South Across France route, or cycle to Blois where you can visit one more château before catching a train to Paris or other points in France.

South Across France

The Loire and Dordogne
valleys to Provence

Distance: 776 km (482 miles)

Recommended touring time:
11–14 days (10 cycling days)

Terrain: countryside riding,
from flat riverbanks to more
challenging hills and
mountains in the south

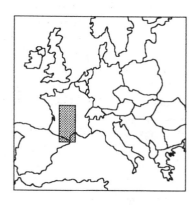

Accommodations: camping
with hostel options

Maps: Michelin 64, 68, 233, 235 in the 1 : 200,000 series

This tour offers a unique ride through some of the quietest and
most relaxed regions of France. It is also a tour of great contrasts: the route winds south from the châteaux of the Loire
Valley through hilly farmlands and little-known towns. As the
miles pass, the scenery gradually shifts from deep green forests to drier fields and open views as you near the Mediterranean-like south. Your journey will take you farther and
farther back into history, from a time of royalty in the Loire to
that of early man in the Dordogne. Vividly painted scenes of
horses and bulls leap out from the walls of caves dating back
17,000 years at Lascaux and Les Eyzies. Above ground again,
you will experience another time transport while visiting medieval towns like Sarlat and la Roque-Gageac, as well as the
cliff-side monastery at Rocamadour.

The last section of the tour visits the hilltop town of Cordes,
with winding streets and red clay roof tiles so characteristic of
southern France. Once over a last mountain ridge, pedal along
the Midi Canal to the bristling fortress of Carcassonne. This
walled city is remarkably well-preserved, its many towers
rising high above the surrounding countryside. Best of all, you
can spend the night at an affordable hostel within the ramparts.

This ride crosses large tracts of rural France and as such, is not for bicycle tourists looking for a concentration of famous sights in a small area. Instead, it takes in extremely varied regions of France at a contemplative pace. On some days, you will spend long hours on your bicycle with few sights along the way, enjoying instead peaceful expanses and long, steady riding. There are inexpensive campgrounds all along the route. This is one of the least expensive sections of Europe to visit by bicycle because of the low prices of these municipal sites. I was able to travel on just five dollars a day here for this reason. The countryside is quiet, but not backward. Every town has the requisite boulangerie, charcuterie, and epicerie. In the Loire and Dordogne valleys there is a particularly wide array of tourist services and facilities available.

You can reach the start of the the tour directly from the Brittany to Loire route or by train to Blois, near Bracieux. From Carcassonne you can take a train to Paris, Barcelona, or other points, or continue cycling eastward across Provence to the Riviera.

Hello: *Bonjour*
Thank You: *Merci*

Chambord (Bracieux) to Buzançais
88 km (55 miles)

Bracieux is the most convenient town to one of the most well-known châteaux, Chambord. The scenic grounds are open to the public and make a great picnic spot (bring supplies from Bracieux as there are few services at the château itself). You must pay a fee to enter the building. This château was used as a hunting lodge by Francois I in the sixteenth century and is one of the most flamboyant of the Loire châteaux. The nearest campground is in Bracieux.

From Bracieux, begin the ride south by following signs for Fontaignes-en-Sologne and then Soings-en-Sologne on D119. You will pass another château in Selles-sur-Cher. The picnic area in the woods just before Valençay is a nice stopping point. Valençay also has a château (and an decent looking campground, as does Selles). There are more châteaux near Veuil and Argy, all modest in scale compared to Chambord. The one at Argy is especially quiet and pretty—a good place to stop for a moment to appreciate a château that retains its original charm without masses of tourists or acres of parking lot.

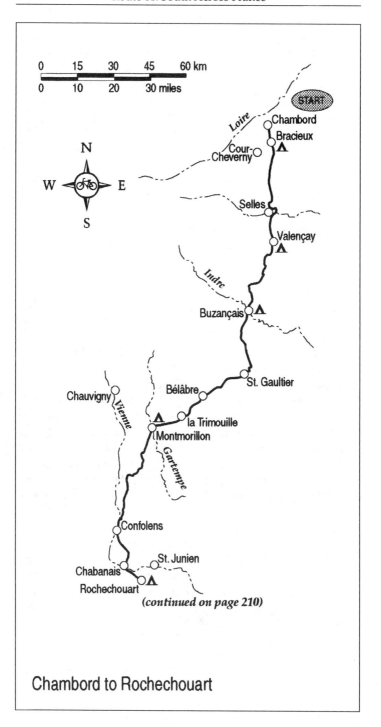

(continued on page 210)

Chambord to Rochechouart

The ride becomes more hilly after Valençay, although it will probably seem worse than it is if you have gotten used to the relatively flat riverside cycling in the Loire. From Valencay follow signs for Veuil on D15, then Lange and Gehee. After Gehee the road numbers change a few times, but keep heading for Fredille (D15 and D7), then Pellevoisin (on D15), and finally Buzançais on D11). In Buzançais head to the center of town and turn right at the T-junction. The campground is to the right after the second bridge, behind the piscine and the stade. This is a good campground on the Indre, right on the edge of the water. There is a supermarket conveniently located directly across from the entrance. I left this campsite early in the morning and since there was no one at the office to pay, I got a free stay.

Buzançais to Montmorillon
84 km (52 miles)

This is the quietest day of the South Across France tour. The route follows a series of secondary roads in a rural area. Settle back and enjoy a relaxed day's ride.

From the campground turn left, cross the bridge over the Indre, and take a right to get on D11 to Vendoeuvres and St. Gaultier. Cross primary road N151 and go straight into St. Gaultier. Ride across the bridge over the Creuse River to Thenay and turn right toward Rivarennes, where you join D927 to Bélâbre. As I cycled on this quiet road, I turned a corner and suddenly came upon a large crowd and a finish line. The people were very surprised to see me pedal by with my heavy panniers, having been expecting the first riders of a bicycle race to pull in. If you hear a whir behind you on this road, watch out.

From Bélâbre turn south for D727 to La Trimouille and Montmorillon. To get to the campground in Montmorillon, head into town, bear left where the road splits, and follow signs to camping. This is the most inexpensive campground yet, at 8F per person (just over a dollar). The site is overgrown, but your tent stakes will not bend in the soft ground—a very important consideration after days of frustrating hard-ground campsites.

Montmorillon to Rochechouart
88 km (55 miles)

From the campground go back to 'centre ville' and follow signs that indicate Confolens to left and Lussac straight ahead. Turn left on unmarked D729, which is opposite the right turn to Chauvigny. This leads you south to the Vienne River's banks via Moulismes, Adriers, Abzac, and Confolens. It is a hilly ride all day, but do not let it get to you. The cycling is especially scenic from Abzac on, as you head deeper into the Mediterranean-like south.

St. Germain is a beautiful old town with a ruined castle on a hill above the gorgeous River Vienne. There is a picnic site here, but you can also eat in Confolens where there is a tamer park right over the river. From Confolens turn on D948 to St. Junien and then right onto D59 for Chirac after about 2 km. This is also a very hilly but extremely scenic road, and you will have more great river scenery. Chabanais is also a pleasant town where you cross the Vienne, and there are beautiful views from the bridge. Next you will encounter a long climb on D29 to Rochechouart. There are Roman ruins 1 km after Chassenon on this road if you feel like stopping off. The campground in Rochechouart is on the D10 (take D10 to the right in the direction of Verneuil) 3 km out of town on Plan d'Eau, a very nice if sometimes crowded small lake. Camping is inexpensive at 10F ($1.50). Rochechouart is a tidy town that also has a castle.

Rochechouart to Périgueux
95 km (59 miles)

The miles you pedal on this day will bring you to the next region to explore, the Dordogne Valley. Périgueux is the gateway to the Dordogne. From this point on the sights are more numerous and concentrated than in the central part of France you have just cycled through. The area is characterized by limestone outcroppings where early man took shelter and created incredibly vivid works of art.

From Rochechouart head south on D675 along the Vayres River to Vayres and St. Mathieu. Continue on to Nontron and Brantôme, which is located along the Dronne River. This is marked as a red road on the map, but it is not a popular route so traffic is light and it is wide enough to cycle comfortably. (On the 1 : 200,000 series maps, roads marked in red are not always true primary roads as marked on the 1 : 1,000,000 map used by most motorists.)

Brantôme is a very pretty town and makes a great lunch spot if you ride this far early enough. I sat on a wall by the river and waited out the midday heat while enjoying the nice view. From here, head south on D939, which is well-marked right into Perigueux. The roads are extremely hilly but quiet all the way to Château-l'Evèque, 6 km north of Périgueux. After this follow the Beauronne River where the terrain is much flatter although traffic picks up considerably and the last few kilometers are uncomfortably busy. Traffic in Périgueux is also bad, but there are few alternatives.

Finding the campgrounds in Périgueux can be difficult. Ride through town and cross over the river on a bridge opposite the Cathedral of St. Font (you cannot miss the cathedral—it looks Byzantine and stands out from the surrounding architecture). Follow signs to Brive and Cite BelAir for a short distance. Once you pass the Michelin station (on your left) look for signs to the left for Camping Bernabe. The campground is in a residential area, right by a quiet section of the river ($3 for one person). I was reluctant to pedal back into busy Périgueux after getting comfortably settled into the campground. If you are not impatient to get to the campground right away, it is a better idea to stop in Périgueux before cycling to the campsite and having a look around the town. There are also rooms for rent in town and a hostel, Foyer de Jeunes Travailleurs off Blvd. Lakanal.

Perigueux to Les Eyzies
76 km (47 miles)

It can be difficult finding road D5 that follows the Auvézère River out of Périgueux. From the campground go back to the main road and turn left toward Brive, then left at each of the next two lights. The D5 is a great road that takes you through some very pretty villages. Follow it as far as Cubjat. This town really is charming. The houses are tidy, the squares perfectly French, and the whole quiet setting is very appealing. From Cubjat, cross the river and take D68 to Ajat. There is a long uphill climb once you leave the river on D68 but it levels out after about 2 km. You will enjoy some very nice scenery along this road, consisting mostly of woods and fields. In the isolated town of Ajat there is also a small castle.

After Ajat cross onto N89 and follow it to Thenon (you will be on this busy road for only 2 km) and then Montignac. The ride from Thenon to Montignac on D67 is very pretty. After Montignac, there is a very long, nasty uphill climb to the site of Lascaux II, which is clearly marked on brown-colored signs to the left. This is the site of the famous prehistoric cave paintings. You can only visit a remarkably well-designed reproduction at a cost of 40F, but it is absolutely worth it for a glimpse of the lifelike animals crowding the cave's walls and ceiling and for the informative talk; tours in English are twice a day. The actual Lascaux cave entrance is about 200 m up the road from the reconstruction. Only five scientists per day are allowed there by special petition only. You can, however, see original rock art in La Grotte de Font de Gaume near Les Eyzies, although the caves may be closed at unpredictable times for testing.

The Lascaux ticket is also good at Le Thot, an indoor/outdoor museum on the way to Les Ezyies. On the way, that is, except for the 2 km uphill climb off the main road to get there. There are also more caves in Rouffignac, about 12 km from Thonac and west of the Vézère River, if you are ready to explore this fascinating area in more detail. If you are not a prehistoric cave enthusiast, visit only the sites of Lascaux and Font de Gaume to get a taste of the Dordogne's impressive history.

When you have finished seeing the Lascaux caves, cycle onward to Thonac and Les Eyzies on D706 south. On the way you will pass la Roque St. Christophe, which is carved into a cliff face. The road (D706) follows the Vezère River but has many gradual ups and downs with one big, long uphill from Tursac to Les Eyzies. Finally you can enjoy a nice cruise down into Les Eyzies, which also has structures carved into the cliffs high above town. The campground has a pool and costs 24F (12F per person, 12F per tent). To get there, cycle through town and cross the river. The campground is to the left.

This turned out to be a very social day for me since the Dordogne is a popular area for cyclists. I rode from Lascaux to Les Eyzies with two Americans and two Danes, and afterward we enjoyed dinner and coffee together. The Americans had cycled to France from Northern Africa via Turkey and Greece—and I thought I was cycling a long way. If you continue cycling south there is always the ferry from Spain to Morocco....

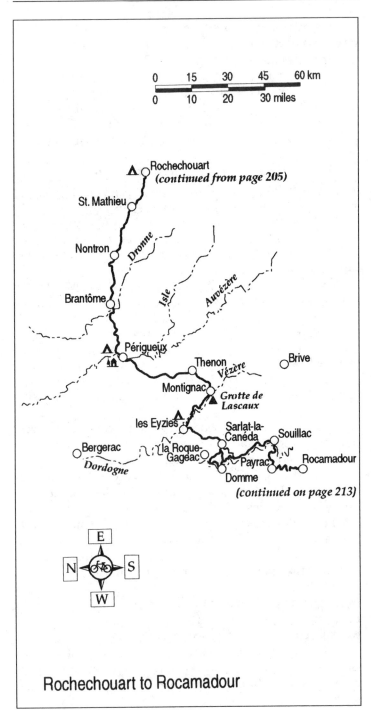

0   15   30   45   60 km
0   10   20   30 miles

Rochechouart
(continued from page 205)

St. Mathieu

Nontron

Brantôme

Périgueux

Thenon

Montignac

Grotte de Lascaux

les Eyzies

Brive

Sarlat-la-Canéda

Souillac

Bergerac

la Roque-Gageac

Payrac

Rocamadour

Domme

(continued on page 213)

Dronne

Isle

Auvézère

Vézère

Dordogne

E

N   S

W

Rochechouart to Rocamadour

Les Eyzies to Rocamadour
85 km (53 miles)

This is a long and sight-filled day. If you like to linger and explore in detail, it is best to make this into a two-day ride by stopping along the way. There are plenty of accommodation options, from rooms in Sarlat or Souillac to any of the camp-grounds along this route.

The caves of La Grotte de Font-de-Gaume are right on the road to Sarlat as you leave Les Eyzies. They only allow 300 people per day into the caves so it is in your best interest to get there early. Although the art is not as renowned as that of Lascaux, you can see original work in this cave.

From Les Eyzies, take road D47 to Sarlat, a well-preserved medieval town especially interesting on market days. Wander the cobblestoned streets and explore Sarlat's many quiet corners at leisure. If you are ready to leave Sarlat, follow signs for Bergenac and Domme, which will lead you to D46 and signs to the right on D703 for La Roque-Gageac. On the way you will pass two pretty riverside campgrounds.

La Roque-Gageac has the distinction of being one of the most beautiful towns in France. The town spreads downward from a sheer limestone cliff to the banks of the Dordogne. Some houses are actually carved from the face of the stone. This town earns its distinctive title in every way. La Roque-Gageac is a great place to have a snack or lunch and wait for the midday heat to ease (buy supplies in Sarlat). The Michelin map seems to indicate la Roque-Gageac farther east than where it actually is. That is only the lettering—the town is 6 km west of the junction of D46 and D703.

When you are ready, double back on D703 toward Souillac and follow the signs for Dordogne. Watch closely for the intersection in Carsac and Vitrac. I almost took 704 south instead of continuing east. There is a big climb to Carsac with great views of the river and the château at Montfort. Most of the terrain, however, consists of easier, rolling hills. You will pass a shady campground along the way in Rouffillac.

Souillac is notable for its Romanesque cathedral. I was pushing to get into Rocamadour, though, and passed through this small city quickly. After Souillac, follow signs to Payrac but turn left onto D43 just before the bridge to big road E09—do not cross the river. D43 is a quiet road. After cycling through Pinsac, cross the river to La Cave and Belcastel and turn on road D247 to Rocamadour and l'Hospitalet. You will enjoy a stunning descent into the canyon around La Cave, but unfortunately there is a 3 km climb back out again. Watch for the sharp hairpin turn as you enter La Cave and start climbing. Luckily, the grade is manageable and the views amazing.

As you approach the towns, turn left at the intersection toward *Medievale Rocamadour*, not to the château. The campground is in l'Hospitalat across another canyon from the monastery and village of Rocamadour. It is close to the scenic overlook in l'Hospitalat, which offers great views across the canyon at night when the whole monastery is flood lit. You can unload your bicycle at the campground and ride to the monastery or hike a trail down. Rocamadour is a small town jammed into a cliff—the streets line up one over the other instead of next to each other. I left my bicycle locked on the lowest street and explored Rocamadour and its many steps on foot.

Rocamadour to Villefranche de Rouergue
79 km (49 miles)

Another sight near Rocamadour is the Forêt de Signes (monkey forest), where you can observe a captive but wild colony of Barbary Macaques, natives of Morocco. You will pass the forest on your way out of Rocamadour.

Cycle toward Gramat by taking D36 for 4 km and then N140. Up to Figeac, this is a big road, but I had no problems on it as traffic was light in the early morning, and there is a narrow shoulder. The alternative is a ridiculous series of side roads. From Figeac, take winding road D922 south across the Lot River to Villeneuve and finally Villefranche. For the last 5 km into Villefranche you can continue on 922 which parallels D1, the bigger road to town for heavy traffic. The campground is located in a residential area next to the public pool that is marked on Michelin maps. To get there follow signs on 922 through Villefranche's industrial area of storehouses and large buildings toward Laguépie. The campground is inexpensive and pleasant, and there is a great LeClerc supermarket within cycling distance back in the 'industrial' part of town. LeClerc is one of the biggest French chain stores and sells everything from hardware to food and comic books. After weeks of cycling with minimal gear, these stores take on a museum-like appeal.

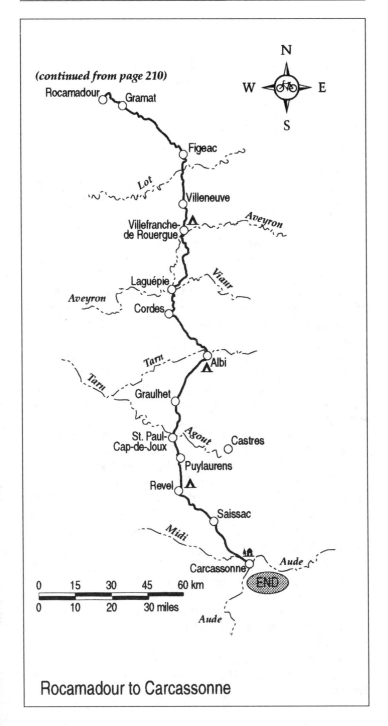

(continued from page 210)

Rocamadour to Carcassonne

Villefranche to Albi
68 km (42 miles)

Maps take on a whole new shade south of Villefranche—brown. This means mountains and canyons as you begin the more challenging portion of this tour. These are not the Alps, however, so there is no need to worry. The new scenery and different sights will keep you inspired as you pedal south toward Carcassonne.

The campground in Villefranche is in a good location. Turn left out of the entrance and you are on D47 to Monteils and Laguépie. This is an excellent road. First you follow the river Aveyron and enjoy an easy flat ride. Then there is a big climb past Monteils, but once at the top you stay high up on the ridge of the mountains with sweeping views of the Gorges de l'-Aveyron and smooth, scenic cycling on a level stretch of road.

Descend into Laguépie and endure another long climb out of the town on D922 south to Cordes. Cordes is a unique, Mediterranean-feeling hilltop town. You can truly start anticipating the sunny south from this point, with red clay roof tiles everywhere hinting of things to come. If you want to call it a day, there is a campground on 922 north of Cordes about 2 km away, and another much farther away on road 600 to the south. The only problem with scenic hill towns is the hill part, but that, as I have said before, goes with the territory of bicycle touring.

Cordes has many art workshops and cafés but few grocery stores, so buy supplies in the modern town at the foot of the hill. Push your bicycle through snaking cobblestone streets to the top of the town. There is an expansive viewpoint over surrounding farmlands from the main square. To avoid the blazing sun, I parked myself in this shady square for several hours, put out some laundry to dry (bicycles make very convenient clothes hangers), and enjoyed a relaxing afternoon. Locals and tourists alike thought this was unusual but no one seemed to mind. After Cordes I became impatient and simply took D600, the main road directly from Cordes to Albi. The traffic was surprisingly light and the lanes suitably wide. You can also wind down a series of side roads if you prefer to avoid this road.

The campground in Albi is on the east edge of town. Cycle across the bridge and all the way into the center of town. Watch for signs here to the left indicating École Infirmieres and

Piscine. The campground is 1.5 km from the center of town and conveniently located across from l'Univers, a huge supermarket that stays open late.

You can leave your gear at the campground and return to the center on an unloaded bicycle for a quick look at some of Albi's sights. The cathedral is a huge brick building that bears more resemblance to a fortress than to anything else. Behind it on the river Tarn are Le Palais and the Toulouse Art museum. In the back of these buildings is a quiet, manicured garden and a vantage point offering pleasant views of the river and town.

Albi to Revel
68 km (42 miles)

Exit the campground and turn right. Follow signs for Toulouse and Castres, which puts you onto the circling highway around Albi. Stay on this road for Toulouse after Castres turns off. On the left 1 km later is an Intermarche supermarket. D84 to Graulhet goes up the hill from just to the left of the Intermarche. Get off the highway here. You will have to take the first possible exit to the right and circle back under the highway to get to the other side of the road and the Intermarche.

Cycle up a long hill on D84 and ride straight through Graulhet. Ignore the signs to St. Paul outside of town, which only lead you onto a loop around town and then back in. It is a shortcut to ride to the center and then follow signs for St. Paul-Cap-de-Joux on D84. There are a few long climbs before St. Paul, but happily the last stretch of ride into St. Paul is along a shady road. *"Vous-y-êtes!"* (you are almost there) yelled a friendly bicycle racer as I sweated up one of the longer climbs. At least someone appreciated my experience.

St. Paul is a nice town with a big church overlooking the river. Continue on to Puylaurens, where you will turn left for Castres and then follow signs right, to Revel, encountering several more long hills along the way. The Montaignes Noirs rise straight up behind Revel, the last obstacle between you and Carcassonne.

The campground in Revel is extremely reasonable at just over a dollar per person. It is on the east edge of town on D85. When you just enter Revel, the road forks. Take the left fork, which brings you against one-way traffic. You can either walk your bicycle here to keep straight or ride parallel side roads for a few blocks until the road becomes two-way again. The campground is on your right as you leave town on this road.

You will also pass a good supermarket as you enter town. I chose to stop in Revel in order to avoid hitting the big climb over the Montaignes Noirs at the end of a day. Revel is a small town of no particular interest but it makes a convenient stopping point where you can rest and catch up on laundry, reading, or writing.

Revel to Carcassonne
45 km (28 miles)

From the campground do not exit back to the D85, but turn left and follow the fishing canal around the first two corners; turn right one block, then left to get on D629, which takes you all the way to Carcassonne. It is uphill to Cammazes, then moderate as you stay on the higher ridges of the mountains, then long downhills until the last hill after Montolieu. In Moussouens and Montolieu especially, take it easy as there are several blind curves with last-minute signs for turns to Carcassonne.

There was a nasty headwind from Saissac on as I cycled and it got worse on the flats coming into Carcassonne. D629 runs into N113, which is full of cars, just before Pezens. Once in Pezens look for the right turn near the far end of town for Caux et Sauzens. This side road doubles back and continues toward Caux. Eventually, you will intersect D33. Turn left and follow this the last few kilometers into Carcassonne.

In Carcassonne head right up into the fortress by following signs for *La Cité*. There is a youth hostel inside the city's well-defended perimeter, an outstanding value at about $9 (compare this to the classy and expensive hotels in La Cité). The hostel is on rue Vicomte Trencavel. Breakfast is included, and there is a kitchen for your use. Other accommodation options include a selection of rooms in the modern town below the fortress and a campground 3 km to the east.

Carcassonne is a medieval fortress—a fantasy castle come true. A massive double wall punctuated by towers protects the inner city, where you can wander narrow streets and treat yourself to an inexpensive crepe at an outdoor snack stand. Carcassonne has a long history, with origins in Roman times. The city puts on a fireworks show during the second week of July and a medieval festival in August. I took a day off in Carcassonne before heading east for Provence and the Riviera.

En Route to Provence and the Riviera

Distance: 686 km (426 miles)

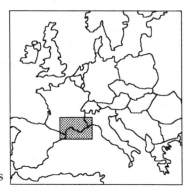

Recommended touring time: 14–16 days (11 cycling days)

Terrain: rolling hills with a few long, steep climbs and occasional flats; crowded roads in the Riviera

Accommodations: camping with hostel and room options

Maps: Michelin 83, 81, 84 in the 1 : 200,000 series

This ride from Carcassonne to St. Tropez crosses some of the most interesting parts of France in a moderate two-week tour. This route offers a wonderful combination of activities and sights to give you a good taste of southern France. It includes the Camargue region, the dry hills, vineyards, and Roman

France: the beach near Adge on the Mediterranean

ruins of Provence, and the ritzy Côte d'Azur. On the way you can explore walled cities, artist colonies, and unique hill-top towns. Favorable weather makes cycling and camping in these regions a pleasure, with plenty of small towns to rest in during the day.

I learned of new sights every day while cycling through southern France. The walled city of Aigues Mortes, the springs at Fontaine de Vaucluse, and the wine center of Châteauneuf-du-Pape kept me pedaling eagerly from one town to the next, constantly making additions to my original itinerary. The wide distribution of campgrounds and other tourist services will allow you to explore these regions easily and add still more detours to the route.

For a shorter ride, this route can be divided into sections. The trip from Carcassonne to Aix-en-Provence can be comfortably completed in eight days and includes rides along the Mediterranean, the Camargue, and historic Provence. Suggested daily mileage on this tour is decreased to 15 to 30 miles for several days in Provence to allow more sightseeing time. If these days are combined into longer stretches, the tour can also be covered in fewer days. Carcassonne and St. Raphael, near the end point of this tour, are both easily reached by train from Paris and other European cities. This tour also connects with the South Across France and Côte d'Azur tours for a more extensive trip.

Hello: *Bonjour*
Thank You: *Merci*

Carcassonne to Narbonne
62 km (38 miles)

Carcassone is the best and most entirely preserved medieval fortress in Europe. The whole complex of double walls and defense towers was preserved or reconstructed and now offers a unique and authentic view of medieval times. Carcassonne is more than simply a skeletal ruin that tourists photograph. I was enjoying a sunset walk along the ramparts when a French army company marched by singing a victory song. Onlookers stood back as the soldiers brought the fortress back to life.

You can stay at the centrally located hostel on rue Vicomte Trencavel or get a room in the modern town below. After a day or two enjoying the city's atmosphere, pack your panniers and begin the ride to Provence and the Riviera.

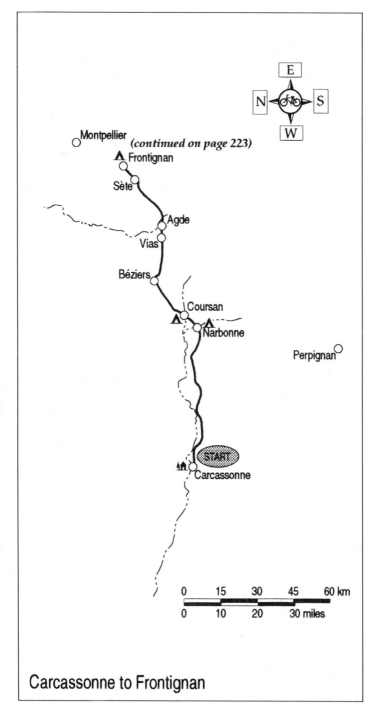

(continued on page 223)

Montpellier

Frontignan

Sète

Agde

Vias

Béziers

Coursan

Narbonne

Perpignan

START

Carcassonne

0	15	30	45	60 km
0	10	20		30 miles

Carcassonne to Frontignan

Find peaceful road 303 out of Carcassonne. Ignore the Narbonne highway signs just outside La Cite and ride toward the Euromarche a few blocks below. Then follow signs to Berriac. From that road take a short hop onto N113, then on to Trebes and Puicheric via D610. You will have attractive views of the Montaignes d'Aleric and surrounding vineyards. In Puicheric take 127 to Roquecourbe, Castlenau, and Escales, where you ride toward Lézignan. Turn left on 611 (no longer in the direction of Lézignan) toward Homps, and make a sharp right onto D11 to Villedaigne. In Villedaigne briefly return to N113 before turning right for Nevian on 118. After Nevian follow signs to Narbonne.

Narbonne is a pretty city of shady streets and wide avenues. The Midi Canal runs through Narbonne, gardens lining its banks throughout the city. The most interesting sight in Narbonne is the cathedral that was never finished on the large scale originally envisioned, with the result that the outside looks like an inside and the inside looks strangely foreshortened. The garden around the building is a wonderfully peaceful place to eat lunch, with a fountain, benches, and plenty of shade.

The nearest campground is 1.5 km away and about $3 per person and $3 per site. Follow the canal south and continue straight on after the canal turns away. There is a slightly cheaper campground 4 km away on the main road to Perpignan. Another option that will shorten the next day's ride is to go 7 km on busy N9/N113—you have not seen the last of this road just yet—to Coursan, where there is a very inexpensive campground ($1 per person and $1 per tent). However, there is a catch—this campground is a dump, complete with ants, Gypsies, and terrible toilet facilities. This site honestly depressed me, but you get what you pay for.

Narbonne to Frontignan
72 km (45 miles)

Take N9/N113 7 km to Coursan, where you switch onto D31 to Salles d'Aude, then to Fleury. This will bring you onto deserted secondary roads through farmlands and hills where you can again enjoy peaceful cycling. Take D618 and D14 to Lespignan and then D37 to Vendres and Serignan. In Serignan follow signs for Béziers and Villeneuve. Cross the bridge, turn right (away from the direction of Béziers), and follow the small track immediately to the left that has a red circle sign indicating

3.2 tons. This goes under the main road to Béziers and winds its way through fields to Portiragnes.

There are no signs here since this is a tiny back lane, but it is simple enough to stay on the main track since the few turnoffs are all clearly smaller roads. The road deteriorates to a lane and finally a small unpaved track, but you should have no problems since the surface is hard and suitable for cycling. It was fun to ride in complete solitude on this road, laughing to myself at the close-up perspective I was getting from this country jaunt. If in doubt regarding directions, aim for the white tower on the hill ahead—it will lead you to Portiragnes.

Cross the Midi canal in Portiragnes and turn left on D37 for about 3 km. Just after the bridge, turn left again past a ranch that you cannot miss—it has a big sign that says *Ranch*. This will put you on another tiny back road through an area chock full of campgrounds. Follow the arrows on the round blue signs. Turn left before the entrance to Méditeranée-camping, then bear right at the next intersection. Now you are on your way back up to the canal. Follow signs for Vias, and from there take N112 to Agde.

Agde is an appealing riverside town where you can explore twisting, laundry-draped side streets and pick up supplies for a picnic. Local kids swim in the river but you can wait for the real thing a few miles later. Follow signs to Séte and ride a sparkling 20 km right along the Mediterranean. At the very least it is worth a quick dip. Better yet, give yourself a picnic break on the beach. So what if you already ate in Agde? I could not resist the temptation to stop, and into the sea I went. Try not to get sand on your bicycle chain. In mid-June the roads and beach were still uncrowded, one of the advantages of touring before tourist season.

At the end of this 20 km stretch keep right to cycle around the coast side of the Corniche (not left for Montpellier). This takes you around the hill and by the port. Then follow signs for Montpellier, which will lead you to more signs for Frontignan on N112. The N112 is a busy road with enough room for you to cycle safely if not peacefully. East of Frontignan 3 km on this road is a big campsite with a not very attentive attendant. I set up my tent between some bushes and a large camper and kept a low profile. There are also several campgrounds at Frontignan-Plage. Buy dinner and breakfast supplies in Frontignan itself, as there is little available outside of town.

Frontignan to Arles
90 km (56 miles)

This day will bring you to the heart of Provence, where a concentration of interesting sights will shorten cycling distances from Arles onward. You will ride past flamingos, through the Camargue, and into Roman Arles on this sight-filled day. The ride is very easy all day and dead flat from Aigues Mortes onward.

Continue up the N112 from the campground until the right turn toward Mireval from where you pick up 116 to Villeneuve. From Villeneuve follow signs for Palavas. You will join D986. There is also a bicycle lane the last few kilometers into Palavas, where you take D62 to Carnon Plage. The city of Montpellier creates extra traffic in this area, but it will ease up again past Carnon. D986 runs past a large, flamingo-specked lagoon. You can get a closer look at the birds from the bicycle lane.

Once in Carnon, stay near the sea with signs for Carnon-Est. In this way you can take D59 to la Grande-Motte and avoid the busier D62 for a stretch. Continue straight through la Grande-Motte and bear right on Rue de Grau-de-Roi. If you ride to Sortie Ville, you will only end up on nasty D62 again. From then on, follow signs to Aigues-Mortes on either D62 or D979. Both are big and busy; 979 is more direct.

Aigues Mortes was built as a defended supply depot and departure point in the time of the Crusades. The city is laid out on a strict grid centered around a church dedicated to the city's patron St. Louis. The ramparts are only accessible from one point, near the main gateway, and a fee is charged to climb up. The town itself is full of souvenir shops and, more importantly, lots of bakeries. You can picnic in the central park or near the walls and spend some time wandering around this interesting town.

From Aigues head north for Nîmes, then turn right onto D58 for St. Gilles. After 8 km continue on road D179 to St. Gilles. This road runs through part of the Camargue, a marshy rural region. There are several ranches along this road where you can see the hardy white horses native to the Camargue. Ride into St. Gilles for a look at the church. Follow signs for *centre ville* and then for *Monument du XIIeme Siècle* to the right. The church is known for its carved Romanesque portals and is worth a look if you are not impatient to get into Arles. Take

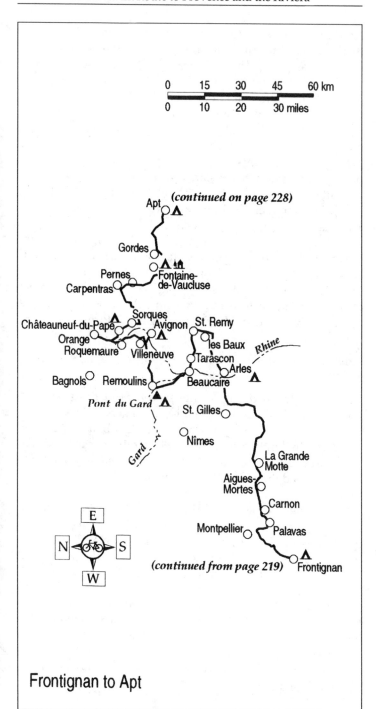

(continued on page 228)

Apt

Gordes

Pernes
Carpentras
Fontaine-
de-Vaucluse

Sorques
Châteauneuf-du-Pape
Avignon
St. Remy
Orange
Roquemaure
Villeneuve
les Baux
Rhine
Tarascon
Bagnols
Remoulins
Arles
Pont du Gard
Beaucaire
St. Gilles
Gard
Nîmes
La Grande
Motte
Aigues-
Mortes
Carnon
Montpellier
Palavas

(continued from page 219) Frontignan

E
N   S
W

Frontignan to Apt

N572 16 km to Arles. You can also wind along a variety of side roads to this city, but if you are impatient at this point in the day as I was, N572 is more appealing. This road is three lanes wide, one lane for traffic in each direction and a passing lane in between, so you will not be crowded off.

The nearest campground in Arles is a quick 2 km from the town center. Ride straight on blvd. Victor Hugo and over the railway tracks, after which the road bends to the right. The campground is on this road, which has become N453. It has a pool and separate areas for caravans and tents. Unfortunately, the tent section is farther from the toilet facilities, but so it goes. The price is moderate at about $2 a person and $2 per site. There is also a hostel on rue Foch.

Arles has its origins as a Roman city. There is an arena right in the middle of town. Cycle a victory lap as a reward for your efforts. The Alyschamps, a shaded promenade on one side of town, is lined with Roman sarcophagi. There are also a number of churches and historic buildings in Arles. Check the tourist bureau on Blvd. Victor Hugo for a map and information on the city's sights.

Arles to Pont-du-Gard
66 km (41 miles)

Another sight-filled day awaits as you prepare to pedal to Pont-du-Gard. The terrain on this ride is generally easy with the exception of the long climb up to Les Baux. The main problem I had in this area was the frustrating headwind that kept up all day. There is nothing to do in this situation but ride low, keep pedaling, and think of the beautiful Pont-du-Gard ahead.

From the campground, ride back toward the center of Arles. After you cross the train tracks, follow signs for Avignon/Tarascon. Turn right after several kilometers toward Les Baux. Just follow clearly marked signs all day. They will lead you over roads D17 and D78F to Les Baux, then D27A and D5 to St. Rémy. Les Baux is a hill-top town built on and carved into cliffs. It is a strenuous ride up but you will lose the headwind for a time. The views from the town to the valleys below are well worth the trouble. Les Baux is very small and full of twisting streets, so leave your bicycle in one place and explore on foot. There are few stores here but many cafés if you are ready for a snack.

The soaring downhill out of Les Baux is fun, although it brings you back into the dreaded headwind. Just before St. Rémy, stop at the site of two more Roman relics—a triumphal arch and a mausoleum that stand in an odd bare place beside the road. St. Rémy is a pretty, shaded town with attractive tree-lined avenues. Van Gogh lived in St. Rémy and created some of his most famous works of that time. The inspiration for his art can be clearly seen in the dry and twisted landscapes of Provence.

From St. Rémy take D99 to Tarascon/Beaucaire. This road is mostly shady, level, and shoulderless. You can parallel this road by taking side roads, although they are less direct; start out on D31 if you wish to do so. In Tarascon follow signs to Pont-du-Gard on D986, which unfortunately is a vicious road full of trucks that enjoy barreling by harried cyclists. There is no way to avoid this but you will get a break after Remoulins when most traffic must follow an alternate route.

Pont-du-Gard is the most impressive Roman construction in Provence. The aqueduct spans a cool, clear river in three superimposed tiers. You can cross to the opposite bank and climb to the tunnel at the top of the hill—a dirt path will lead you right to the top tier. In some places you can climb out of the waterway and sit on the very top of the aqueduct. It is high and scary, but you will earn thrilling views of the river and surrounding countryside.

There is a huge shady and grassy campground right near the aqueduct. Due to the popularity of the Pont-du-Gard, the campground is expensive, but the staff will undoubtedly give you at least a small reduction for being a poor and tired cyclist. There are few stores and services in this area, so shop in Remoulins before riding to the aqueduct.

Pont-du-Gard to Avignon
28 km (17 miles)

Cycle back to Remoulins and follow signs to Avignon. After the railroad overpass, turn right and follow signs the rest of the way, through Fournes, Theziers, and Aramon. At the T-junction in Aramon, turn left and watch for signs for Avignon. This is a mostly level ride. D2 along the Rhône has fast cars but the cycling is all right since the shoulder is wide, and there is not much traffic. You will more likely face the problem of headwinds as you cycle upriver toward Avignon. Cross the last bridge over the Rhône and Avignon awaits. A wall and defense towers surround the city. Avignon was home to seven successive popes for a time when the papacy left Rome. Modern and somewhat startling influences are everywhere in this historic city. Kids on skateboards practice in front of the Palais-du-Papes, and there is a McDonald's a few blocks away. The large hill-top park near the Palais is nice, although you are not allowed to sit on the grass. I was happily reading under a tree when I was kicked out (the French have strange ideas about parks). The park also offers good views of the Rhône and the unfinished bridge that ends only half way across the river. At first glance it is hard to realize what looks wrong with it.

There are several campgrounds on Ile de Barthelasse, the island beside Avignon in the Rhône. Cross the bridge toward Villeneuve to get there. Camping Bagatelle also offers indoor dormitory rooms.

Avignon to Châteauneuf-du-Pape
37 km (23 miles)

Continue over the bridge from Ile de Barthelasse to Villeneuve (opposite Avignon) and get on D980 in the direction of Bagnols. The ride is level all day and from this point on I was no longer bothered by headwinds. Get off D980 after Roquemaure, following signs for Orange. This puts you on D976, which is quiet due to the proximity of a big road that most cars take. In Orange, cycle out to one end of town to see the triumphal Roman arch. It is set in a traffic circle ,but if it is a quiet time of day, this can be a nice picnic area. This arch and the arch near St. Rémy are actually entry archways to Roman cities, but people like to consider them triumphal structures and the term has stuck. The open air Roman theater in Orange is the best preserved in France (an admission fee is charged).

After Orange, continue past the Roman theater, heading back toward Avignon. Turn right at the sign for Châteauneuf-du-Pape. This town is 10 km away on D68, a slightly hilly road with nice views of the endless fields of grapes that make the area famous. I cycled alongside a group of Swiss cyclists heading for Châteauneuf-du-Pape. This is a popular area for bicycle touring.

These vineyards belonged to the popes during the Avignon papacy. Châteauneuf itself is located just outside the town. Finding the campground from town can be tricky since it is poorly marked. To get there, take the right fork into *centre ville*—the left fork is also marked for *centre*, but don't take it—and bear right through town. Ride down a road that runs between a restaurant and a fountain. Turn right at the first intersection and continue straight for about 2 km out of town. Cycle straight through the roundabout that is in the middle of nowhere, past vineyards and over a river into the campground. It is a nice site, if a bit removed from the center of wine action in town. Do not spend too much time tasting in the caves (wine cellars) before you ride out to the campground, or you may never get there.

Each cave charges a fee that includes samples of the various wines offered for sale (by the bottle or the case). Châteauneuf-du-Pape has a small grocery store and the campground has some supplies, but to save money and be safe, shop while in Orange.

Châteauneuf-du-Pape to Apt
65 km (40 miles)

The ride from Châteauneuf-du-Pape to Apt covers a good deal of rural scenery. The cycling is challenging at times, but stops at Fontaine de Vaucluse and Gordes will break up the day comfortably. Cycle back into Châteauneuf-du-Pape from the campground and follow signs to Avignon and Sourgues (D17). In Sourgues keep looking for signs for Entraigues, which you pick up as you leave town. Keep following these signs as you take a roundabout course behind Sourgues. This part of the ride rambles around a series of small towns where the roads are all well marked. In Entraigues follow signs for Carpentras and Althen. Ride over the overpass and turn right for Althen and Le Thor (D16). Keep riding toward Le Thor after passing Althen.

There is an intersection for Pernes 2 km after Les Valayans. Go straight and then take the first left for Velleron, abandoning the road to Le Thor. There is a fork after 2 km on this road, and either way will take you to Velleron, but the one on the right is more direct. From Velleron ride on D31 to Isle-sur-la-Sorgue, then follow signs to Fontaine-de-Vaucluse. Take D25 to Fontaine de Vaucluse, where there is camping and a hostel. It is advisable to arrive as early as possible, before the tourists and opening times of souvenir shops that spoil the brilliant scenery with their gaudy displays. This is the site of a beautiful natural spring and a pretty town. Petrarch lived in Fontaine de Vaucluse for many years, having followed Laura to this town (I

0 15 30 45 60 km
0 10 20 30 miles

St. Raphaël
Fréjus
St. Tropez
Ste. Maxime
END
Le Muy
le Luc
Carcès
Brignoles
St. Maximin-la-Ste. Baume
Aix-en-Provence
Marseille
Apt
Cadenet

(continued from page 223)

E
N S
W

Apt to St. Tropez

still don't know who Laura is). A pillar in the center of town commemorates the poet.

From Fontaine it is another 14 km to Gordes, which involves the only hilly section of the day. Take D100a to Cabrieres and D100, followed by D110 and D2 into, and up to, Gordes. There are great views across the valley to the Montaignes-du-Lubéron from Cabrieres, a very small and tidy town. Gordes is worth the big climb for its spectacular vantage point and sand-colored stone buildings. Gordes is a great place to stop for lunch and while away a few hours in the afternoon heat. When you are ready to leave for the last part of the ride, continue down through the other side of town and follow signs to Rousillon and Le Saturin on D2. The ride is very flat and very pretty, with dry fields of herbs and scrub all around. The towns of Joucas on the left and Rousillon on the right add to the scenery, each being smaller hill-top versions of Gordes. You can easily take short detours to visit them if you wish. After passing the turnoff for Rousillon, stay on D2 until the clearly signed intersection for Apt and Le Chene on D4. Follow this road right into Apt.

The campground in Apt is a bit on the dingy side, but adequate and inexpensive. To get there, turn left after crossing the bridge by the third light in town, then left again over another bridge at the next light. The campground will be immediately to the right after you ride under an overpass. If this will not do, there are also two other campgrounds, both well-marked from this area. One is 1.5 km away and the other is 8 km away. Apt itself is an uninteresting town that the majority of traffic passes directly through.

Apt to St. Maximin
93 km (58 miles)

From the center of Apt take road 943 to Aix-en-Provence. This road will lead you over the mountains, a steady climb of several kilometers. You will, however, enjoy great views behind and ahead, and as a reward, there is a beautiful 5-km cruise down the other side of the ridge 25 km farther. Ride through Cadenet toward Rogues on road 543 and keep following signs for Aix. South of the Duranc River the terrain is mildly hilly, but not much to worry about. Cross straight over the N7 and go on to Equilles, where you take quieter D17 the last 10 km to Aix. There is a good Office de Tourisme right in the center of town by the large fountain. They can give you exact directions to the campground (3 km south of town in the direction of Nice) or information on alternate accommodations.

Aix is best known for its sidewalk cafés and people-watching. If you are on a tight budget, you can still enjoy the atmosphere. Get a small soda or milkshake and relax on the terrace of McDonald's, which is situated right in between two classier restaurants and offers just as good a view for people-watching as any other terrace in town.

You can find accommodations in Aix and call it a day. I was ready to move on after a few hours, though, especially with the enticing prospect of the Riviera ahead. In order to shorten the next day, you can cycle on to St. Maximin, where there is a campground. To do so, go down Cours Gambetta in Aix and follow signs for Nice and St. Raphael. Do not take the A road (blue signs) but take red N7 for 38 km to St. Maximin. This ride offers striking views of a white cliffy ridge (Montaigne de Cangle) to your left, and later the gorgeous Mt. Aurelien (880 m high) on the right. There is no shade and only a narrow shoulder on this road, but I found it nearly deserted even on a summer afternoon. This is probably due to the proximity of the faster A road, which takes the brunt of car traffic. The N7 is a rolling road of gradual ups and downs.

In St. Maximin, ride into town and then skirt around its edge to the right, following signs for Nice. Turn off to the right for St. Zacharie and follow signs to Camping Provençal. The other campground, Nans Les Pins, is straight down this road and has a pool but is more out of the way. For Provençal, turn left after the underpass, continue straight ahead across the intersection, and continue 1 km more on a small winding residential road. It is a quiet campground, costing about $2 each per person and tent.

St. Maximin to St. Raphaël
93 km (58 miles)

I took the large and busy N7 out of St. Maximin. In the early morning it was still quiet. Depending on how patient you are, an alternative to this large road is to follow a series of side roads to the north (D28 to Bras and le Val; D224 to Vins; D24 to D13 and Cabasse).

To take the more direct route, proceed as follows: From the Provençal campground in St. Maximin, turn right at the yield sign at the first intersection. When you are on the overpass, turn left to get on the road below which is the N7. You will ride through Tourves 7 km later (not around it) to save some distance. Do the same later in Le Muy. Once you pass Brignoles, turn left for Cabasse, just where the N7 becomes two lanes and a divided highway. Turn left off N7 for Cabasse on D79. Cabasse, a picturesque town with tiny narrow streets and sidewalk gutters, is 14 hilly kilometers away. Turn left toward Carces at the T-junction in town, not right for N7. Then take the first right and cross the river for D33 to Le Luc. Happily, this part of the route follows quieter roads and is not longer than N7 because that road dips south.

After Le Luc, rejoin N7 where traffic picks up considerably and you will have to endure an uncomfortable ride for the last miles into St. Raphaël. Unfortunately, there are no secondary roads in this area that lead even somewhat directly into St. Raphaël. Keep following green signs for Fréjus and St. Raphaël. Once in Fréjus, follow signs that bear right toward St. Raphaël and Fréjus-Plage. Do not continue on N7 to Cannes when you get outside of Fréjus because it goes inland and you will miss St. Raphaël. There is a Roman arena in Fréjus, but it was so difficult to concentrate on the busy roads that I did not even try to find it.

St. Raphaël offers an exciting introduction to the Côte d'Azur as a city complete with a harbor, promenade, and umbrella-specked beaches. St. Raphaël is not the most glamorous Riviera city, but it is a good starting point, being of manageable size. There is a reasonably priced Monoprix supermarket in town. It looks like a clothing store from the outside, but they have food in the back section. The public beach shower on the promenade near the large fountain is great for a cooling splash. Finally, there is a free toilet in the peach-colored building by the eastern marina—it is actually for marina use but no one seems to mind landlocked cyclists using it occasionally.

The nearest campground is 4 km east of St. Raphaël. The next is beyond Boulouris, and there are more on the way to Agay and inland. The one at Agay is right on the beach. All are terribly overpriced (about $10 a person in summer), but you may be able to get a slight cyclist's discount. Buy food in St. Raphaël before heading out to these sites.

St. Raphaël to St. Tropez
37 km (23 miles)

From St. Raphaël you have a few options. This tour continues into St. Tropez, one of the most attractive Riviera resorts. You will have to do a return trip back to St. Raphaël eventually since this is virtually a dead end unless you plan to cycle westward toward Marseilles from St. Tropez. Another option is to cycle east and ride the Côte d'Azur tour to Italy. If you are ending your ride in St. Raphaël, however, you can ride or take a train to Cannes from which point there are very easy train connections to Paris. You can even take the high-speed TGV on this route, and your bicycle will be shipped on the same train.

From the center of St. Raphaël cycle westward, following signs to St. Tropez. There is only one road (N98), which is in bad repair and a bit bumpy but not crowded in the off-season. The advantage of these roads and St. Tropez's location is that it restricts the number of visitors to a degree, not being on the main Riviera drag. Unlike most Riviera cities, St. Tropez has retained its small fishing harbor charm. Colorful buildings and flags ring a sheltered harbor and brighten the town while impressive yachts will tempt you to trade in your bicycle for a seafaring life. St. Tropez is perhaps the most easily appreciated and beautiful of the famous Côte d'Azur resorts.

The campgrounds are all located in the west. As you take D93 toward Ramatuelle you will encounter a barrage of signs. Unfortunately most are closed in the off-season. Croix de Sud Camping, 8 km away from St. Tropez but only 1 km from the beach, is open until the end of October. A few other campgrounds operate year round, although they are practically deserted very late in the season. Rooms in town are scarce and expensive.

Once you have had enough of St. Tropez's harbor and beaches, such as La Tahiti, you can ride back to St. Raphaël and continue touring along the Côte d'Azur. There is no train service to or from St. Tropez.

Côte d'Azur: French and Italian Rivieras

Distance: 239 km (148 miles)

Recommended touring time: 7–8 days (6 cycling days)

Terrain: from easy, level riding to long but moderately graded hills on twisting and often crowded seaside roads

Accommodations: camping and hostels or private rooms

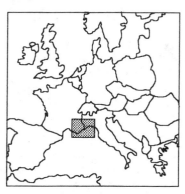

Maps: Michelin 84 (includes St. Raphaël to Bordighera, Italy)

This tour visits the famed Riviera, land of yachts, beaches, casinos, sports cars, and a number of less advertised elements. Cycling in this highly populated area is not the quiet, meandering experience it is in rural areas such as the Provence. However, since distances are short and enjoyable distractions abound, cycling offers a flexible and inexpensive alternative means of visiting the Côte d'Azur. The distances on this route are purposely short to maximize sightseeing and sunbathing opportunities. If this pace is too slow, however, combine two days in one to make better time.

The cities of St. Raphaël, Cannes, Nice, Monte Carlo, and Menton are highly developed, glitzy resorts. Their yacht harbors and sweeping promenades are exciting to wander around, as are the well-preserved *Vieilles Villes* (old towns). The winding streets in these quarters are filled with fruit stands and small shops, offering quiet, shady refuges from the intensity of the sun and the city scene. Smaller resorts such as Antibes and St. Tropez preserve a feeling of the classic Riviera. Here you will find stone-walled harbors and pastel-colored buildings. Just inland, the tiny hilltop town of St. Paul de Vence merits a side trip for its calming effect and Provençal character.

East of Menton, the tour follows the coast to the Italian Riviera. Although this is also a resort area, the feeling is markedly different. The towns and cities are smaller and less developed here, and the lifestyle is very Italian. This tour offers a look at the natural beauty of the Rivieras as well, particularly in the secluded coves and beaches of the Corniche de l'Esterel, dramatic red cliffs that plunge into the Mediterranean.

It is particularly important to use safety precautions when cycling the crowded Côte d'Azur. To keep safe and maximize your appreciation of the area, ride early in the morning when traffic is light. This will also help you to get to your destination early, leaving plenty of time for sightseeing. In Italy you will encounter several unavoidable tunnels, an unpleasant experience. Just before and after the peak summer months, the area is still very warm and attractive, with the additional advantages of less traffic, fewer tourists, and lower prices.

There are very easy train connections to and between many Riviera cities. The high speed TGV train from Paris to Nice and Cannes will accept your bicycle, without the delay and trouble often experienced on other train lines. From Finale Ligure you can cycle eastward to Genoa and the Riviera di Levante, or ride a train back to France or to other points in Italy. This tour also connects with the Provence to Riviera route.

	French	Italian
Hello:	*Bonjour*	*Buon Giorno*
Thank you:	*Merci*	*Grazie*

St. Raphaël to Cannes
40 km (25 miles)

St. Raphaël is a small city, representative of most of the Côte d'Azur, with a typical harbor ringed by a wide promenade. The beaches are sandy, unlike the rocky sites farther east, and crowded but most are free. There are rooms available in town and the nearest campgrounds are located a few kilometers to the east on N98. St. Raphaël offers a good, manageable introduction to the Riviera lifestyle.

The ride from St. Raphaël to Théoule along the beautiful Corniche de l'Esterel, road 98, is all ups and downs. The scenery is unforgettable, with dramatic red cliffs towering high over and plunging down into the turquoise waters of the Mediterranean. This section of the coast has not been developed, leaving plenty of unspoiled bays and small inlets to

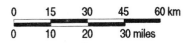

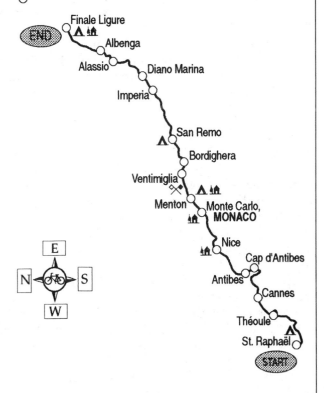

St. Raphaël to Finale Ligure

tempt you with a swim at your own private beach. It is best to get early starts to avoid traffic, since this is the one and only road in a highly traveled area.

There is a nice campground 7 km west of Cannes in Mandelieu. There are signs for Camping Les Pruniers from N98 in La Napoule. Turn inland along a river inlet and watch for more signs. This is a good budget option since Cannes does not have a hostel, and rooms are expensive. You can enjoy the rest of the day on the nearby beach or ride farther east to spend time or get a room in Cannes.

Cannes, host city of the famous film festival, is one of the prettiest Riviera cities. The palm-lined Promenade de la Croisette sweeps along a yacht-packed harbor. The best thing to do in Cannes is to settle on a bench with some pastries and watch the world go by. I thoroughly enjoyed the view from my bench—the azure Mediterranean to one side, and a row of flashy sports cars being towed away on the other. This was my visual revenge for all the exhaust fumes I had put up with during my ride.

Cannes to Antibes
17 km (11 miles)

From the the center of Cannes, ride along the Promenade de la Croisette on trusty N98. After you ride past the center of town, go along the sea to Pointe de la Croisette for a break from the traffic and then continue *par la mer* with signs for Antibes. From Juan-les-Pins you can cycle around the Cap d'Antibes, a promontory looking out over the sea. This ride of 6 km takes you past mansions and rocky beaches. After you round the point and begin heading back inland for Vieille Antibes, you will pass the youth hostel (blvd. de la Garoupe). It is not open year round, however. You can get a room in Antibes or ride east to the nearest campground, 7 km to the east in Biot. To give you an example of rates, I was able to talk the price of a double room down to $30 in the off-season. This is about as inexpensive as it will ever get for indoor accommodations.

Antibes, like St. Tropez, has retained its original charm. The Old Town and harbor are surrounded by high stone walls punctuated by defense towers. Antibes is also home to a renowned collection of Picasso's works at the museum in a castle within the city walls. Antibes has a fine public beach that offers views of Nice and inland mountains. For appropriate beach reading, F. Scott Fitzgerald's *Tender is the Night* provides a good taste of classical Riviera style.

Antibes to Nice
46 km (29 miles)

Leave Antibes by heading east on N98. At Villeneuve-Loubet-Plage follow signs for Villeneuve-Loubet-Village to the left and cross over a confusing series of intersections. You will briefly take N7 toward Nice, and then turn off for Villenueve-Loubet-Village again. From there, signs will guide you to the hilltop town of St. Paul de Vence. There is a 3 km uphill climb to St. Paul, but you will quickly forget about it once you reach the cool, narrow streets of the tiny town. Every winding lane opens unexpectedly onto small squares, each with a different moss-covered fountain. The bustling world of Riviera tourism seems hundreds of miles away from this sheltered enclave in the hills.

Reverse your route back to the coast. Cycle through Cagnes on the way and follow green signs for *Autres Directions* to take to a seaside route to Nice. As you approach Nice, traffic becomes much heavier. On the outskirts of the city there is a tourist information office, right off N98. You can get a map of the city and information on accommodations here. There are no campgrounds anywhere near Nice. If you want to stay in town, there are several official and unofficial hostels and a wide selection of chambres (rooms). Any indoor accommodation in Nice will be expensive. The International House for Young People (22 rue Pertinax, near the train station) is an unofficial hostel that is worth a stay just for the experience. For $10 a night, it offers peace, love, and granola in an international style.

Nice is the largest city on the Côte d'Azur. The vieille ville and the Promenade d'Anglais are the best sights in Nice. There are also many gardens and parks throughout the city that offer a shaded break from the blazing heat. While in Nice, be cautious and keep your valuables well protected as pickpockets and camera snatchers abound. I was targeted twice in one day but managed to snatch my wallet back in time.

Nice to Menton
30 km (18 miles)

Ride east on the Promenade d'Anglais until it runs out. Here you will have to rejoin road 98 and wind around hills and cliffs

22 km to Monte Carlo. You can spend the whole day here and ride the last 9 km into Menton in the afternoon. The only affordable place to stay in Monaco is the perfectly situated hostel, the Centre de Jeunesse Princess Stephanie on avenue Prince Pierre, near the train station (about $9 a night, open July to September only). Leave your bicycle in the train station baggage room instead of walking it around all day.

Monte Carlo is an overbuilt, congested city, but fun all the same. The vieille ville and palace at the top of the hill are the best sites. There is a nice park at the tip of the old town with wonderful views of the sea. In the modern part of town is the classy Casino, the main source of Monaco's revenue. Monaco is famous for its unique postage stamps, which are available at the post office in the vieille ville. There is also a reasonably priced supermarket directly across from the pool in the harbor.

In Menton there are a variety of accommodations available, but the most inexpensive options are the most challenging to reach. The hostel and campground of Menton are situated next to each other on the top of a mountain ridge high above the city. You will have to sweat to get there, or you can pay for a room in town. The easiest way to find the site is to check one of the Menton city maps posted along the sidewalks.

Menton to San Remo
30 km (18 miles)

Follow green signs to l'*Italie* from Menton. The border is only 4 km away. The relaxed border guards will probably not even want to look at your passport. You will be introduced to a common element of the Italian road system as soon as you cross the border: tunnels, long, dark, and frightening. Wear bright clothing, turn your lights on, and pedal fast. The tunnels sound scarier than they are because engine noise echoes so much, but this is of little comfort while you are riding through them.

The coast road that you will follow to Finale Ligure is SS1. Michelin map 84 ends at Bordighera, 18 km east of the border. SS1 goes straight through every coastal town with no confusing turns or intersections. It is so clearly marked all the way to Genoa that you do not even need a map. One thing to note is that signs are the reverse of the French system—follow blue-backed signs (the green signs are for the main autostradas) to Génova (Genoa). From west to east, the prominent towns are: Ventimiglia, San Remo, Imperia, Alássio, Albenga, Savona, and Génova. This is all you need to know to easily ride around this corner of Italy. All the signs are based on destinations rather than road numbers so you can get by with an understanding of which town comes after which. If you plan to cycle beyond Genoa, however, get the 1 : 300,000 Touring Club Italiano map of Liguria.

You will reach Ventimiglia, a somewhat grubby and crowded but classic Italian city, 8 km east of the border. Watch out for killer mopeds—everyone in Italy seems to drive one, and no one seems qualified. Signs for Genoa are easy to follow through town. Bordighera is 6 km later, and 2 km farther east is San Remo.

There is a very overpriced campground 3 km west from the center of San Remo (about $15 a person with no discounts for cyclists) and two more farther to the east. There are also *pensiones* in San Remo, however, and you may be able to bargain for a reasonable price if you are traveling with two or more people.

San Remo is called the 'Riviera of Flowers' by enthusiasts. The town is not as built-up as French cities of the Côte d'Azur although it retains that ever-present element, the seaside promenade. San Remo's has a checkerboard design well-trod by fashionable Italian women towing little dogs.

I found the sudden transition from France to Italy difficult for several reasons. There were such abrupt changes in mannerisms, customs, language, and scenery that my first day in Italy was a hard one. Everybody seemed to be yelling at me. Worst of all, I was subjected to the sudden loss of French bakeries. Italian bread, sadly, is a poor substitute. I was tempted to cycle back to familiar France after just a few hours in Italy. Being alone exaggerated the difficulty of the transition since I had no one to speak to or help me find food, find the campground, etc. However, these feelings soon passed as I continued cycling eastward and became accustomed to the country and its people. Three days later, I was haggling with vendors in Italian, following directions with little difficulty, and happily cooking huge tortellini dinners. The moral of my story is that it pays to be patient and give yourself a chance to enjoy Italy on its own terms.

San Remo to Finale Ligure
76 km (47 miles)

Continue riding east from San Remo, following green SS1 signs to Genoa. The terrain is generally more level than that of the French Riviera, but you will still find yourself cycling a series of gradual hills, especially between Imperia and Albenga. Here you must climb up and edge around each seaside cape, descend into the sweep of the town, then climb back up and around the next bend.

East of San Remo 8 km is Bussana (ignore signs to Tággia), then Diano Marina. Next it is 15 km to Alássio, 7 km to Albenga, 14 km to Loano, and 6 km to Finale Ligure. I pushed on straight into Finale Ligure, anxious to get settled in, but many of these seaside towns would make good stopping points. There are coastal campgrounds near every town. Albenga has a hellish tunnel, but you can avoid it by swinging right just before the tunnel and taking the seaside road.

Finale Ligure is a nice town, more so if examined in detail. All the buildings in the waterfront area have faded but beautifully painted facades. The beach in Finale Ligure is crowded on summer weekends but appealing all the same. The youth hostel located in the upper part of town on Via Generale Caviglia is a real castle with dragon-shaped doorknobs and torch holders on the walls. A cold breakfast is included. Head up Via Torino to reach the *ostello*. There are also pensiones in town and a campground to the east.

From Finale Ligure you can keep cycling eastward to Genoa or turn north for Milan, over an inland mountain range. Another option is to take the train to Milan and then tour the flat Po Valley or mountain lakes such as Lago di Como. This 'valley' is an expansive, sometimes featureless, plain that covers most of northern Italy. Traveling by train can be a challenge if the employees do not feel like letting you ship your bicycle. Ask several different people at the station well ahead of time to avoid problems. I would not recommend shipping your bicycle on a separate train and traveling ahead. In Italy, who knows when it will arrive at whatever destination it chooses.

Catalonia and Aragón

Aragón to Catalonia, the
Costa Dorada, and Barcelona

Distance: 350 km (217 miles)
total; Lleida–Barcelona:
194 km (120 miles)

Recommended Touring
Time: 7–8 days (6 cycling
days) total; 4–6 days (4
cycling days) Catalonia only

Terrain: a challenging tour,
with some long climbs inland and along the steep coast;
possibility of severe heat

Accommodations: hotels, hostels, or camping

Maps: Michelin 443 (1 : 400,000)

Spain is one of the most challenging countries for bicycle
touring due to a combination of difficult terrain, extreme heat
in summer, and a lack of facilities for travelers outside major

At a beach on the Spanish Costa Dorado

tourist areas. For this reason only those with a specific interest in cycling in Spain should consider this tour across the plains of Aragón to Catalonia. Having said that, I must also note that I covered this route with my mother, who was on her first bicycle tour. The point, therefore, is not to say that Spain is impossible, but that cycling here is not the leisurely pursuit it may be in other areas.

This tour, if undertaken from Lleida to Barcelona, is a short, enjoyable ride through one of the most interesting parts of Spain, the province of Catalonia. However, if you begin the tour two days further west, from Zaragoza, you will be more harshly exposed to some of the conditions that make cycling in most of Spain a great challenge. Therefore, this tour is organized in two parts, the first two days recommended only to those with a specific interest in cycling that region.

Two days of cycling will take you from Zaragoza, once the residence of the kings of Aragón, across high, hot plains to the province of Catalonia, where you pedal through orchards, quiet mountain villages, and to the Cistercian Monastery of Poblet. It ends on the beautiful Mediterranean coast in Barcelona, one of the most dynamic and exciting cities in Spain, which host to the 1992 Summer Olympics. There are train connections between all these points, and your bicycle can be shipped overnight at no extra charge.

Though it can be said that this tour covers two provinces, crossing into Catalonia is truly like entering another world, and most Catalonians would insist the tour includes two countries. Catalonia has a very strong sense of self-identity, an autonomous and even secessionist province with its own language, culture, and history. This sentiment is observed in graffiti on the walls, a firm adherence to local tradition, and even on cars, which sport the red and orange flag of Catalonia with a letter C in place of an E for España. Partly as a result of booming tourism, Catalonia is also one of the wealthiest parts in Spain, another factor fueling the secessionist fire of the province.

While the growing tourism industry may be responsible for driving prices ever higher, it has also created a good infrastructure for travel in Catalonia, making the region much more accessible and more easily enjoyed by cyclists than other parts of Spain. For this reason you should consider following the tour only from Lleida to Barcelona, by far the most interesting and welcoming portion of the trip, taking more time to explore

Catalonia in detail, and perhaps extend your ride to the north afterward. Whereas in other parts of Spain you will often have no choice but to cycle on large roads (for the ride from Zaragoza to Lleida, for example, you have virtually no choice but to cycle the wide shoulder of a major road) and be confronted with a lack of accommodations, in Catalonia there are not only more quiet side roads, but also more shops, hotels, and campgrounds, as well as extra luxuries such as public swimming pools. In short, I would recommend the Catalonia portion of the tour to almost anybody, and the Aragón section only to those who are truly determined to bicycle there.

Only mad dogs and Englishmen would continue cycling at midday (Spain seems to have its share of both, plus a few overdetermined American cyclists). If you must cycle in the summer, observe the local siesta; either get to your destination early or wait out the scorching afternoon heat in a shady place. Be aware that dehydration and overexposure are real threats. Carry plenty of water and drink constantly.

Note: Catalan is the first language of Catalonia, but almost everyone also speaks perfect Castillian (which is what we call Spanish). Though it is said that Catalonians often refuse to speak Castillian, this is usually only the case when they confront other Spaniards. I used Castillian throughout Catalonia and most people were very friendly and helpful, respecting my efforts to at least try something understandable.

Hello: *Hola*   (also *Bom Dia* in Catalan)
Thank you: *Gracias*

Zaragoza to Bujaraloz
72 km (45 miles)

The first two days of the tour should only be undertaken by those determined to cycle across the plains of Aragón. There is plenty of wide open space in which to free camp in this region, but as there are few tourists it is an uncommon and perhaps unwelcome practice. The only campground between Zaragoza and Lleida is in Mequinenza, 25 km south of Fraga. Otherwise, lack of accommodations severely limits your route. There are hotels in Bujaraloz, a few kilometers later in Peñalba, and in Candasnos, Fraga, and Caspe, to the south. Most cater to truckers, not tourists, and cost $20 or more for two people. For complete listings, check the guide to accommodations in Spain, a book most tourist offices have. Tourist offices also

243

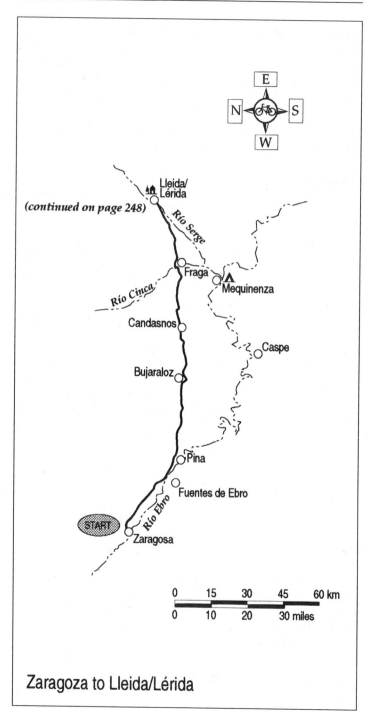

(continued on page 248)

Zaragoza to Lleida/Lérida

have pamphlets listing campgrounds (the Aragón pamphlet is about three pages long, giving you a clue as to the scarcity of these budget-saving sites).

There are few choices in this area but to cycle along the very wide shoulder of busy Route Nacional 2 (written in Roman numerals as NII). This is perfectly safe but not pleasant, as an endless stream of trucks and cars will accompany you throughout your ride. There are smaller roads farther to the south but few accommodations options there. Where possible, detours off NII are noted.

Zaragoza, once the seat of the kings of Aragón, is an un-touristed treasure (and the best reason for you to undertake these two optional days). Though most of the modern town is uninteresting, the main Plaza del Pilar is nothing short of magnificent. Grouped around the unique square are the domed Cathedral, Town Hall, and a number of monuments, with modern and ancient elements blending unexpectedly well. Nearby are ruins of the original Roman town walls. All the most interesting sights of the old town lie in this area, except for the Castillo de la Aljaferia, a Moorish fortress closer to the train station to the west. Near the fortress are a number of small side streets with less expensive rooms. Casablanca campground is at km 316 off NII in the direction of Madrid.

Leave Zaragoza on road N232 toward Alcañiz. This busy road with a wide shoulder becomes much quieter as you ride away from Zaragoza. The road parallels (but has no views of) the Canal Imperial de Aragón, originally dug in the sixteenth century. The road passes through a number of interesting towns in the vicinity of Zaragoza, such as Cartuja, El Burgo de Ebro, and Fuentes de Ebro. Turn right 6 km past Fuentes on a well-marked road to Pina de Ebro and NII. Connect to NII and follow it east (direction of Barcelona) the rest of the day. If it is late and time to siesta, Pina has a good shady park and some bars in which to refill your water bottles.

Bring plenty of water on this ride, which passes through a region of hot, open plains with few towns or even patches of shade. At midday the area resembles Death Valley. The ride is mostly flat, with a slight incline most of the way from Pina to Bujaraloz and possibly some strong winds. At km marker 369 there are two small trees with some shade, and there is a bar at km 372 where you can get cold water and more shade. There is absolutely nothing the rest of the way to Bujaraloz, which has three hotels ($25 and up for two) and a few grocery stores, but not much else.

Bujaraloz to Lleida
83 km (51 miles)

Within 20 km of Bujaraloz there are two towns, Peñalba and Candasnos, and then only one gas station before Fraga. Continue a long, slight incline toward Fraga, until 5 km before that town where you will suddenly reach the end of the plateau and have a sharp 5 km downhill to the Río Cinca area. To avoid a tunnel and gain quieter side roads, cycle up the steep hill past Fraga and turn right at the second intersection for Seròs. The ride becomes hilly; cycle straight through Seròs and to Aitona, where the turn for the bridge across the river is unmarked. After the colegio (school) to your left and before the bus stop, turn right to cycle down a one-lane road to the bridge; turn left after the bridge and continue east to Torres de Segre, 7 km further. On the outskirts of Torres do not turn right for N230 up a hill; the road is unpaved. Go straight to the blue arrow and through town until the roundabout where you will go straight, for Sudanell.

From Sudanell you can see Lleida (Lérida is the Castillian name). At the unmarked junction outside Sudanell turn left. Follow signs for Lleida, N230, and Albatàrrec to join N230 straight into town. Head straight, across the Segre River (not the canal) for the center and the old town within the city walls. There are a number of nice and reasonably priced hotels there. The tourist office is on the left side of the main gate into the old town. Like most tourist offices in Catalonia it can provide a wealth of information on the local area and the entire province. They can also direct you to camping Les Basses, 5 km away from the city center (400 Ptas. per tent; 400 Ptas. per person) and the youth hostel in town.

Lleida to Montblanc
63 km (39 miles)

Lleida is an interesting city and a good introduction to Catalonia. The old town is undergoing reconstruction at a spirited pace; around town you will see old and new architecture being mixed with great results. Head to the castle above the old town for great views over Lleida, the flat plains of Aragón, and the mountains of the coastal ridge lying ahead.

The day's ride is hilly and sometimes windy, taking you to the mountain valley where both the Monastery of Poblet and Montblanc lie. Leave the city by pedaling straight out of the old town, over the river and the canal, to follow signs for N230 to Albatàrrec. On the outskirts of Lleida, take the left turn for Castelldans (18 km away) to join quiet side roads to this town, passing through Artesa and Puigverd on the way. Unfortunately, the road unnecessarily runs up a long hill to reach Castelldans, only to descend again at the other side. However, there are good views back to Lleida and the surrounding plain from the hilltop town. Bear left into town and follow signs for 'Les Borges Blanques.' Go straight to the Spar supermarket and turn left to find these signs. Then it is a quiet 10 km ride through fields of apricots and pears to Les Borges Blanques, with a few more hills on the way.

Turn right onto N240 to cycle through Borges. The small park in the middle of town has some interesting historical artifacts and ruins, a good excuse for a water break. N240 is not as busy as NII, with much lighter traffic and very few trucks, but it has no shoulder. There are two long difficult climbs along N240, and virtually nothing until Vinaixa, 15 km later. This pretty town has an interesting old town gate and a sparkling blue public pool that will lure you for a quick dip (250Ptas. per person).

Continue on N240 past the exit for Tarrés and exit a few km later for Vimbodí to regain side roads. Cycle into the town and watch for signs for Poblet to the right. Cycle 6 km on this winding, practically deserted back road. The ride is hilly as you cycle to the Monastery of Poblet on the edge of the valley, near the mountains' edge. Signs will lead you directly to the entrance.

Refreshing shade and cool, clear-running water in fountains and pools makes the Monastery of Poblet one of the best lunch spots you could ask for. It was originally founded by Benedictines and is famous as the burial place of the kings of Aragón. The monastery is beautiful to view even from without, and you can also visit the interior (by guided tour only). Spend some time in this beautiful place to recover from the ride and the sun, and see another part of Catalonia's history in one of the most important Cistercian monasteries in the province. There is also a snack bar and toilets at this popular tourist destination.

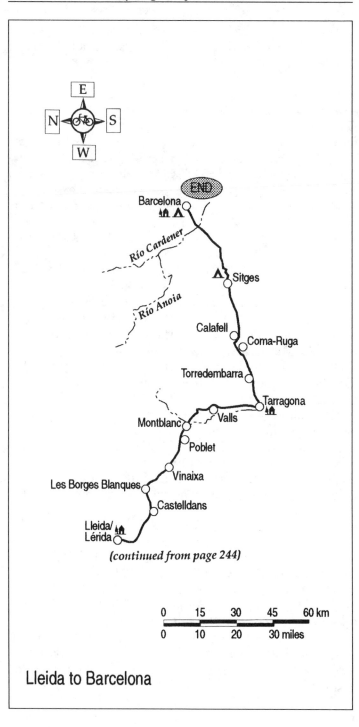

END

Barcelona

Río Cardener

Sitges

Río Anoia

Calafell

Coma-Ruga

Torredembarra

Tarragona

Montblanc Valls

Poblet

Les Borges Blanques Vinaixa

Castelldans

Lleida/ Lérida

(continued from page 244)

| 0 | 15 | 30 | 45 | 60 km |

| 0 | 10 | 20 | 30 miles |

Lleida to Barcelona

Turn left out of the Poblet gates and follow signs the last 8 km to Montblanc, first along side roads and then back on N240 for 4 km. Along the way, about 2 km from the monastery in the small town of Masies, there is a hotel and campground (on the left) that is sometimes open only for groups. Ask at the Lleida tourist office for more information. There is also a youth hostel in Masies. Montblanc has only three hotels (Ducal in the modern town, Hostal Colom, and Fonta Angele in the old town) and there are no campgrounds. The town is fascinating, modern life continuing with great vivacity within the ancient walls. Climb to the top of the hill in the center of town to best appreciate the layout of Montblanc, where spires of small churches and the larger cathedral point up between narrow rows of balconied houses. The hill also offers good views of the surrounding area, with mountains and the pass ahead. This quiet, untouristed town is a welcome surprise, its charm growing with each hour spent in the plazas of the old town.

Montblanc to Tarragona
35 km (22 miles)

This short ride brings you from the mountains down to the azure coast on mostly flat or downhill terrain. Leave Montblanc on road C240 to Reus (at a corner near the Ducal Hotel). The Michelin map erroneously marks this road as 'paved but in poor condition.' It is actually in good condition, and in fact freshly paved after the first few km. Happily, there is no pass to climb over, only a few short uphills. Otherwise, it is a smooth downhill ride all the way to Tarragona.

Stay on C240 until the exit for Picamoixons and Valls. Take this quiet side road until the signposted right for Picamoixons (not straight for Valls). After the turn, follow signs for Rourell and Tarragona. There is one unmarked intersection where you should go left. If you turn around, this road has a yield sign, while the other intersecting road that runs uphill has a stop sign. Cycle down a long, gradually sloping grade to Rourell, Vilallonga, Morell, and Poblet (a different Poblet) through miles of orchards and vineyards. In Morell keep left for Constantí/Tarragona to stay on side roads longer.

From Constantí follow signs for Tarragona. You will eventually join a very large road into the city but the shoulder is very wide and safe. Stay left for *Tarragona* and then follow signs for the city center. The road will put you directly onto Nova Ramblas, the main avenue. If you cycle to its end you will come to a high balcony and promenade overlooking the Mediterranean and the Roman amphitheater. There are tourist offices all over town, one on the right as you cycle down the Ramblas to the sea. They can give you a list of hotels and campgrounds, the nearest being Las Palmeras in Playa Larga, just to the north. The youth hostel is on Av. President Companys in Tarragona, and there are two more hostels in Altafulla and Vendrell.

Tarragona is a very interesting old city with Roman ruins, including an amphitheater and Roman city walls, and a large cathedral. The evening scene on the Ramblas and seaside promenade is not to be missed in this lively city on the Costa Dorada (Gold Coast).

Tarragona to Sitges
53 km (33 miles)

Leave Tarragona on N340 toward Barcelona. Traffic is heavy to moderate, and there is a suitable shoulder except when passing through towns like Altafulla and Torredembarra. After 16 km the traffic parts around a Roman arch, another relic of the empire that once stretched as far as this coast. Watch for the right turn after 4 km into *centre* at an exit for Urbana. Take the one-lane road that closely parallels N340 and passes a statue of men forming a human pyramid.

The side road will lead to Comaruga and then Calafell. These are towns with beautiful seaside promenades and sandy beaches. Follow the waterside roads and walkways as far as possible (at one point in Cunit, all paths seem to end but you can push your bicycle over a dirt path on the edge of the beach for about 20 m, where the road continues). Cycle into Vilanova and try to find the secondary coastal roads to Sitges. Due to road construction all over the area I got completely lost and ended up on the main road, C246, for an uncomfortably busy 7 km to Sitges.

Sitges is a very pretty harbor town reminiscent of those on the Riviera—the Riviera, that is, before it was spoiled by rampant commercialism. It is a pleasant, quiet stop before heading on to urban Barcelona. Walk along the promenade, past the old church overlooking the harbor, and through the old town, to get a better feel for this lovely place. The old town is chock full of hotels and cheaper hostels (lower grade hotels), and there is a campground 2 km west of town off the main road.

Sitges to Barcelona
43 km (27 miles)

The best way to get from Sitges to Barcelona is actually by train. The road (C246) running east from Sitges, crowded with car and truck traffic and without a shoulder, runs several kilometers along a steep cliff. Nearing Barcelona, traffic increases even more and could become dangerous. There are several trains a day from Sitges to Barcelona. Your bicycle may only be shipped on certain trains, but it will arrive the same day (30 min; 250Ptas).

Not convinced? Go ahead—carefully. The beautiful coastal views along the road are the only good thing about this ride. Head northeast on C246 out of Sitges. There is a long, twisting climb of about 4 km. When trucks pass (they will be going almost as slowly as you) it is best to pull off the narrow road and onto the even narrower, sandy side. After the long climb, ride downhill to Garraf, a small town, then climb again (not quite as long as the first time). From the top it is downhill or flat all the way to Barcelona. If the new autopista being built in 1991 is finished when you are cycling through, much of the traffic should be eased off the crowded coastal road.

There is a shoulder along C246 from Castelldefels on, but it runs out just when you need it near the center of Barcelona. For this reason it is much better to take the secondary road C245 into Barcelona. Watch for the left turn to Gava from Castelldefels. C245 runs straight into the heart of Barcelona.

Try to have a city map of Barcelona if cycling in. There is a tourist office in the Termino Station (Estacio de la Franca), the train station, and branch offices all around town, well-signed from the street. It is a large, busy city, and the 1992 Olympics will only make it busier, but Barcelona seems to thrive on the attention. The Ramblas is crowded with vendors and pedestrians, but the many public parks remain quiet, a haven from the bustling streets. There are cheap rooms for rent all over town. Ask for a listing at a tourist office. The area off the Ramblas near the seafront and statue of Cristóbal Cólon (Columbus) is not the best neighborhood at night, but has many hostels on the cheap side. For camping, stop at one of the countless coastal sites outside Barcelona. Most have good bus connections into the city. The sheer number of these allow you to be choosy, as some have better facilities than others (such as pools; prices vary greatly). There are a number of official and unofficial youth hostels in Barcelona as well.

The principal site of the 1992 Olympic Games is Montjuïc, the castle-topped hill south of the city center. It is worth getting to the top, whether on foot, by bus, or the cable car, for the tremendous views over the city, the mountains, and the endless blue of the sea. The reverse view, from the distant Parque Güell, is also worth the trip. This park is full of buildings in Gaudí's bizarre architectural style. Bizarre is the word for another one of the architect's works, the Templo de la Sagrada Família, in the north part of Barcelona. Whether you like it or not, the Templo will certainly make a strong impression on you. Barcelona is also dotted by countless plazas, large and small, each with its own character. Ask at the tourist office for more information on this dynamic city.

Barcelona is a major stopping point on the main train route between Madrid and France, with overnight connections to the French Riviera, Paris, and Madrid. To continue cycling, head north toward the French border and the Pyrénées. Consider, however, that coastal traffic is likely to be heavy. Another good way to continue cycling is to connect with the Provence to the Riviera Tour in Carcassonne, France, either by cycling or catching a train. Your bicycle can be shipped at no charge and should arrive on the first night train to your destination.

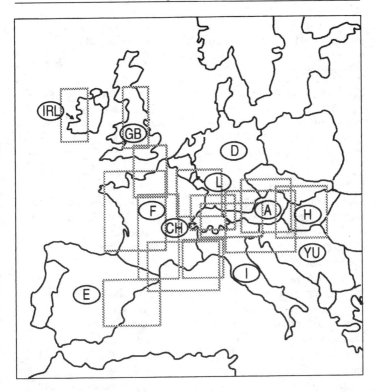

Mapping Notes

☐ The route maps in this book are based on the Michelin Europe Road Atlas at 1:1,000,000 scale.

☐ The actual scale used varies on account of space limitations.

☐ The scale does not always allow accurate location of route; maps are for orientation only. Use the maps indicated in the text.

☐ Refer to the legend below for the symbols used.

☐ Symbols used on maps do not always indicate exact locations, but only availability at the town shown.

☐ North arrows with boxes around cardinal point letters indicate maps that are rotated (i.e. North is not at top of page).

Legend

    ♠ Hostel   ✖ Border Crossing

    ▲ Camping   ▲ Mountain Peak

    🚶 Hiking   ■ Point of Interest

List of Titles Available from Bicycle Books

Title	Author	US Price
All Terrain Biking	Jim Zarka	$7.95
The Backroads of Holland	Helen Colijn	$12.95
The Bicycle Commuting Book	Rob van der Plas	$7.95
The Bicycle Fitness Book	Rob van der Plas	$7.95
The Bicycle Racing Guide	Rob van der Plas	$16.95
The Bicycle Repair Book	Rob van der Plas	$9.95
Bicycle Technology	Rob van der Plas	$16.95
Bicycle Touring International	Kameel Nasr	$18.95
The Bicycle Touring Manual	Rob van der Plas	$16.95
Bicycling Fuel	Richard Rafoth	$9.95
Cycling Europe	Nadine Slavinski	$12.95
Cycling France	Jerry. H. Simpson, Jr.	$12.95
Cycling Kenya	Kathleen Bennett	$12.95
The High Performance Heart	Maffetone/Mantell	$9.95
In High Gear (hardcover)	Samuel Abt	$21.95
In High Gear (paperback)	Samuel Abt	$10.95
Major Taylor (hardcover)	Andrew Ritchie	$19.95
The Mountain Bike Book	Rob van der Plas	$12.95
Mountain Bike Magic	Rob van der Plas	$14.95
Mountain Bike Maintenance	Rob van der Plas	$7.95
Mountain Bike Maint. and Rep.	John Stevenson	$22.50
Mountain Bike Racing	Gould/Burney	$22.50
The New Bike Book	Jim Langley	$4.95
Roadside Bicycle Repairs	Rob van der Plas	$4.95
Tour of the Forest Bike Race	H. E. Thomson	$9.95
Tour de France (hardcover)	Samuel Abt	$22.95
Tour de France (paperback)	Samuel Abt	$12.95

Buy our books at your local book shop or bike shop.
Book shops can obtain these titles for you from our book trade distributor (National Book Network for the USA) and from Ingram or Baker & Taylor, bike shops directly from us. If you have difficulty obtaining our books elsewhere, we will be pleased to supply them by mail, but we must add $2.50 postage and handling (as well as California Sales Tax if mailed to a California address). Prepayment by check (or credit card information) must be included with your order.

Bicycle Books, Inc.
PO Box 2038
Mill Valley CA 94941
Toll free tel.: 1-800-468-8233

In Britain: Bicycle Books
463 Ashley Road
Poole, Dorset BH14 0AX
Tel.: (0202) 71 53 49